Railroads Past and Present • George M. Smerk, Editor

VISIONARY
RAILROADER

Jervis Langdon Jr. and the Transportation Revolution

H. Roger Grant

Indiana University Press   BLOOMINGTON · INDIANAPOLIS

This book is a publication of

Indiana University Press
601 North Morton Street
Bloomington, IN 47404-3797 USA

http://iupress.indiana.edu

Telephone orders	800-842-6796
Fax orders	812-855-7931
Orders by e-mail	iuporder@indiana.edu

The paper used in this publication meets the
minimum requirements of American National
Standard for Information Sciences—Permanence
of Paper for Printed Library Materials,
ANSI Z39.48-1984.

Manufactured in the United States of America

Library of Congress Cataloging-in-Publication Data

Grant, H. Roger, date
  Visionary railroader : Jervis Langdon Jr. and the transportation revolution / H. Roger Grant.
    p. cm. — (Railroads past and present)
  Includes bibliographical references and index.
  ISBN 978-0-253-35216-3 (cloth : alk. paper) 1. Langdon, Jervis, 1905–2004. 2. Railroads—United
States—History—20th century—Biography. 3. Railroads—United States—History—20th
century. 4. Baltimore and Ohio Railroad Company—Biography. 5. Executives—United
States—Biography. I. Title.
  HE2754.L32G73 2008
  385.092—dc22
  [B]   2008004740

1 2 3 4 5 13 12 11 10 09 08

For "Jerv's boys"

CONTENTS

In the early 1960s, Jervis Langdon Jr. (1905–2004) emerged as a nationally prominent railroad official, and he continued to receive acclaim for his executive skills and imaginative thinking. In a professional career that spanned more than 50 years, this Cornell University–educated railroader served as a tax and commerce lawyer, lobbyist, president of three major railroads, a bankruptcy trustee, and industry consultant and commentator. Jervis became a person worthy of scholarly attention.

Jervis Langdon consistently revealed a strong, imaginative bent; he was a visionary railroader at a time when there were few others. Throughout his involvement with the industry, he advocated fairness of regulation, especially greater rate-making freedom for rail carriers. This perspective ultimately became accepted public policy, notably demonstrated in the Staggers Act of 1980. Jervis also reacted against the ossification and the lack of creativity that had become a hallmark of railroad leadership. With his ascendancy in 1961 to the presidency of the Baltimore & Ohio Railroad (B&O), Jervis gained the opportunity to revolutionize a company, even though the fetters of regulation and tradition remained. The B&O rapidly became a changed property. This renaissance came about in part because Jervis gave a new breed of "young Turks" from both within company ranks and outside the industry the chance to alter the status quo. He attracted bright, energetic men who generated new ideas in operations, marketing, and business practices. The flow of red ink ended through various Langdon administration–inspired responses, including unit coal trains, customer-oriented intermodal services, and corporate profit centers. When at the throttle of the faltering Chicago, Rock Island & Pacific Railroad (Rock Island), Jervis continued to employ progressive methods. Unit grain trains, for example, bolstered freight revenues. Failure, however, of industry leaders and regulators to develop a workable strategy on railroad mergers derailed a beneficial Rock Island marriage with Union Pacific. His efforts to establish a dialogue or machinery for arbitrating internal disputes came to naught. This widely acclaimed "doctor of sick railroads" worked more magic initially as lead trustee and then president of the tattered and bankrupt Penn Central Transportation Company (Penn Central), setting the stage for the ultimately prosperous Consolidated Railroad Corporation (Conrail).

A theme of this Langdon biography is that personal skills can contribute greatly to success as a railroad leader. Jervis possessed qualities that revealed modesty, honesty, generosity, and a deep concern for others. And he loved trains, an affection that began in childhood. Although a difficult quality to describe, Jervis had what might best be called charisma. Employees wanted to work for him, even though they might earn higher salaries elsewhere and have more comfortable work assignments. Some railroad executives collected enemies like barnacles, but this was not the case for Jervis Langdon. No wonder so many co-workers, "Jerv's boys" as they called themselves, adored him and remained close to him throughout his long life.

Although there exists an extensive literature on American railroads, there are few studies of railroad leaders, especially for those men who came to the forefront after World War II. Hopefully, this examination of the life and times of Jervis Langdon Jr. will prompt scholars to consider book-length biographies of distinguished contemporary executives. Perhaps others might want to examine in greater detail the histories of the B&O, Rock Island, and Penn Central, railroads that this visionary railroader made better.

ACKNOWLEDGMENTS

I never expected to write a biography of railroad executive Jervis Langdon Jr. or anyone else. The focus of my recent scholarship has been on company histories, including studies of the Chicago & North Western, Georgia & Florida, and Wabash railroads and a general history of railroad technology. The closest that I ever came to writing a biography was a book on a small New Thought utopia, the Spirit Fruit Society, which required a careful examination of Jacob Beilhart, the group's founder. Needless to say, when Herbert H. Harwood Jr., a retired CSX executive and accomplished railroad historian, contacted me in early 2005 about this project, I was both surprised and intrigued.

As with every scholarly endeavor, numerous individuals have given me enormous assistance. Irene Langdon shared her memories about her husband and family and provided a wealth of materials, including personal papers, business documents, and photographs. Then there were "Jerv's boys," mostly former associates from the Baltimore & Ohio Railroad, who raised money to cover my research expenses. It was Kent Shoemaker who was the primary force in initiating the project and spearheading the fund-raising. And E. Ray Lichty served effectively as the "point" person for a variety of tasks, ranging from processing expense reports to making appointments for interviews. While not really Jerv's boys, there were other railroad people who contributed generously of their time to respond to my questions. These individuals whom I interviewed in person, by telephone, or through e-mails are noted in my chapter notes, and the list is extensive.

A memorable event in preparing the manuscript was my overnight stay at Quarry Farm on East Hill outside Elmira, New York. Irene Langdon and Barbara Snedecor, who directs the Center for Mark Twain Studies at Elmira College, made this a special experience. It is important for authors to visualize their subject, and Quarry Farm contributed much to my understanding of Langdon's sense of place and family pride.

As with all books, archivists and librarians aided me in examining various resources. I thank the staffs at the Baltimore & Ohio Railroad Museum, Baltimore; Hagley Library, Wilmington, Del.; Mercantile Library, St. Louis; University of Iowa Special Collections, Iowa City; and Western History Collections, University of Oklahoma Libraries, Norman. And Pat Aftoora, who oversees records for CSX in Jacksonville, Florida, kindly made available B&O corporate minute books. The Baltimore & Ohio Railroad Museum also processed the paperwork involved with the research expenses.

Several individuals kindly read all or portions of the manuscript, including Keith L. Bryant Jr., Bill Collins, Herb Harwood, Don L. Hofsommer, Irene Langdon, Ray Lichty, and Kent Shoemaker. Collectively they improved the work immensely, finding errors, contradictions, and inconsistencies and adding to the content.

As with previous books, my wife, Martha, has been my foremost critic, offering solid advice about coverage and style. She graciously allowed Jervis Langdon to become an extended member of the Grant household. In the long run, I imagine, all the assistance that I have received from others would have counted for little had it not been for Martha's encouragement.

VISIONARY **RAILROADER**

1 The Making of a Railroader

The Langdons of Elmira

On the morning of April 3, 2004, a cool, damp Saturday, several hundred family members and friends of Jervis Langdon Jr., some of whom had come from great distances, gathered at historic Park (Congregational) Church in downtown Elmira, New York, to celebrate the life of an exceptional individual. Six weeks earlier, on February 16, 99-year-old Jervis had died peacefully in his sleep of congestive heart failure following a brief illness. His ashes were placed in the Langdon family burial plot in Elmira's spacious Woodlawn Cemetery, resting only a few feet from his famous great-uncle, Samuel Langhorne Clemens (Mark Twain).[1]

The mood of the memorial service was upbeat. By this time everyone had recovered from the shock of Jervis's death; moreover, there was the realization that he had achieved an unusually long, productive, and rewarding life. Carl Hayden, an Elmira attorney and family friend, offered a thoughtful and at times moving eulogy. "But even the most comprehensive obituary fails to capture the complexity which lies at the core of a great man like Jervis Langdon. It fails, for example, to record that he was proud and humble, serious and witty, tenacious and gentle, sober and sweet." Appropriately Hayden noted the strong relationship of the Langdon family to this Congregational house of worship. Jervis's great-grandfather, the first Jervis Langdon (1809–70), although raised a Presbyterian, played an instrumental role in founding this independent church in 1846, and Jervis's grandfather, Charles Langdon, helped to finance the present edifice in the 1870s. It had been through the longtime minister, Thomas Kennicut Beecher, that this progressive religious body had contributed to the antislavery and women's rights movements and reflected the Langdon family's deep commitment to social justice and civic betterment. In no way did the Langdons feel superior, spiritually or socially, to their neighbors.[2]

Jervis had a powerful sense of place. Home was Elmira, New York. Since before the Civil War the family had been a part of this vibrant "Southern Tier" community. In 1845 Jervis's 36-year-old great-grandfather and his wife, Olivia Lewis Langdon (1810–1890), moved from Ithaca to Elmira with their adopted daughter, Susan (1836–1924). This Jervis Langdon represented the successful businessman of the period. Following the death of his father, Andrew Langdon (1774–1811), who had farmed and managed a small hotel, at times he had struggled. Although he lacked extensive formal education, he possessed basic skills in reading, writing, and arithmetic; furthermore, he was sharp-witted, hard-working, and exceedingly kind. "The ordinary life of a country boy at home and at school was his until he passed 16, when he went into a common country store in Vernon [New York] kept by a Mr. Stevens," observed the Reverend Beecher at Langdon's funeral in August 1870. "Langdon was a quick, intelligent, slender, fair-haired, diffident youth: better esteemed by those he served than he was by himself—a trait which he never outgrew." And Beecher observed an enduring family trait: "Mr. Langdon was often-times too tender-hearted."

That same theme of generosity came from the pen of his son-in-law, Samuel Clemens, in a memorial tribute that appeared in the *Buffalo Express*, a newspaper that Langdon had financed to allow Clemens to become an editor. Langdon "spent more than one fortune in aiding struggling unfortunates in various ways, and chiefly to get a business foothold in the world. He had so charitable a nature that he could always find some justification for any one who injured him; and then the forgiveness freely followed."

It was understandable that the Elmira community expressed deep sorrow at Langdon's passing. "In response to a common sentiment, the business places of our city were generally closed," observed the *Elmira Weekly Advertiser*. "The business portion seemed almost as deserted as though it were Sunday, and a quiet pervaded the streets, as though a calamity had befallen us, during the ceremonies at the house and the grave." Added the newspaper, "Seldom does a man, whose munificence has been so unosten-tatious and private, and whose life has been so far removed from public and prominent ways, go to his long awaited home with more evidences of a public appreciation of his loss than signalized the funeral of Mr. Jervis Langdon." Even months after Langdon's death, individuals continued to express their condolences. In a November 9, 1870, letter to Olivia, Freder-ick Douglass, the famed abolitionist, who as a runaway slave had been given shelter and medical care in the Langdon home, wrote: "I beg you to allow me to enroll myself among the many who today hold [your hus-band's] name and history in grateful memory. The record of his life as given in the address of his Pastor has touched me deeply—and hence these few words."[3]

Once Jervis's ambitious great-grandfather mastered business matters and accumulated some capital through employment in several rural mercantile stores, he left the retail trade for lumbering, initially in Millport on the Chemung Canal and soon thereafter in nearby Elmira, seat of Chemung County. Elmira proved an excellent choice. Described as a "lumbering vil-lage," Elmira abutted large stands of commercially valuable pines and hard-woods and benefited from exceptionally good transportation facilities. Not only was there the Chemung River, suited for the floating of logs to neigh-boring sawmills, but in 1833 the Chemung Canal (1833–78), one of several state-sponsored lateral or feeder canals to the Erie Canal, opened for traffic, extending from Seneca Lake to Elmira. Then the companion Junction Canal (1854–71), built with private capital, became a link to the network of Penn-sylvania canals and railroads, the so-called State Works.

About the time that the Langdons made Elmira their home, the broad-gauge (six feet between the iron rails) New-York & Erie Rail Road, later the Erie Railroad, built through town, and in 1851, after several interruptions, it com-pleted its 447-mile line between the New York communities of Piermont on the Hudson River, 25 miles north of New York City, and Dunkirk on Lake Erie about 40 miles southwest of Buffalo. The Erie proudly boasted of being the first carrier "Between the Ocean and the Lakes," and its length was widely acclaimed. And local transportation options got even better. After the Civil War Elmira enjoyed access to the main lines of the Delaware, Lackawanna & Western Railroad (Lackawanna) and the Northern Central Railroad. The former operated between Hoboken, New Jersey (New York City), and Buf-falo, and the latter, an affiliate of the Pennsylvania Railroad (PRR), connected Baltimore, Maryland, Harrisburg, Pennsylvania, and Canandaigua, New York. A branch of the Lehigh Valley Railroad (Lehigh), constructed in the mid-1870s as the independent Utica, Ithaca & Elmira Railroad, tied Elmira to

Van Etten, New York, on that carrier's main line between Jersey City (New York City) and Buffalo.[4]

No wonder Elmira developed a strong, diversified economy. By the 1860s the town's leading products were axes, barrels, boots and shoes, iron, and woolen cloth, and the industrial tradition, albeit with other manufactured goods, remained strong. These activities prompted a New York City journalist in 1871 to call Elmira "this over-head-and-ears busy little city." By the turn of the twentieth century, local firms like Elmira Iron and Steel, Howell's Box Factory, LaFrance Manufacturing (firefighting equipment), and Thatcher Glass contributed to the general prosperity. Residents also took pride in being the home of the progressive, nondenominational Elmira College (nee Elmira Ladies' Seminary), which offered young women an education that "shall compare favorably with the best institutions for the other sex," and the popular Gleason Health Resort, a private clinic on Watercure Run. Some residents, though, may have been less pleased with the massive New York State Reformatory facility, although this public institution bolstered the local economy.[5]

Jervis's great-grandfather, who resembled so many contemporary entrepreneurs, opted for a business partnership. This gave him more capital and managerial help. The Elmira lumber firm of Andrus and Langdon prospered. But timber reserves were finite, and that prompted Langdon to turn wisely to coal, a fuel that was rapidly gaining widespread use. He now dubbed his business J. Langdon, Miner & Dealer in Anthracite & Bituminous Coal. In 1855 Langdon entered the field on a large scale by contracting for the entire output of two anthracite or "stone coal" mines in the Shamokin District of Northumberland County, Pennsylvania. Direct railroad service on the Northern Central from the diggings to Elmira and then by rail and water to markets in western New York, Canada, and the Midwest, especially Chicago, Milwaukee, and St. Paul, led to handsome profits. Yet the disastrous Panic of 1857 struck the business hard. "My father was on the verge of failure," remembered his daughter Susan, "which was afterwards averted." With the slow return to more prosperous conditions, expansion followed. In time Langdon controlled some of the choicest coal lands in Northumberland and Schuylkill counties, and eventually two of these Pennsylvania properties were sold at a hefty price to the Philadelphia and Reading Coal and Iron Company.[6]

In 1870, Langdon had launched J. Langdon & Company. This partnership consisted of his son Charles, son-in-law Theodore W. Crane (1831–89), and John De La Fletcher Slee (1837–1901), former professor of German and Greek at Fally Seminary in Fulton, New York. In time Langdon family interests controlled a number of valuable mineral holdings, including the Shamokin Coal Company of Pennsylvania and properties in Nova Scotia. In 1871 the Shamokin operations produced 900,000 tons even as production rose. The firm played a key role in the sale of these black diamonds through the Anthracite Coal Association, a marketing pool based in Buffalo, where the talented Slee served as the company's coal agent. "Jervis Langdon made a great deal of money," recalled his great-grandson.[7]

Without question, the life of the Langdon patriarch reinforced the "rags-to-riches" rise of so many contemporary native-born businessmen for whom seizing individual opportunity emerged as a central theme in their lives. It was hardly surprising, especially in frontierlike environments, that the chance for unprivileged, gifted, and industrious young men to succeed was celebrated in literature, newspapers, and political rhetoric. Unlike the formula employed by the prolific writer and self-help advocate Horatio Alger Jr., Langdon did not need to marry the boss's daughter; he was truly a self-made man. Langdon's life could be displayed as testimony to the dream of success.

The Langdons of Elmira were a closely knit family. In addition to Susan, they had a daughter, Olivia (Livy) (1845–1904), and a son, Charles Jervis (1849–1916). The Langdons lived a conventional Victorian-era life. Most of their cherished moments took place in the expensive (initially valued at $25,000) Italianate-style house and surrounding grounds situated on the corner of West Church and North Main streets directly across from Park Church. "The acreage around [the house], which included fully half the block, with the vine-covered stable standing on First Street, was planted with some rare and many fine native trees; supplied with greenhouses (one of them for plants and flowers, the other mainly for grapes, but sheltering also a mammoth night-blooming cereus given to prolific blooming at twilight) and bright and formal flower beds and dotted with fountains and canopied iron garden-seats," remembered Langdon's granddaughter, Ida. "Hammocks and birdcages, their occupants only mildly disturbed by an occasional passing [street railway] horse-car, hung on the front porch." The three-story house featured a tasteful fourth-level tower, an ornate parlor and dining room, a large library/music room, and multiple bedrooms for the five family members and house staff.[8]

Since Olivia Langdon was "socially inclined and socially gifted," the Langdons did extensive entertaining. Guests, though, were not always business associates of Langdon and friends of Olivia. Occasionally, famous visitors paid calls, including abolitionists Frederick Douglass, Henry Lloyd Garrison, and Gerrit Smith and politicians Chester A. Arthur, James G.

Blaine, Roscoe Conkling, and Ulysses S. Grant. As with so many upper-middle-class Victorians, the Langdons used their "much loved house" to the fullest.[9]

While the Elmira home was the scene of pleasant times, Langdon had sought to create a personal utopia of sorts, really a retreat from the stress of daily business life. In 1847 he acquired seven acres on the crest of East Hill about 2.5 miles from the center of town that featured commanding views of Elmira, the meandering Chemung River, and the distant hills of Pennsylvania, and here he had constructed a modest summer cottage. The pleasure obtained from this convenient getaway led to the purchase of more land in 1869, approximately 250 acres, and the building of a larger, year-round dwelling.

Named Quarry Farm at the suggestion of the Reverend Beecher because of an abandoned stone quarry on the property, this beloved family place gained lasting fame. Beginning in the early 1870s, Langdon's son-in-law, Sam Clemens, spent considerable time at the farm, especially during the summer months. He often used a detached writing study, built in 1874 under the supervision of Susan Langdon Crane, to pen a variety of books, plays, and essays, most notably *The Adventures of Tom Sawyer, A Connecticut Yankee in King Arthur's Court,* and *The Adventures of Huckleberry Finn.* "My study is a snug little octagonal den, with a coal-grate, 6 big windows, one little one, and a wide doorway" is how Clemens described this distinctive building, allegedly (and appropriately) designed in the shape of a Mississippi River steamboat pilot house. Initially this study even included dual fireplace chimneys, reminiscent of the double stacks commonly found on river boats. "The study is nearly on the peak of the hill; it is right in front of the little perpendicular wall of rock left where they used to quarry stones. . . . It is remote from *all* noises." Like the Langdons and others of their socioeconomic class, Clemens valued privacy as never before. He would add that Quarry Farm was "a foretaste of heaven."[10]

Following the death of Jervis Langdon in 1870, Charles became the "titular head of J. Langdon & Co." With other men of business, including his brother-in-law, Theodore Crane, he focused on the daily operations of the coal-mining properties. Charles resembled his late father by possessing a similar character, including that get-up-and-go spirit. Although lacking a college experience, he had attended the Gunnery School for Boys, a respected preparatory academy in Washington, Connecticut, that had been founded at midcentury by abolitionist, educator, and outdoorsman Frederick William Gunn. Charles also benefited from two extensive overseas trips. Since his

Elmira, N. Y. Mark Twain's Summer Home, Quarry Farm.

Public interest in Quarry Farm, which overlooked Elmira, New York, is reflected in this commercial picture postcard, ca. 1910, which shows the main structure from the west. In the mid-1920s, Jervis's father had the house remodeled, altering the exterior appearance. (Author's collection)

"inclination for traditional schooling was not too strong," supervised travel abroad became an effective and undoubtedly pleasant way to expand his general education. He was accompanied by his tutor, Darius Ford, an ordained Baptist preacher and teacher of astronomy and mathematics at Elmira College. The first tour centered on the Mediterranean and the Holy Land, but the second was truly global. It would be during the initial journey that Sam Clemens met Charles and became fascinated by a small daguerreotype that he carried of his sister Livy. Clemens's interest in Livy intensified, leading to a brief formal courtship and then to their wedding in February 1870, shortly before her father's death.

Charles Langdon, the seasoned world traveler, performed well in the business world. An early triumph involved a joint venture with Vanderbilt family members to obtain a dependable and reasonably priced supply of locomotive coal for their New York Central System. At first their actions centered on production from the MacIntyre Mine, located near Ralston, Pennsylvania, which initially produced "enormous tonnage." About 1880, however, the usable coal supply became exhausted, and so Charles relocated mining operations to the Clearfield area, about 100 miles to the west, within the great hills of western Pennsylvania. With continued backing from the Vanderbilts, who believed that the PRR monopolized the eastern coal market, the Clearfield Bituminous Coal Company became a thriving concern, operating at one time 58 mines and claiming to be the largest single coal producer in the region. Charles served as chairman and his bank, Chemung Canal Trust Company, acted as a depository for the CBC.[11]

But Charles became involved in more than coal and banking. In order to move the black diamonds to market, including sites along the sprawling Vanderbilt transportation properties, he joined the Vanderbilts in 1883 in financing a connecting railroad, the Beach Creek, Clearfield & South Western Railroad, which linked Williamsport (and a friendly interchange with the Reading Railroad) with Clearfield, a distance of 104 miles. The carrier also operated several coal-gathering appendages. Although the PRR was hardly pleased by this incursion into its coveted territory and even attempted to take control, the Beach Creek remained a busy shortline and independent of the PRR. In time, New York Central interests acquired the Langdon stock in these coal and rail operations.[12]

Yet Charles had hardly retired from business. There continued to be substantial family holdings in the anthracite and bituminous coalfields of Pennsylvania and investments in Elmira firms, including the Thatcher Glass Company and the Chemung Coal Company, a retail seller of hard coal. And he remained active in the dominant local bank, providing a source of investment capital and personal income.

Politically Jervis's grandfather upheld the Republican Party allegiance of his abolitionist father. But Charles became more involved in party activities, emerging as a recognized force in New York Republican circles. He was a member of the powerful Stalwart or pro-business faction headed by Roscoe Conkling, and as a delegate to the Republican National Convention in 1876, Charles backed the faction's unsuccessful efforts to nominate Grant for a third presidential term. Thereafter, Charles treasured ownership of a "306" medal, recognition for having been one of the 306 delegates to have backed the former president. Governor Alonzo Cornell, a member of the Stalwart machine, rewarded his party loyalty and business talent in 1880 by appointing him commissary general of the state militia. Charles often used the title of "General," a vain action uncharacteristic for a male Langdon. Yet like nearly all members of the Langdon clan, Charles embraced a capitalistic, individualistic, and nationalistic worldview, sentiments shared by so many white Anglo-Saxon Protestants.[13]

When Charles Langdon died in 1916, sadness swept the community. After all, he was known for his good works, including the "secret charities" that quietly provided financial assistance to deserving individuals. The *Elmira Star-Gazette* commented that Charles was a "man of integrity, character, unselfish spirit, broad sympathies and unstinted generosity" that made him "a citizen beloved by all." These words could also have described his father and subsequent members of the Langdon family. Obituary writers noted, too, that Charles was the "Charley" mentioned frequently by Mark Twain in his highly acclaimed book *The Innocents Abroad* (1869).[14]

Charles left a widow, Ida Clark Langdon (1849–1934), whom he had married in 1870, and three children: Julia Olivia (1871–1948), Jervis (1875–1952), and Ida (1880–1964). Both girls did well, one following Victorian customs and the other leading a less conventional life. In 1902 Julia married Edward Eugene Loomis, a rising railroad executive, and in 1905 she gave birth to a daughter, Olivia, and three years later to another daughter, Virginia. Ida never married. After graduating from Bryn Mawr College and earning a doctorate in English literature from Cornell University, she spent her academic career on the faculties at Bryn Mawr, Wellesley, and Elmira colleges. She particularly enjoyed her class offerings, which included the works of John Milton, the seventeenth-century English author and the subject of her scholarly interests. In 1920 Ida returned to Elmira to head the Department of English at the college in order to be at home to care for her ailing mother. This response, though, was typical, even expected, from a single woman of the time. In this case Ida's commitment was wholly practical; Ida's sister lived with her husband and children in New York City.[15]

Charles and Ida's son, Jervis, did more than carry on his grandfather's name; he participated in the family businesses with his father and then took charge. But before he entered the workaday world, he received a superb education. Like his father, he benefited from foreign travel, specifically a European trip with his mother and sisters that consumed most of a year. Then in 1893, following two years at Ithaca's Cascadilla School, he entered Cornell University. Opened in 1868, Cornell operated privately and also publicly as the land-grant college of the state of New York. Following his graduation in 1897, he joined J. Langdon & Company, where he attended to an array of business interests, ranging from the hometown Chemung Coal Company and Chemung Canal Trust Company to the Lackawanna Coal Company, an affiliate of the Lackawanna Railroad.

He also devoted his time and resources to Park Church, Arnot-Ogden Hospital, and Community Chest. "The impression of his work for Elmira is left on many phases of the city's church, civic, business, and social life," editorialized the *Elmira Star-Gazette* at the time of his death. "To every cause in which he worked . . . he gave leadership, counsel, and quiet, unstinted devotion that earned the respect and the affection of those with whom he was associated."

Langdon also volunteered outside Elmira. Most significantly he became an active alumnus of his alma mater, serving for years on the Cornell Council, the university's fund-raising body, and also as a trustee from 1930 to 1940. He made a substantial contribution for the purchase of timber lands to be used as a teaching laboratory by the highly acclaimed Department of Forestry. And during the administration of Charles Evans Hughes, New York's renowned progressive-era governor, Langdon received an appointment as a trustee of the Binghamton State Hospital (today's Binghamton Psychiatric Center). His interest in this position may have stemmed from a personal concern for the mentally ill, since there was a family history of depression.[16]

Resembling other family members, especially his abolitionist grandfather, Langdon exhibited a staunch respect for all human beings. Understandably, he did not care for those who showed resentment and prejudice toward others. An illustration of his enlightened attitude can be found in his diary entry for July 4, 1925: "Big Ku Klux parade in late afternoon. Very discouraging sight. 'Organized Ignorance.' Rain came down in torrents before it was over."[17]

Langdon gave considerable time to his growing family. On October 2, 1902, he had married Elmira native Eleanor Sayles (1878–1971), daughter of Henry Halsey Sayles and Ellen "Nellie" Boardman Smith Sayles (1853–1936). Known affectionately as Bob, Bobby, and later Lee, she was a loving wife. Lee's father, Henry Halsey Sayles (1845–83), operated a local family-owned "wholesale house." But following Henry's sudden early death, Lee's resourceful mother took Eleanor and her two brothers and sister to live in France "where the over-all cost of living was cheaper." In time the Sayles returned to America, and it would be in Elmira that Langdon and Lee met and courted. Within a few years after their marriage, they became parents of two children, Jervis Jr., born on January 28, 1905, and Eleanor, called Polly, who arrived on March 15, 1906.[18]

The birth of Jervis, which took place in the family's rented house at 362 West Church Street, was heralded with much joy. "It began about 1 AM," wrote his father in his diary for Saturday, January 28, 1905. "Telephoned Dr. Stuart and then went to Miss Nisumno at the Whittiers. Lee [Eleanor] had

Three-month-old Jervis Langdon Jr. and his father at the family home in Elmira, New York, in April 1905. (Irene Langdon)

a hard 12 hours being delivered at 12:35 [PM]. Dr. Stuart in charge, Dr. [Arthur] Booth assisting. The youngster—a 8¾ to 9 lb boy—taken with instruments finally. Great rejoicing. Lee doing beautifully." The following day, the proud father noted that "everything going well. Went to church and was a hero!" Then on Monday, he observed that "Bobby [Eleanor] and 'Jervis' still getting on nobly. The town has named him 'Jervis' and that agrees with Lee's [Eleanor] wish, so it goes." A few days later, he wrote: "Lee and her boy doing admirably. Letters and telegrams continue to come. Presents arriving." These delighted new parents had daily assistance from their two maids and family cook, a graphic indication of the family's solid socioeconomic position.[19]

Although Jervis and Polly grew up in large rental properties on West Church Street and then in the ancestral house across from Park Church, the family spent summers at Quarry Farm. When Langdon's great-aunt Susan Crane died in 1924, Jervis's father inherited the property and made it the permanent family residence. The subsequent remodeling of the historic house, which included a major addition that contained a teak-paneled library with an imported Italian marble fireplace, created a comfortable, modern dwelling, and Jervis's own attachment to this historic place increased.[20]

In addition to a loving family life, another pleasurable diversion for Jervis's father involved hiking. As a young man he joined an informal group known as the Rambling Club, led by Elmira resident Rufus Stanley and sponsored by Park Church. "Jervis was full of zest for the long country walks," recalled his sister Ida, "and very happy in the companionship of the other young 'Ramblers' and their unique leader." And there were always those invigorating walks between Quarry Farm and downtown Elmira. There is little doubt that Jervis's lifelong enjoyment of walking came through his father.[21]

The blue-eyed, dark-haired Jervis entered a family that was functional, prosperous, civically involved, and thoroughly respected. As a result of either genetics or social conditioning, but likely both, he displayed personal characteristics that resembled his father, fraternal grandfather, and great-grandfather. Early on, Langdon became "extremely proud of his family," and for good reasons.[22]

Days of Youth

All evidence indicates that Jervis enjoyed his childhood. He benefited from doting parents who provided love, encouragement, structure, and financial security; it was a stable, nurturing family atmosphere. There were walks with his father, canoeing on the Chemung River, raising chickens in the backyard, playmates, including sister Polly, time with the relatives, especially "the cousins" and friends at Quarry Farm, and trains. Late in life when Jervis wrote an autobiographical sketch (in the third person), he recalled that "his home town of Elmira was a railroad center in the early days of the twentieth century, and even at night he could hear the freight trains making their passage through the valley with steam whistles protecting the many highway crossings." In this same piece he admitted that "the arrival of a freight train from the West, carrying perhaps 50 to 60 refrigerator cars loaded with California fruits and vegetables destined for the East Coast, was a real event, which young Langdon would take his father to witness—an occasion even

As a youngster Jervis played with his younger sister, Polly (left), and their first cousins, Olivia and Virginia Loomis. (Irene Langdon)

more important than the summer arrival of the circus train." At an early age Jervis loved trains.[23]

Although Jervis was close to his father, he became fond of several other older men, and they had "an enormous influence on him." One was Merle Dow Thompson (1879–1970). This prominent and popular resident of Elmira, who had graduated from Princeton University in 1902, spent much of his business career in banking, becoming a Marine Midland Trust Company executive. He also served as a director of the locally based Insular Lumber Company, a firm that had extensive interests in the Philippines. At the close of World War II this business connection gave Thompson an opportunity to spend time in Manila with Jervis, a meeting that both men cherished. Jervis related the story that Thompson enjoyed playing poker with him and fellow officers and "proceeded to take all to the cleaners!" Added Jervis, "Very popular with everyone. . . . For me he put my home town on the map!"[24]

And especially close to Jervis were Halsey Sayles (1876–1958), his mother's brother, and Edward Loomis (1865–1937), an uncle by marriage.

A successful and highly respected attorney in Elmira, Uncle Halsey came from a distinguished local family and had been educated at Princeton and the Columbia University Law School. "Although his practice was primarily trial and appeal work," noted the *Elmira Star-Gazette* following his death, "Mr. Sayles was an excellent lawyer in every field." Like others who influenced Jervis, Uncle Halsey was a kind, compassionate, and generous individual. "His pro bono work was legendary," and he was a pillar in Elmira's First Presbyterian Church, the Young Men's Christian Association, and the Arnot-Ogden Memorial Hospital. Moreover, Uncle Halsey "possessed a sharp wit, and whenever he was present there usually was much merriment." He and his wife, Julia, had two children, Henry and Ellen, but Jervis became an integral part of the immediate Sayles family.[25]

Uncle Edward had followed a considerably different career path than Uncle Halsey. Even though he also had formal legal training, having earned a law degree from Lafayette College, Uncle Edward became a railroader. He entered the industry as a member of the law department of Jay Gould's Denver & Rio Grande Railroad, but in 1894 he joined the Erie Railroad, where he took charge of the company's bituminous coal and lumber interests. Later he moved to the Lackawanna in a similar capacity, and in 1902 he became senior vice president at the Lehigh. "As vice president of the Lehigh, he established himself as one of the country's great, practical railroad executives," commented the *Elmira Star-Gazette.* "He became distinguished as a man who could think quickly and accurately and was just in his dealings with all his employees." Then in 1917 Uncle Edward assumed the Lehigh presidency and continued to excel as a railway executive.[26]

Jervis relished time spent with his kindly Uncle Edward. He eagerly anticipated trips with his family to New York City to visit the Loomises. At times Jervis and his father used the Loomis Manhattan apartment as a base for their activities, although the Loomises also had a home in suburban New Jersey. Jervis, though, particularly liked his uncle's railroad connections, most of all to the Lehigh shops and yards in nearby Sayre, Pennsylvania. Being closely tied to a top official gave Jervis special access to these teaming facilities. His repeated visits to Sayre allowed him "to become friendly with most of the employees and usually [he] could catch a ride [to and from Elmira] on a Lehigh train."[27]

Jervis also admired his Uncle Edward's commitment to the study of railway economics. In the 1930s the Edward Eugene Loomis Foundation at Lafayette College brought to campus distinguished speakers in the field. In

ABOVE: "Off to a picnic" is how this ca. 1912 photograph is labeled. Jervis joins his sister and the Loomis cousins, perhaps at Quarry Farm. Jervis said the girls always bossed him around, yet they were always close. (Irene Langdon)

LEFT: Jervis and his grandmother, Ida Clark Langdon, about 1915 in Elmira. (Irene Langdon)

1939, for example, William James Cunningham, the James J. Hill Professor of Transportation at Harvard University, presented a public lecture that the University of Pennsylvania Press subsequently published as *The Present Railroad Crisis,* a thoughtful analysis of industry finance and surely one that Jervis would have endorsed.[28]

Much of Jervis's formative life involved education. He first attended Elmira's Public School No. 2 (later named Booth School after the physician who had assisted in his birth), but at age 14, he went to boarding school. Rather than selecting either the Gunnery or Cascadilla, continuing family connections, his parents chose The Hill School in Pottstown, Pennsylvania. Noted his father in his diary entry for July 7, 1919: "Wrote Hill School asking admittance for Jervis Jr." While not the most prestigious boarding school in the Northeast, this institution, founded in 1851 by the Reverend Matthew Meigs, at the time offered a solid, personalized nondenominational education to approximately 500 young men.

On September 23, 1919, Jervis began his four years at The Hill. On that day his father wrote: "Jervis and I got breakfast at Bellevue Stratford [Hotel in Philadelphia] and went up to Pottstown on 10:30 train from Reading Terminal. Fine reception at 'The Hill.'" Before leaving home, Jervis's parents had outfitted him with the proper wardrobe, including a stylish Brooks Brothers suit that his father helped to select. Since the school required a coat and tie for classes and most other functions, Jervis started his lifelong habit of wearing such attire and being particular about his clothes and overall appearance.[29]

The Hill School was a positive experience. Some boys who attended boarding school suffered severe homesickness, but that was not the case for Jervis. Perhaps the reason for the easy transition from Elmira to Pottstown was that "he was a self-contained person," able to cope with separation from family and hometown friends and the trials and tribulations of private-school life. Furthermore, The Hill offered a supportive environment, being the first school in the country to have faculty live with students in their campus housing. And the Langdons paid visits, often taking Jervis and classmates to Philadelphia for dinner and the theater.[30]

Jervis flourished in his new educational environment. Bright and conscientious, he excelled in the classroom, especially enjoying history, language, and literature courses. "He had an exemplary record at The Hill." Moreover, this tall and lanky lad participated in various athletic endeavors, including basketball and tennis. He won a silver trophy in The Hill School spring tennis tournament in 1920. He lived up to the school's ideal of preparing "mind, body, and spirit."

The football team at The Hill School is captured by a photographer, ca. 1920. Jervis is the team manager, dressed in white, on the far right. Competitive tennis, however, was his favorite sport while a student at The Hill. (Irene Langdon)

But Jervis's last days at The Hill were hardly happy. The school had a practice of excusing its best students from final examinations, and Jervis was one of several boys winning this privilege for the spring 1923 term. Some of his friends decided to celebrate while other colleagues studied for their tests. When Jervis arrived at the party, he discovered that there had been champagne toasts. Alcohol was strictly forbidden at The Hill; after all, national prohibition had been in effect since passage of the Eighteenth Amendment a few years earlier. Unfortunately for Jervis and those in attendance, a school official discovered what had transpired. Although Jervis had not touched a drop of champagne, he was sent home with the others and not permitted to participate in the graduation ceremonies. Jervis was devastated. And his parents, who were "strong on discipline," were not pleased either when they learned what had happened, first from a telegram sent by

Jervis and then another communiqué from Dr. Boyd Edwards, the school's new headmaster. Edwards quickly followed with a full letter of explanation. When Jervis arrived back in Elmira, he father noted that he looked "terrible." After learning the details, the family felt that the punishment was wholly unjustified based on the degree of Jervis's involvement. "His [Jervis's] story shows the school taking an incomprehensible position," wrote the senior Langdon in his diary for June 1, 1923. Although he protested, the ejection decision stood, even though the headmaster admitted that "Jerv did not belong to [the] drinkers."[31]

He had ended his secondary education on a sour note, but he was fully prepared for higher education. Although the number of men and women who entered college remained relatively small, despite having increased dramatically during the 1920s, Jervis had the ability, training, and financial support to attend any top-level college or university. He entered Cornell in the fall of 1923 and would join other freshmen who wore the little numeral beanies with 1927 emblazoned on the visors. Cornell was a growing Ivy League school, with its more than 5,000 students and an institution that his father so loved.[32]

The Langdons worried about what impact Jervis's failure to attend graduation at The Hill would have on his admission to Cornell. But his father was proactive, noting in his diary for June 10, 1923: "Talked with Mr. Van Cleef about Jerv's trouble and how it would affect his getting into Cornell. He wants a statement of the facts." Apparently no further problems developed with the admissions process. The senior Langdon's forthright attack nicely revealed a common family trait.

College life went smoothly, although at times the senior Langdon rightly worried that his son was stretching himself too far. Early on, Jervis was assuming the role of "big man on campus," and that meant involvement in a variety of activities outside the classroom. A liberal arts major, he was mostly an average student, although he earned some high marks. Yet the 1920s was not a time of rampant, even shameless grade inflation, as it would become in the 1960s and later, and the granting of the "gentleman's C" was common in elite schools. Jervis's best subjects were government and history; his worst were geology and physiology. He also heightened his academic experience by attending the London School of Economics in the summer of 1925 and Dijon University in France the following summer, where he earned six hours of French-language credit. During Jervis's senior year at Cornell, a professor observed that "Langdon is a young man of push, of initiative and of a markedly radical bent in all his thinking." The latter comment suggests that the Cornell experience had caused Jervis to question some of his assumptions about life, although he remained committed to the family heritage of concern for the worthy underdog and dedication to bringing about societal uplift.[33]

As a recognition for his innate intelligence, stellar character, and prowess on the tennis court, having won several tennis championships his freshman year, Jervis was nominated by Cornell for a Rhodes Scholarship. A faculty committee believed that Jervis was fully qualified for this prestigious honor. If selected, he would continue his studies at Oxford University. Created by the will of the British entrepreneur, colonial pioneer, and philanthropist Cecil Rhodes (1853–1902), this scholarship was awarded based on "academic ability; sporting activity; qualities of personal rectitude, strength and compassion; and sense of the public good." This criteria transcended the purely academic. On October 30, 1925, Jervis had a formal interview with representatives of the Rhodes Trust in New York City, but in December he learned that "a boy named Chase of Hamilton College" had won the appointment.[34]

Jervis was at a disadvantage in the competition being a Cornellian, not because of the quality of the institution but rather due to the plentiful supply of outstanding candidates in New York. Under terms of the Rhodes Trust, each American state and territory was eligible to have an annual recipient. New York, with its large number of prestigious schools, both public and private, made for keen competition among nominees. Indeed, the power of states to select inhibited domination by students from elite eastern colleges and universities. "Because of the inequality of population between the different states," observed the American secretary of the Rhodes Trust, "each year many were rejected in populous states who would have been better scholars than those selected for other states." Jervis was one such person.[35]

Just as he had done at The Hill, Jervis became involved in nonacademic endeavors. Perhaps his lackluster grades during his sophomore year reflect a preoccupation with extracurricular interests. Following World War I, college fraternities nationwide experienced considerable popularity; existing Greek organizations expanded, and new fraternities appeared. Jervis became a member of the New York Gamma Chapter of Kappa Alpha, the nation's first collegiate social fraternity, founded in 1825 at Union College in Schenectady, New York. Understandably this organization would appeal to Jervis; his father had been a Kappa Alpha member "to the core," and this selective fraternity always sought an aristocracy of merit rather than merely an aristocracy of privilege. Apparently Jervis enjoyed his campus associations with his fraternity brothers, and several were frequent guests at Quarry Farm. For years Jervis attached his solid-gold Kappa Alpha key to his favorite pocket watch, but in time he relegated the key to a dresser drawer. Later in life, unlike most railroad executives who had belonged to collegiate fraternities, he failed to list his Kappa Alpha affiliation. Similarly, Jervis never bragged about being a popular student at Cornell. For example, he was one of five members of his junior class to be elected to the prestigious student council, and he was named to Sphinx Head, an organization reserved for the most respected men of the senior class.[36]

While an undergraduate at Cornell, Jervis experienced lighter moments. He enjoyed sporting events, especially football games at Schoellkoph Field, the annual Spring Day festival, and fraternity and all-college social events. Jervis took pleasure in the ownership of a car, although he described the vehicle as "an ancient Dodge runabout." Shortly after his death, a son told a reporter from the *Elmira Star-Gazette* that his father "was something of a party boy at Cornell," and added that "they had two competing drinking societies and I think he joined them both," perhaps a garbled reference to Jervis chairing the Sophomore Smoker Committee. But remembrances of his final days at The Hill may have meant that Jervis was a member who largely abstained. There is no evidence that alcohol ever became a problem for Jervis. He may have been merely caught up in a widely accepted culture of drink. "Jolly journeys were made to the wine country westward, where gallon jugs were passed out of vineyardists' back door," commented university historian Morris Bishop about student life in the 1920s. "In the fraternities the no-liquor rule, hitherto respected, went the way of the law of the United States. Previously drinking and dancing had been rigorously separated; now they were blent, and even the girls had their nips from the boys' hip flasks." Jervis also began to date, which really would have been much more challenging at The Hill but not at the coeducational Cornell with its conducive atmosphere for social interactions.[37]

The nonacademic activity that likely produced for Jervis the greatest satisfaction involved his association with the campus newspaper, the *Cornell Daily Sun*. Although failing to gain a Rhodes Scholarship during his junior year, toward the end of his sophomore year he had won election as an associate editor. "The competition is a short one, lasting about eight weeks, and depending upon the ability shown and the closeness of the leaders, one or more men will be recommended to the Board of Directors [of the *Sun*] for election to the editorial board as associate editors." At the start of fall semester 1925, Jervis became one of eight associate editors, joining three others from his class.[38]

The *Cornell Daily Sun* was not the typical collegiate newspaper. Most campus papers were published on either a weekly or semiweekly schedule during the school year, but the *Sun* appeared every weekday throughout the academic semesters. More significantly, the *Sun* developed a readership beyond the immediate campus community. "The *Sun* was the morning newspaper of Ithaca, N.Y.," wrote Jervis for a presentation to a class reunion in 1992. "And as a member of the Associated Press, [the *Sun*] had a circulation among the townspeople as well as students and faculty members." As such the newspaper developed a sizable number of diverse advertisers, ranging from local clothiers who catered to students (at times offering pricy raccoon coats and dress suits) to railroads that served the Cornell community. The *Sun* grabbed the opportunity to take large (and presumably profitable) advertisements from the passenger department of the Lackawanna when in the fall of 1926 the railroad introduced the *New Whitelight Limited*, which linked Buffalo and New York City "with drawing room sleeping cars for Ithaca."[39]

Most of the contributions that Jervis made to the *Sun* as an associate editor involved news reporting, although he may have written an occasional editorial. The newspaper was hardly a radical publication, taking a consistently moderate position on national, state, local, and campus issues. Whether it was the desire to boost school spirit for the Big Red Team's gridiron clash with Dartmouth or Pennsylvania or to scold students for their poor attendance at public lectures, the *Sun* performed its mission well. And news from the wires of the Associated Press informed all readers, student or otherwise. The tone of the *Sun* properly reflected the incumbent administration of President Livingston Farrand, for "the faculty was happy during this era of good feeling, under the benevolent gaze of the President, and the generally benevolent gaze of the Deans." Students also felt good about being a part of Cornell's life.[40]

Jervis emerged as a star member of the *Sun* staff. In the spring of 1926, he won election as editor-in-chief, a campus job that provided prestige and a modest income. Langdon remembered this position offering "compensation for those essentials of student existence such as a car and a very occasional week-end trip to the Big Apple." At the time of the personnel change, the incumbent editor-in-chief wrote: "To the new editors and managers we . . . save a parting wish for their success and the hope that they will continue to attempt to serve the Ithaca-Cornell community as best they may even as we have tried, even though imperfectly."[41]

And that is what happened under Jervis's leadership. The *Sun* continued with its hard news content supplied by wire service dispatches, commentary from collegiate exchange newspapers, and editorials about often mundane campus matters. Even though personally part of the Greek community, Jervis thought that there was an excessive focus on fraternity life and a critical need to create a "dignified and academic atmosphere" on campus. "Everyone talks, eats, and sleeps [fraternity] rushing," he observed on September

23, 1926. "In fact, this occupation seems almost to be our one excuse for collegiate existence."

But Jervis realized correctly that there was a problem with traditional collegiate-based editorials. "There were student concerns to be discussed, but there was a limit to these," he recalled. "World affairs and national and local politics could also be tackled, but the efforts were usually too amateurish for adult consumption and the students did not care." Still Jervis was responsible for producing an editorial page five times a week. He thought that a solution might involve stirring up controversy and receiving letters-to-the-editor that would not only fill space but that would provoke students, faculty, and townsfolk.[42]

Near the end of the fall semester Jervis and his associates at the *Sun* struck gold. What became known as the "Five Bewildered Freshmen" letter appeared in the issue of December 6 and "gave rise to one of the grandest philosophical discussions that Cornell University has ever had":[43]

We are five freshmen who live in a boarding house together. We are students in the College of Arts and Sciences, and as Christmas draws near, and we are about to pack up and go home for the holidays. We've been wondering just what progress we could report to our parents. We are all taking about the same courses—the regular ones for incoming students, but in a bull session we had last night we all discovered that we were suffering from a common ailment. We hadn't found out what it was all about. And by that we mean that we don't see why we should be taking the courses that we are. We don't see any connection between them. We don't see where they are going to lead us, we are just fulfilling certain hour requirements, it seems. What's it all about?

And as a last resort we decided to write The Sun in an appeal to discover just what all these courses mean and how they fit together in what is generally termed the educational process.

—*Five Unhappy and Bewildered Freshmen*[44]

The letter caused a modest sensation. "It inspired a flood of responses to fill vacant spaces on the editorial page," happily remembered Jervis. "It also served as 'indisputable' evidence of the crying need for an 'orientation course' to be provided by the University for the enlightenment of freshmen and their guidance in picking elective courses of instruction—a popular subject for *Sun* editorials for several years."[45]

In addition to creating opportunities for writing editorials, a delightful controversy ensued. Responses came from a variety of readers and included a thoughtful reply from a distinguished Cornell scholar, historian Carl Becker:

> I was interested in the letter of Five Bewildered Freshmen and in the discussion it gave rise to. The freshmen say they have been engaged in the intellectual life for more than two months and don't know what it's all about. This is bad, but who is to blame? Some say the students are to blame, and some say the professors. What is to be done about it? You suggest a foundation or an orientation course such as is given in other universities.
>
> For my part, I don't blame anyone—not freshmen, certainly. It's not especially the student's fault if he doesn't know what it is all about. If he did, he wouldn't need to come to college. That's why, I have always supposed, young people come to college—to get some notion, even if only a glimmering, of what it's about. They come to get "oriented." But why expect to be oriented in two months or a year? The whole four years college course is a course in orientation. It isn't a very satisfactory one, indeed. Four years isn't enough. Life itself is scarcely long enough to enable one to find out what it's all about.
>
> The Five Bewildered Freshmen have got out of their course more than they know. It has made them ask a question—What is it all about? That is a pertinent question. I have been asking it for 35 years, and I am still as bewildered as they are.[46]

Jervis probably received an adrenalin rush with the instant hit of the "Five Bewildered Freshmen" letter. But working on the *Sun* also allowed him to meet intellectually stimulating individuals who came to campus. In the spring of 1927, he had an opportunity to talk with Walter Lippmann (1889–1974), commonly hailed as the greatest journalist of his age. At the time of their meeting Lippmann regularly wrote editorials for the *New York World* and made masterful contributions to other thought-provoking publications, including the *New Republic* and *Vanity Fair*. The contact with Lippmann excited Jervis. When his father came to campus on April 28 to have dinner with him in the elegant dining rooms at William Straight Hall, the University's student union which had recently opened, Jervis praised Lippmann to the hilt, announcing that he would like to attend graduate school at Columbia University, where he could study "American history, Politics and Economics, etc." About the same time Jervis contemplated a journalistic career with the *World* or some other New York City newspaper. He seemingly longed to become part of the intellectual life that Columbia and Gotham offered.[47]

The last days for Jervis as a Cornell undergraduate came in June 1927 and would be far different from those at The Hill. On June 10 he participated in

Class Day exercises, taking an important role, in part because he had been named class historian. His proud father pronounced the program as "very good." Three days later, the lengthy and stately graduation ceremonies took place, attended by his parents, family, and friends. And in the midst of these pleasurable activities, Robert Cushman, a professor of government, wrote to provide constructive criticism of a senior paper, noting, "I have given you an A on this paper which seems to me an excellent piece of work. It is interesting, well organized and well written and seems to me to be a really valuable survey of the field covered."[48]

The Cornell years had been good for Jervis. He extracted a solid, well-rounded education, and he received much-deserved recognition. Arguably Jervis left more of a mark as editor-in-chief of the *Sun* than most of his immediate predecessors and successors. At least, in the words of Wallace Notestein, a renowned historian of seventeenth-century Europe, "he has made that paper an interesting and lively sheet." Looking back, Jervis cherished his foray into journalism. Moreover, the opportunity to develop and express thoughts while associated with the *Sun* became valuable skills in his future role as law student, commerce lawyer, and railroad president. "He understood the power of words," a friend once recalled. Surely, too, the leadership experience at the newspaper paid additional dividends; after all, as editor he needed to judge an individual's ability and reliability and to encourage teamwork.[49]

Developing Career

With sheepskin in hand, Jervis needed an occupation. He might return to Elmira and work for his father, but that option was probably never seriously considered. There were the possibilities of graduate school at Columbia University or maybe a newspaper job in New York City. Then there was the railroad industry, and that would be his career path. In the entry of his father's diary for September 28, 1927, there is this brief statement: "Jerv wants to change plans—No Columbia but to work at Lehigh." Surely, the Langdons did not fret about their son's decision, knowing that there existed a close family connection to the company and that the railroads, although heavily regulated and starting to feel the sting of motor vehicle competition, remained an essential national industry that benefited a vast array of shippers and travelers. For most Americans up until the immediate post–World War II period, railroads were a visible and vital part of their lives.

In November 1927 Jervis accepted an entry-level position with the Lehigh in New York City. This 1,362-mile railroad served New Jersey, New York, and

Pennsylvania with a heavy-duty main line that stretched between Jersey City and Buffalo. Long backed by the investment banking house of J. P. Morgan, the road functioned independently of other carriers, although by the 1930s the powerful PRR owned a substantial block of Lehigh stock. Throughout this time the Lehigh hauled an impressive volume of coal, grain, building materials, and high-grade merchandise, and before the 1930s it experienced considerable profitability. Unlike scores of railroads during the Great Depression, the property avoided bankruptcy.[50]

When Jervis became a Lehigh employee, he started at the "very bottom" of the corporate ladder, a long-standing tradition in the railroad industry. As he told David Vrooman in 1996, "I was a clerk in the Office of the Foreign Freight Agent . . . in the Produce Exchange, the lower part of Manhattan; it was just off Broadway." These duties, however, hardly required a Cornell education. "My job was to be an errand boy and also [work] on the bills of lading and all paperwork in connection with the inbound export traffic. I was to just make sure that it was in order and to classify it in certain very elementary ways that didn't require any knowledge other than an ability to read." Next Jervis became a clerk in the office of the operating vice president at company headquarters at 143 Liberty Street.[51]

Jervis was hardly paid handsomely. His salary of $20 per week was barely enough to survive in New York City, and Jervis and his apartment mate, a friend from Cornell who worked for the telephone company, eagerly anticipated parental visits that inevitably included a hearty dinner in a good restaurant. Otherwise, the two roommates would take most of their meals at a local beanery. He told Vrooman, "You'd get a meal for 60 or 70 cents and the reason they were so cheap was because there was no meat." Yet Jervis liked his entry-level position, being intrigued by the heavy volume of grain that moved from Canada to the Port of New York over the Canadian National Railways through the Buffalo gateway connection with the Lehigh. "It was very interesting and instructive."

In Jervis's mind the only negative aspect of the clerk's job involved neither salary nor assignments but rather that Edward Loomis was president. Jervis's colleagues in the downtown freight office knew about the family connection, and "I didn't like that." Admittedly, Jervis was in an awkward position in the workplace, but, of course, he still adored his uncle.

The Loomis relationship, though, provided positive dimensions. One involved a long-remembered encounter. A close friend of his uncle was George F. Baker, who headed the mighty First National Bank of New York. Knowing of Baker's financial ties, Jervis decided to take his modest paycheck to the bank, "physically just a very small bank . . . on the corner of Wall Street and Broadway," and open an account. Much to Jervis's surprise and embarrassment, this was not a typical banking institution, since it required a minimum deposit of $10,000 to start transactions. While in this "very important financial institution," Jervis encountered Baker, and the kindly president offered to open a special account, but "I told him no. I didn't want that because I couldn't see doing business with a bank where the minimum was $10,000."

Jervis became "friendly" with George Baker, and this connection had a profound impact on his professional life. During a conversation with an assistant of Baker's, Jervis was reminded that the railroad industry was heavily regulated and that "if you wanted to get ahead fast in the railroad business," an individual needed legal training. Initially receptive to the suggestion, Jervis still gave the matter considerable thought. Predictably he talked with his Uncle Edward about law school, and "he thought it was not a bad idea," although Jervis once recalled that "my uncle advised me to be either an engineer or a lawyer if I wanted to succeed in railroading." (Much later in life, Jervis suggested that there were three ways to prepare for a career as a railroad executive: "Be a certified public accountant, study engineering, or study law.") Furthermore, Uncle Edward had told Jervis that "he could not remember a year in his career when railroads did not seem to be on the brink of collapse," and that observation made Jervis wonder "whether I had made a mistake." And he doubtlessly consulted Uncle Halsey, that skilled attorney. In late spring 1928, the Lehigh granted Jervis a leave of absence, with the expectation that with diploma in hand and the New York state bar examination passed, he would join the company's legal department. So law school it would be.[52]

Rather than seek legal training in New York City or nearby, Jervis returned to the familiarity of his alma mater. Cornell offered a solid law program and had received attention for admitting women, an admissions policy that began when the school opened in 1887. Still, law schools in the late 1920s, including Cornell, were mostly male preserves.[53]

Jervis encountered no difficulties with his professional schooling. Indeed, he earned a top grade in a transportation and communications course in the fall semester of 1929, surely an offering that he enjoyed. As with his earlier secondary and collegiate education, the senior Langdon agreed to finance law school. But Jervis went through the program rapidly, reducing costs somewhat. At that time the Cornell Law School allowed students to take an accelerated schedule. "In those days they had a method in which you could save a year by going to three summer schools, not just six weeks, but really the whole summer," he later related. "Three of those whole summers were the equivalent of a year and I got through in two years and a third and was assigned to the class of 1930." Specifically, Jervis took law classes during the first and second session of summer school in 1928, attended full time during the academic years 1928–29 and 1929–30, and enrolled in the second session of the 1929 summer school and both summer sessions in 1930.

With his second degree from Cornell, officially awarded on September 24, 1930, Jervis returned to the Lehigh. Shortly thereafter he passed the rigorous New York State bar examination. This newly minted lawyer received as his principal assignment in the railroad's New York City general offices the complicated and always vexing New Jersey tax cases.[54]

Not only did Jervis have a new job and career path, but his personal life changed considerably. While at Cornell he had fallen in love with Jean Gordon Bancroft, who was also a Cornell graduate, Class of 1930, and a resident of Ithaca. As a student, Jean joined Kappa Kappa Gamma sorority, served as women's editor for the *Cornell Daily Sun,* and played golf. Her father, Wilder Dwight Bancroft (1867–1953), a chemist trained at Harvard College and the University of Leipzig, had been a member of the Cornell faculty since 1895. He became a renowned scholar and was widely considered to be the founder of physical chemistry in the United States. As a lieutenant colonel in the U.S. Chemical Warfare Service during World War I, he helped to perfect the gas mask and aided in the development of poisonous gases. And Jean's fraternal great-grandfather was the distinguished American historian, presidential cabinet officer, European diplomat, and founder of the U.S. Naval Academy, George Bancroft (1800–1891).

The Bancroft-Langdon wedding became a social event in Ithaca, bringing together two prominent area families. On September 19, 1931, at 7:30 PM, a large number of family and friends gathered at Sage Chapel on the Cornell campus to witness the exchange of marriage vows. Jervis's sister, Polly, a recent Smith College graduate, served as a bridesmaid, and George Bancroft, Jean's older brother, performed the honors of best man. A reception followed in Willard Straight Hall, and soon the newlyweds left for their honeymoon in Hot Springs, Virginia.[55]

The future for Jervis Langdon seemed promising, indeed. Although the worst depression of the twentieth century was taking hold at the time of his marriage, he had a secure and rewarding job with the Lehigh. He possessed an impressive Ivy League education and all of those personal characteristics that would contribute to his success in the railroad industry. No one would deny that he was smart, diligent, resourceful, principled, honest, even-tempered, and considerate of others. As for the latter, "There was an inherent kindness in the male Langdon genes." Jervis's personal lifestyle pointed toward longtime good health; he continued to enjoy tennis and walking, maintained his weight (approximately 165 pounds on his 6'2" frame), gave up his earlier smoking habit, and exhibited moderation with intoxicants. But surely in 1931 Jervis had no idea how his life would unfold.[56]

2 Railroad Lawyer

Getting Started

The decision to pursue legal training at Cornell University satisfied Jervis Langdon; he had no regrets about temporarily leaving the Lehigh Valley Railroad (Lehigh) and resuming academic life. Still, even without a law degree, Jervis could have climbed the corporate ladder at the Lehigh or at some other railroad. A contemporary, Milton McInnes, for one, who also came from an upper-middle-class family and graduated with a liberal arts degree from Dartmouth College in 1930, immediately thereafter took an entry-level position with the Erie Railroad in New York City and advanced steadily through the operating department, eventually becoming a high-ranking official. In 1961, the same year that Jervis became head of the Baltimore & Ohio Railroad (B&O), McInnes assumed the presidency of the recently formed Erie-Lackawanna Railroad.[1]

The principal assignments that Jervis received on his return to Lehigh headquarters involved contentious and detailed tax matters, although until he passed the New York state bar examination, he served as a law clerk. With professional certification in hand, Jervis took on more important tasks. An eager learner, he mostly wrote first drafts of pleadings and

29

briefs. As Jervis told David Vrooman in 1996, "This was time well spent."[2]

In the early 1930s the Lehigh and most railroads and utilities in New Jersey faced hefty tax obligations, based on high rates of property assessments. They confronted assessments of 100 percent valuation whereas other firms usually had just 65 percent. This seemingly unfair policy resulted in these quasi-public corporations annually paying millions of dollars more than most other large businesses. Part of the explanation involved the result of the state's potent progressive movement early in the twentieth century. Perceived tax dodging committed by railroads and utilities, particularly the Public Service Corporation of New Jersey, an electric power, interurban, and streetcar combine, aroused the citizenry to demand stronger regulation. Alert politicians signed on, realizing that if they ignored the matter, there might be negative consequences at the polls. But for some railroads, including the Lehigh, the problem involved more the actions of the flamboyant and all-powerful "boss" of Jersey City, "I am the law" Frank Hague, who for 30 years ruled with an iron fist. During the Great Depression, the Hague organization reached the zenith of its influence, causing Jersey City to become widely (and correctly) known as "Hagueville." This dynamo in Jersey City, Hudson County, and New Jersey politics pushed for increased taxation on rail properties, focusing on those located along the city's busy waterfront on the west bank of the North (Hudson) River. Hague sought to generate as much income as possible for city coffers, allowing him to please his constituency, most of all small homeowners who benefited from low property assessments, and to lubricate his political machine. His political clout permitted him to select loyal members of the Hudson County Tax Board, the State Board of Tax Appeals, and the New Jersey Public Service Commission.[3]

Although railroads that operated in the Jersey City area continued to face excessive taxation until the 1960s, the Lehigh and affiliated Lehigh Valley Harbor Terminal, through assistance provided by Jervis, joined forces with the Central Railroad of New Jersey (Jersey Central) to charge discrimination, the first serious challenge made by railroads to the tax policy. In 1932 the companies, confronting sharply reduced income from their freight and passenger operations, refused to pay taxes levied on "second-class" property, namely, docks, terminals, and rail yards. Attorneys for these carriers had attempted to have the Pennsylvania Railroad (PRR) join the suit, but "with their usual arrogance they stayed out." Remarked Jervis: "I worked on that [case] almost exclusively for the first year and a half . . . and then after that periodically from time to time." Shortly before Jervis left Edward Loomis's road for the New York Central Railroad (NYC) in 1934, the Lehigh and Jersey Central succeeded in having the federal court temporarily enjoin the collection of those property taxes. But ultimately the railroads lost. In the early 1940s, though, some tax relief occurred during the governorship of Charles Edison, who bravely asserted his independence from the Hague machine. Still, as late as the 1960s, railroad property taxes in New Jersey were about five times the national average.[4]

In the summer of 1934, Jervis joined the New York Central System, whose five principal units—New York Central; Michigan Central; Boston & Albany; Cleveland, Cincinnati, Chicago & St. Louis (Big Four); and Pittsburgh & Lake Erie—offered extensive interregional freight and passenger service. Compared to the Lehigh, the NYC was a giant. This New York City–based railroad, with more than 11,000 miles of line, linked Boston, Buffalo, Chicago, Cleveland, Cincinnati, Columbus, Detroit, Indianapolis, New York, Pittsburgh, and St. Louis and served hundreds of lesser cities. From the standpoint of mileage, the NYC was the largest of the eastern trunk systems, although in terms of revenues it was second to the PRR. Only the major coal-carrying roads of the region exceeded NYC's freight tonnage. The traveling public knew the NYC for its crack passenger service, which featured such legendary name trains as the *Empire State Express, Southwestern Limited,* and the *Twentieth Century Limited,* and marveled at the road's long stretches of four-track main line, rolling stock characterized by muscular Mohawk-type (4-8-2) steam locomotives and that imposing monument to the railway age, Grand Central Terminal in New York City.[5]

Through his developing legal contracts among New York City railroads, Jervis learned that the NYC sought a commerce counsel at corporate headquarters on Lexington Avenue. By having friends who knew Jacob "Jake" Aronson, vice president of law at the NYC, Jervis obtained an interview and subsequently received an attractive offer. No doubt his expanding legal skills, positive personality, high moral standards, and Cornell pedigree collectively helped to advance his professional career.

The position that Jervis took at the NYC focused on regulatory issues, particularly freight rates; tax matters would not be involved. By the 1930s, American railroads had been heavily regulated since the progressive era and needed to cope with a variety of statutes administered by the Interstate Commerce Commission (ICC), most notably the Hepburn Act of 1906 and the Mann-Elkins Act, passed four years later. Steady federal intrusion into the affairs of the carriers had created a regulatory environment where the NYC and other railroads found themselves in straitjackets. Moreover, the industry faced the tortuous maze of state regulation.[6]

Jervis was pleased with his new post, wanting the job for several reasons. The subject of freight rates was close to railroad operations and much different from property taxation, which really had nothing to do with the day-to-day functioning of the rail industry. Furthermore, the NYC nearly doubled his salary, and even though New York City and the nation remained in the depths of the Great Depression, living expenses were far from dirt cheap in the better sections of Gotham.

On May 17, 1933, his wife, Jean, gave birth to their first child, a daughter, Lee. With increased family responsibilities, the added income was appreciated. Then there was that relationship with Uncle Edward, who remained Lehigh chief executive until shortly before his death in 1937. "I was old enough to realize that I shouldn't stay at the Lehigh," Jervis remembered. "If anything, the dice were loaded against me because my uncle would make sure I didn't get any special favors."[7]

Initially the NYC legal department did not give its new hire much responsibility. After all, Jervis had hardly grasped the complexities of ICC rate-making. "At first I had the smaller rate cases where the complaint was for unreasonableness of the rate in the past, and they [shippers] wanted reparation. I tried those cases almost by the dozen and fairly successfully." But as Jervis became better versed in ICC affairs, more important assignments followed. And on May 15, 1935, he strengthened his position by becoming licensed to practice before the U.S. Supreme Court.

Since the ICC affected all aspects of the railroad enterprise, carriers, including the NYC, worked closely with other roads, even their principal competitors. The ICC held firm to the principle that each commodity required its own rate, which was subject to public approval. Once Jervis had cut his teeth on basic regulatory matters, the NYC named him to a variety of regional and interregional rate committees. Since freight traffic might move over long distances, whether from a manufacturing plant on NYC rails to a city in the South or from a grain terminal on the Great Plains to the Port of New York, companies collectively needed to figure out precisely what the tariffs should be in order to attract the business and to make a reasonable profit. Railroads did this in the face of growing opposition from a maturing motor carrier industry that frequently protested these interstate rates, prompting the ICC to suspend increases until an investigation was held. This process might take a year or longer. Usually several attorneys from the affected carriers would serve on these ad hoc rate committees. "One lawyer or two had the chief responsibility and had to put the case together and write the briefs and make the oral argument," related Jervis. It was detailed and painstaking work, albeit essential for the well-being of the NYC and the industry. Moreover, volume was enormous. Commonly, though, representatives from the traffic department gave pointers to the legal personnel on which rate cases were the most pressing, and a prioritization occurred.

Although for most of Jervis's career at the NYC he was involved in a succession of rate cases, there were other duties to perform, ranging from service orders to operating contracts. He was also assigned to participate in several line abandonment petitions. During the 1920s and 1930s, a number of financially troubled shortlines folded and larger roads started to shed little-used and money-losing appendages. In 1916 the scope of the national railroad network, including steam and electric interurbans, had peaked. That year steam carriers operated 254,251 miles, and once the federalization of World War I ended in March 1920, contraction accelerated. By 1936, steam-road mileage stood at 240,104, and on the eve of World War II it would drop to 231,971. The NYC focused its downsizing on trackage in Upstate New York, including the Thendara–Old Fort, Carter-Raquette, and Tupper Lake Junction–Helena lines. "They were originally built for [the] lumber [market], but lumber had all moved," Jervis told Vrooman. "There was very little of anything at all left up there, about 100 miles of line that they wanted to abandon." In an imaginative move, Jervis had the shipping sites extensively photographed, revealing graphically that there were no sound economic reasons to retain this trackage, that this was "empty territory." The hearings conducted before ICC examiners went smoothly, and the NYC received permission to retire the unwanted trackage. Jervis recalled, "The New York Central was so pleased because this reduced their mileage [and] . . . all the factors that were done on a mileage per road basis were increased because the total was less."[8]

The final assignment that Jervis received at the NYC involved some of the company's largest and best customers, mainly steel mills. As with the majority of rate matters, more than a single road was affected: "A lot of Chicago railroads [were] involved in this." This litigation, known as Ex Parte 104, was watched closely by both carriers and shippers. The ICC decided that the current practice of roads bringing and picking up inbound and outbound cars at customers' gates and then having these firms spot this equipment on the appropriate private sidings with their own locomotives violated commerce statutes. What troubled the ICC was that the NYC and other carriers gave customers generous allowances for performing these switching chores. Regulators considered the pricing to be beyond the scope of the line-haul rate, contending that these financial arrangements were illegal rebates. Again working with the NYC legal staff and representatives from other roads and American Steel Foundries, a trade association, Jervis wrote the principal brief. The railroads lost before the ICC, however, and that eventually caused the U.S. Supreme Court to consider the case, with Jervis preparing part of that all-critical legal document. Jervis, though, left the NYC before the high court sustained the ICC's decision.[9]

The skills that Jervis displayed in Ex Parte 104 brought him to the attention of other railroad executives. Silas Good, who served as vice president of traffic for the Chesapeake & Ohio Railway (C&O), was one individual who found Jervis's work impressive. His railroad faced similar problems with rates charged to large manufacturers, in particular a steel plant located in Ashland, Kentucky. "So I guess . . . [Good] persuaded somebody in the Law Department of the C&O to get in touch with me and offer me a job and . . . soon the C&O . . . wanted me to . . . be [an] assistant general attorney." The offer, Jervis told Vrooman, came "one day out of the blue." In October 1936, George Doswell Brook, the C&O president "and a very fine guy," officially extended the offer. Jervis quickly accepted. The explanation was simple. "I was asked to do essentially the same thing for [the C&O]. . . . And it paid three times what I was getting with the Central." He added, "I was very fond of the Central, but I couldn't get them to match what the C&O was offering. This was in the Great Depression, and the C&O was a rare thing at that time—a very prosperous railroad." Jervis again made a crucial career decision. After accepting the C&O invitation, he relocated his family to Richmond, Virginia.

At the NYC Jervis had had a rich variety of job assignments. He benefited from his repeated exposures to the complexities of the regulatory process and how he might best defend his employer. "I had a chance to see and study and deal with almost every phase of the overall operation." The nearly two years at the NYC contributed considerably to Jervis's developing career as a railroad lawyer.[10]

C&O Lawyer

In 1936 when Jervis accepted the C&O appointment as a commerce lawyer, he joined a railroad that was experiencing a host of internal and external problems, yet had a bright future. While avoiding receivership during the Great Depression, the C&O suffered from the economic disruptions caused by the financial and related problems associated with the Alleghany Corporation. This giant holding company controlled the property and was the handiwork of two talented Cleveland brothers, Oris Paxton and Mantis James Van Sweringen, who were known as O. P. and M. J., always in that order, or the Vans.[11]

For more than a decade before Jervis's employment, the Vans had played a vital part in the life of the C&O, having gained working control in the early 1920s. This largely coal-hauling railroad (about three-quarters of its freight tonnage were mine products) stretched from the Atlantic tidewater to the Great Lakes. Specifically, the C&O main line connected Newport News, Virginia, with Chicago, and served such cities as Richmond, Virginia, Charleston and Huntington, West Virginia, and Cincinnati, Ohio. And the C&O operated a major line between Ashland, Kentucky, and Toledo, Ohio, via Columbus, Ohio, part of which belonged to the former Hocking Valley Railroad. Then there was a cobweb of branches that served the rich bituminous coal mining belt of Kentucky, Virginia, and especially West Virginia, as well as a secondary line to Louisville, Kentucky, making for a network of nearly 3,000 miles. The public, though, generally associated the C&O as the railroad that served the popular and exclusive resorts at Virginia Hot Springs, Virginia, and White Sulphur Springs, West Virginia, situated near the Virginia–West Virginia border in the beautiful central Allegheny Mountains.[12]

Through the creative use of holding companies, including the Alleghany Corporation (the uncommon spelling commemorated the Alleghany, Virginia, summit on the C&O's main line and highest point on the Vans' sprawling rail empire) and financial backing from the J. P. Morgan investment-banking house, the Vans controlled an impressive system by 1930. Included in their holdings were the C&O, Chicago & Eastern Illinois (C&EI), Erie, Missouri Pacific (MOP), New York, Chicago & St. Louis or Nickel Plate (NKP), Pere Marquette (PM), and Wheeling & Lake Erie. Even though the ICC in 1926 had rejected the Vans' petition to merge the C&O, Erie, NKP, and PM, the brothers had developed what was essentially a fourth system in the East, competing with the B&O, NYC, and PRR. They did win regulatory approval in 1930 to have the C&O absorb the Hocking Valley, and that provided several strategic benefits, most significantly access to the Toledo coal docks. Soon, though, hard times damaged, even threatened, the existence of the Vans' empire and forced several units, most significantly the MOP, into bankruptcy. Still, the Vans' shaky corporate structures remained mostly intact. In 1935 a partial reorganization of assets, which involved creation of the Midamerica Corporation, another holding company, offered hope for solvency. But then on December 6, 1935, M. J. died, and less than a year later, on November 23, 1936, O. P. passed away. Thus at the time of Jervis's arrival at the C&O, the brothers' Alleghany Corporation remained together, although there was an air of uncertainty about its fate.

Fortunately, a measure of stability developed for the C&O. A syndicate, headed by business-executive-turned-stockbroker Robert R. Young, became interested in the Alleghany Corporation and acquired it on May 5, 1937. Yet all was not well for the new investors. In the fall of 1937 the national economy turned sharply downward, the so-called Roosevelt Recession, the worst economic slide since 1933.[13]

Although the C&O's cash and credit supported that unit of the Alleghany Corporation, the historically weak Erie, another component, "took a beating" as its freight revenues plummeted. "It became necessary on January 18th [1938] for the Erie Railroad Company to file a petition under the Federal Bankruptcy Act," related Erie president Charles Denney to his nearly 21,000 employees. "The shortage of funds was primarily due to a marked decline in earnings during the latter part of 1937 and increases in expenses beyond our control."[14]

Erie management had made a concerted effort to avoid bankruptcy. The hope was to obtain immediate funding to pay vouchers, taxes, and interest on maturing bonds and equipment trusts. So the carrier asked the Depression era's banker of last resort, the federally operated Reconstruction Finance Corporation (RFC), for a loan of slightly more than $6 million. But first the ICC had to approve the request. The decision, which came swiftly, was both good and bad news for the Erie. The company could have the ICC endorsement, but the C&O, Erie's principal stockholder, must either guarantee payment of the loan or deposit collateral, which, taken with Erie's collateral, would satisfy the RFC. The C&O board of directors refused, contending that "its first and most important duty to the public and to security holders is to maintain unimpaired the C&O resources, especially in view of the uncertainties of business conditions, and their relation to the railroad situation."[15]

President Denney did not surrender; instead, he took the loan matter directly to Jesse Jones, the dynamic head of the RFC. Although Jones was supportive, he still demanded C&O backing. Yet determined to assist, Jones informed the C&O leadership that "in my opinion your Board can do no greater dis-service to the railroad situation, including the systems of which your road is the principal, than to refuse help to the Erie at this time." Soon thereafter, Denney and Charles Bradley, chairman of the Erie board, met with C&O directors, but these men refused to extend any aid. "In 1937 . . . the C. & O. declared cash dividends of $20,000,000 and also a 4 per cent preferred stock dividend of $15,000,000," recalled Jones in his memoirs. "Probably if the directors had been less interested in fattening the Alleghany Corporation, the holding company which received a large part of the road's dividends, their course with the Erie might have been different."[16]

The bankrupt Erie was hardly the only American railroad that faced receivership. The Great Depression sent scores of carriers into bankruptcy; mileage under court control peaked at a record 77,013 in 1939, or nearly a third of the nation's trackage. In time, though, the Erie could claim the distinction of being the last major railroad to go into reorganization and the first to emerge. Compared with the Missouri Pacific, another property under the Alleghany Corporation banner, this seemed only momentary. In 1933 the MOP became the first major railroad to file for legal protection, and 23 years later it was the last to be reorganized from a Depression-era bankruptcy.[17]

Word of Erie's financial plight produced an almost immediate response from investors. The first body of security owners to organize was the Group of Holders of Erie Refunding and Improvement Bonds. "The Group," as it became known, consisted of more than a dozen financial institutions that held the less secure bonds, or about $100 million of the company's nearly $270 million of debt. These investors feared that unless they took the initiative, they would be forced to make substantial sacrifices. Henry Sturgis, an aggressive vice president of the First National Bank of New York, became the chief spokesman for the Group.

Before submitting a proposal to the ICC, a necessary part of the reorganization process, the Group prudently discussed the overall situation with large holders of the senior Erie bonds, namely, four giant life insurance companies. After intense negotiations the Group soon scored its first triumph when these firms agreed to cooperate.

The Group worked diligently, taking six drafts to reach a proposal that the dominant junior and senior bondholders could endorse. Then on October 18, 1938, exactly nine months after the filing of the bankruptcy papers, the ICC received this document. The plan represented what mostly became the financial reorganization of the "new" Erie Railroad Company. Not long thereafter, the two court-appointed trustees submitted their proposal to the

Commission. While these two plans differed on the proposed capital structure, they resembled each other on the treatments of the underlying bonds.[18]

The C&O leadership did not fret much about the overall debt structure in a reorganized Erie, but worried rightly about the fate of the existing common stock. After all, the C&O held approximately 56 percent of the outstanding shares, and this represented an investment of between $70 million and $80 million. In most railroad bankruptcies, common stock became worthless or nearly so following a reorganization.

Jervis became intimately involved in the Erie bankruptcy case. In fact, this assignment prompted the C&O to move the Langdons from Richmond to Cleveland where the C&O, Alleghany Corporation, and Erie each had their corporate headquarters. Jervis found himself working in the Terminal Tower complex, an imposing office-shops-hotel-station legacy of the Vans, located on Public Square in the heart of the city. "The C&O asked me to represent them before the Commission in this bankruptcy proceeding and see if we could finally get any value out of that [stock] investment," recalled Jervis in 1990. "So for two years that's all I did was try to work on that."

Being involved with a major railroad bankruptcy was a different experience. Now Jervis would have a hand in more than tax, rate, and abandonment matters. "I encountered an entirely different crowd of people," he explained. "In the first place, the Interstate Commerce Commission treated this not as a rate case but as a case where the commissioner himself on whose docket it was took part in the actual proceeding. . . . He wanted to talk with the lawyers. They were groping their way because they hadn't much experience in this area before. And, of course, all of the people who were involved represented the interests; the bondholders had a committee and we represented the stockholders largely."[19]

Efforts to reorganize the bankrupt Erie moved with dispatch. The Group and most other investors believed that some bonds should not be disturbed, and the remaining debt and equity owners should receive a combination of securities. Those who held better-grade bonds would be awarded the consolidated mortgage and income bonds and preferred stock, while those with less valuable securities would be issued mostly common stock. Existing common stockholders, including the C&O, would not have their equity destroyed; both they and junior bondholders would get an attractive and ingenious offer. "The refunding and improvement bondholders, who were to receive common stock to the extent of roughly 70 percent of their claim, would place their stock under option to the stockholders for a reasonable period at the price at which they [bondholders] were taking it in satisfaction to their claim," explained Sturgis. "In effect, the owners of the property [stockholders] were being given an opportunity to redeem their property by the payment of a part of their junior debt." Later the Group endorsed the proposal that old stockholders should be given 20 percent of their holdings in new common stock in addition to the stock warrants.[20]

The Group showed considerable shrewdness with its offer to stockholders. Since the C&O owned a majority of Erie common, the Group rightly feared that unless it could win support early on from this powerful investor, reorganization might be delayed for years. "Sturgis was an able negotiator, and the Erie wanted a settlement," recalled Jervis, "and so he brought in the opposition [C&O]." Jervis, of course, was pleased with the unfolding of events, and so were his superiors. The overall strategy that Sturgis employed worked. After some disagreements, the C&O endorsed the Group's plan, and for this cooperation the railroad, Jervis reckoned, "came out about $35 to $38 million ahead."[21]

The reorganization process had hardly ended. On January 4, 1939, formal hearings began before the ICC. Following initial testimony, the presiding commissioner called a short recess to permit discussion between the various parties. The Group surrendered little, as this coalition of bankers and insurance executives remained committed to its course of action. Several weeks later, the proceedings reconvened. Jervis and his associates argued that the Erie was of "considerable value," which was the basic principle that the C&O had always contended. After three days, the commissioner adjourned the hearings, and the participants awaited the report.[22]

But Jervis had not merely formulated a legal argument; he also had made certain that he had given the ICC ample evidence to support the C&O position. At the heart of his case was that business on the Erie had rebounded nicely from the recession of 1937–38 and that future earnings looked promising. At Jervis's suggestion the C&O hired William Wyer, a skilled railroad financial specialist who shortly would form the highly respected consulting firm of William Wyer & Company, later Wyer, Dick & Company and an organization that Jervis would depend on in the future. Wyer possessed considerable talents: he was bright, well-educated, and knowledgeable about railroading, having served as statistician to the president and assistant to the chairman of the board of directors of the Vans' MOP. "He helped assemble a lot of the evidence that we needed to support the fact . . . that a lot of the stock had value," Jervis related. This was critical

"because automatically when you go into bankruptcy, the stock is traditionally wiped out."[23]

The wheels of the federal regulatory machinery now turned somewhat
slowly, a course of events that surprised no one, including Jervis. Not until
August 21, 1939, did the ICC reveal its hand. The ICC modified or opposed
several features, but after rebuttal arguments in November, the Group's plan
largely prevailed. In early 1940, the ICC formally endorsed a reorganization
scheme that satisfied the principal parties.[24]

Additional steps remained to be taken. The Federal Court in Cleveland
needed to endorse the ICC's actions, and on August 12, 1940, the judge
held the prescribed hearings. The C&O, the Group, and the Erie offered
no objections, although a protective committee, which represented some
junior bondholders, protested that they would not escape the bankruptcy
unscathed. Following several more minor legal hurdles, the court, on December 17, 1940, deemed the reorganization to be "fair and equitable."
About two months later, Erie security holders received ballots on the reorganization document, and by mid-April 1941, they had completed their
voting, expressing their overwhelming approval. The final legal paperwork
followed. Then on December 22, 1941, the Erie Railroad Company, its corporate name unchanged, emerged from bankruptcy protection, delighting
Jervis and most everyone else. In the final analysis, the C&O had protected much of its multimillion-dollar investment, since every five shares
of old Erie stock became a share in the reorganized company. Moreover,
the "new" Erie, with its debt level reduced, had the potential of becoming
a viable property and therefore enhancing the value of the C&O's financial
stake.[25]

It was while immersed in the Erie reorganization that Jervis made a decision that would greatly affect his life, both personally and professionally.
He decided to take up flying. From his 32nd-floor office window in Terminal Tower, Jervis enjoyed watching seaplanes on Lake Erie, being especially
impressed with the Taylorcraft seaplane. "I could look down and see this
seaplane operation on the lake, and I used to go down at noon with a sandwich and a cup of coffee to watch them." His second wife, Irene, explained,
"He told me that it looked like fun." On September 29, 1941, Jervis began
his flying lessons in a model BC-65 Taylorcraft that had been built in Taylor's nearby plant in Alliance, Ohio. Once he decided to pursue his new
love, Jervis used his lunch break to take flying lessons first at the seaplane
base and later at nearby Lost Nation Airport, but he kept quiet about his
newfound interest. "A lawyer wasn't supposed to fly; it was like riding a
motorcycle." Jervis soon mastered the art of flying, although he found

Jervis stands on the right, wearing a business suit, in this September 1941 photograph of his first series of flying instructions in Cleveland. During his lunch hour, Jervis slipped away from the nearby headquarters of the Chesapeake & Ohio Railway, located in Terminal Tower, to take lessons. (Irene Langdon)

making spins the most challenging. Not long after he obtained his pilot's license, he acquired a four-passenger airplane, a Stinson Voyager. On April 26, 1941, Jervis traveled to the Stinson factory in Wayne, Michigan, and flew back to Cleveland in Voyager No. 32201. This was a good choice, for of all the larger personal planes of the day, the Voyager was among the least expensive to purchase and operate, and it could be flown and landed with ease.

Notwithstanding possible criticism from colleagues (or anyone else), flying became Jervis's passion. He wrote, "When you are up there in the air, you are on your own," and he loved this feeling of independence. Later, as the pressures of work increased, he flew whenever possible "in order to get up there away from it all and clean out the cobwebs." Any danger that was involved failed to bother him, although he was an "extremely careful pilot." That, of course, was good; for one thing, his family responsibilities had increased. Jervis "Jerry" Langdon III was born on June 14, 1937, in Richmond, and on July 14, 1941, Bancroft was born in Cleveland. So Jervis was a husband and a father of three active youngsters.[26]

Later in his life Jervis revealed another reason for taking flying lessons and earning his pilot's license. He sensed that the nation might find itself involved in world war, as the Germans, Italians, and Japanese had made incursions into formally neutral nations. By the late 1930s, the seeds of chaos had been sown and threatened a harvest of worldwide discord and strife. Then after September 1, 1939, much of Europe erupted into armed conflict, and war intensified in Asia. Jervis was hardly an isolationist; in fact, he was an ardent internationalist. If the United States entered the fray, Jervis could rally to the colors and contribute his flying skills.[27]

Until December 8, 1941, America remained officially at peace, and Jervis continued his promising career at the C&O. Although he had focused much of his daily labors on the Erie reorganization, since March 1938 he formally had served as a general attorney for the C&O and Alleghany affiliates NKP and PM, collectively the "Chesapeake & Ohio Lines." His work activities varied and included such matters as attempting to win approval from the ICC for a reduction of freight charges for iron and steel billets and skelp between Youngstown, Ohio, and Chicago. Then on April 1, 1941, Jervis took on a fresh assignment in a newly created position, namely, that of assistant vice president of traffic for the C&O and PM. This dramatic shift from law to traffic indicated that the C&O was preparing Jervis for a major executive role. In fact, he would serve as an understudy to the head of the traffic department. There is no indication, however, that Jervis objected to the transfer. After all, he had a vast range of experiences with traffic matters at the NYC, and "at least I knew what I was supposed to be doing." Such a job potentially gave Jervis excellent employment options. His professional life was just beginning to reveal its possibilities. Jervis celebrated by buying that new Stinson Voyager 25 days later![28]

Wartime Interlude

Then war came. Because of his age and family status, Jervis could have avoided military service. But like so many other men and women, he eagerly joined the active military, explaining that "I simply couldn't keep from volunteering." Jervis would have loved to become a military pilot. "I tried hard to get in as a pilot, but I couldn't pass the 20/20 eye test or even come close." He enlisted in the U.S. Army Air Corps, and in the fall of 1942 this 36-year-old railroad executive found himself in an officers training school in Miami Beach. Soon he would become part of the "G.I. Generation," or as media journalist Tom Brokaw has called it, "America's greatest generation."[29]

Much to Jervis's happiness he was not stuck "state-side" during World War II. After four months of intense training, now Captain Jervis Langdon Jr. asked for and received assignment to the Air Transport Command (ATC) that the War Department had recently established. In late 1942, Jervis reached the headquarters of the China-Burma-India Theater wing of the ATC in Chabua, Assam, India, strategically situated in the extreme northeastern part of this British possession and near the eastern Himalayan foothills. In this isolated locale, "populated by a handful of British tea planters and lots of tigers and elephants on the loose," the ATC sought to supply the embattled forces of the Republic of China in their efforts to wage a more effective ground war against a million Japanese troops in China and Southeast Asia. Indeed, there was no other practical way to aid the Chinese. By this time the enemy had gained control of Burma, the Dutch East Indies or officially the Netherlands East Indies (NEI), French Indo-China, Malaya, Siam (Thailand), and most of the islands of the western Pacific. The Japanese even threatened Australia. Because of the Japanese military presence, the famed Burma Road, constructed in the late 1930s and briefly a vital supply route that connected the Irrawaddy River north of the Burmese port of Rangoon with China's Yunnan province, could not be utilized for ground transport to assist the government of Chiang Kai-shek. Until the 1,079-mile Ledo Road between

Shortly after the start of World War II, trainees in the U.S. Army Air Corps in Florida assembled for a group portrait. Jervis is third from the left in the front row. Several of these men became lifelong friends. (Irene Langdon)

Ledo, Assam, India, Myitkyina, Burma, and beyond could be built and pro-tected, flying the "Hump" over the towering Himalaya Mountains became the only practical way materially to assist the Chinese.[30]

Jervis would quickly contribute to the war effort in Asia as a cog in what was essentially an airline in military dress. Early on, he volunteered to assist in the construction of airfields in Assam and China. And at last he could fly. Using an old biplane trainer ("It wasn't very new or very good"), he traveled between these emerging landing strips. Soon Allied planes were able to use airfields at Jorhat, Mohanberi, and Sookerating and then Masamari and Tezpur. And bases appeared rapidly on the Chinese side of the Himalayas, including Yangkai and Yunnani. "The result was excellent runways," opined Jervis, and these betterments would stand out as a major engineering triumph in this theater of the war.[31]

Once the construction phase had ended, Jervis participated in the task of overseeing the loading of aircraft. In reality, he became a traffic manager, hardly an unfamiliar role. There were several constituencies to serve with these Hump flights. Jervis recalled a constant battle among "(1) General [Clair] Chennault of the China-based 14th Air Force demanding more avgas [aviation fuel] and bombs to drop on Japanese facilities in China as well as shipping on the South China Sea, (2) Chiang Kai-shek . . . screaming for more lend-lease material—not to use against the Japanese but to store against the day when the Communists would move to overthrow him, and (3) General [Joseph] Stilwell with more modest requirements as the theater commander with no American troops." Initially the military cargo version of the highly successful DC-3 passenger plane, the C-47, served as the principal transport aircraft. Then the much larger C-46, known as the Curtis Commando and affectionately described as "one tough lady," appeared, as did converted B-24 bombers, called C-87s. Some of the latter aircraft served as fuel tankers. In all, several hundred cargo planes were assigned to this mission. Jervis remembered that overloading became a common practice and that "there was many a prayer on initial takeoff when everything was, or seemed to be, hanging on the props."[32]

As a military traffic manager, Jervis participated in a variety of activities. The ATC utilized a large force of native workers to load aircraft with a range of cargoes. And Jervis oversaw two or three officers at each of the airfields who personally supervised the actual shipping process. But the logistics were not limited to one side of the Himalayas. "When cargoes got over to Kunming, in Yunnan, and the other fields in western China, I had to make arrangements with the Chinese to unload and deliver the material further on in certain cases," Jervis explained. "At many of the fields we could make direct delivery, but certain Chennault units were based at forward strips beyond the round-trip range of our transports. We had to have the Chinese make overland delivery by broken-down trucks [and] you were lucky if 50 percent [of the goods] got through."[33]

As Hump flying progressed, Jervis spent more time in the cockpit, often serving as the co-pilot in transport runs. Every mission was an adventure. "Minimum altitudes ranged between 20,000 and 24,000 feet. Severe turbulence was inescapable. Cross winds from the south, unless recognized and countered, could blow you into the much higher mountains to the north. A lost engine, particularly on the heavy east-bound trips, meant an immediate bailout." And when weather conditions were good, the aircraft became "sitting ducks for Jap fighters based below in Burma." Jervis made 23 flights, either in the jump seat or as co-pilot, and these trips were "always tense."

Yet there were lighter moments. As an ever-increasing volume of freight moved to China, Lieutenant General Stilwell wanted to bring young Chinese recruits to India to be trained for combat assignments. And this happened; thousands of men were transported on return flights. "On one of these trips, when I was serving as co-pilot, there were over 70 Chinese boys in the cabin in their underwear (uniforms to come, thanks to Uncle Sam, upon landing in India)," related Jervis. "On takeoff roll the boys started to roughhouse, and after takeoff it got worse affecting the stability of the plane. The answer: up to 25,000 feet without oxygen, and the situation took care of itself." Then upon landing, "these young men were all smiles again and jumping to the ground promptly lined up to vomit."[34]

Jervis's commanding officers recognized his organizational talents. In early 1944, the wing received orders to plan for the future development of Hump operations. The job was given to Jervis. By this time the airfields in Assam and China were operational and rail supply routes to Assam from Indian ports had been significantly strengthened, mostly by improving operations on the principal bottleneck, the narrow-gauge Bengal & Assam Railway. And there were ample aircraft, parts, fuel, and personnel. But Jervis determined that more airfields were needed in India. "I found suitable sites near the Burma border in the vicinity of Chittagong." His report went to Washington, and it was approved without change and "to my astonishment, fully implemented." By late 1945 the monthly transport totals exceeded 45,000 tons, a dramatic increase from the 2,000 to 3,000 tons a month in late 1942. Jervis's demonstrated skills predicted what he later would do as a senior railroad executive, namely to make sense out of impossibly chaotic problems.[35]

After serving 19 months in the China-Burma-India wing of the ATC, Jervis won a transfer to its Southwest Pacific wing. Most of all, Jervis, now a colonel, wished to continue working with his much admired commanding officer, General Herald Alexander, who earlier had received this posting. Once reassigned, he served as Alexander's chief-of-staff. "My job was to run the place when the General was away and he was away most of the time." Furthermore, the nature of the operation was "entirely different," and Jervis relished variety in his duties. Specifically, he became involved in military tasks that focused on using a fleet of nearly 100 C-47s ("comparable to a medium-sized American airline") to supply troops and materials to the forces of General Douglas MacArthur. "Whenever there was any need for air transportation of the ground forces, along with troop carrier units, we supplied it." Between late 1944 and 1945, Jervis moved with General MacArthur from Australia to New Guinea, then to the Philippines and Okinawa. He was especially proud of the ATC's performance. "Although most of the flying was over the South and Southwest Pacific, we never lost an airplane." This was a remarkable record, indeed.[36]

Even after V-J Day (or Victory in the Pacific Day) on August 15, 1945, Jervis remained busy. His final major assignment in the ATC involved closing 30 U.S. bases in New Zealand, Australia, the Philippines, and assorted Pacific islands. With his usual efficiency, Jervis effectively handled the work, duties he thoroughly enjoyed. "I'd arrive and get hold of the CO [commanding officer] and [say,] 'It's all over and make your arrangements to go home.' I had some orders to sign and then they'd have a small little party and the war was over for them. Then we'd go to the next place. That was fun!" In October 1945 he wrote to his mother in Elmira, "How would you like to have been with me on a personally conducted tour in your own airplane leaving Manila one fine morning and visiting in turn—Biak (N.E.I.), Admiralties, Bougainville, Treasure, Guadalcanal, Spiritu Santo (New Hebrides), Tontoreta (New Caledonia), Norfolk Is. (of "Mutiny on the Bounty" fame), Auckland, New Zealand, Lord Howe Is. (from the air), Sydney, Brisbane?" Jervis vividly recalled his last flight into Sydney. "Our approach this time was of course from the east and we broke out, just at sunset, over that glorious harbor filled with the British Navy! It was really a sight I shall *never* forget." Jervis returned to spend Christmas with his family in New York State.[37]

The war had a pronounced impact on Jervis. He seemed to have become even more patriotic as a result of his experiences. There is no question that he willingly risked his life for his country; he had no love for the "Japs" and what the empire of Japan had done in Asia and the Pacific. He took great pride in his military record and was honored to have been awarded the Legion of Merit with oak leaf cluster for "exceptionally meritorious conduct in the performance of outstanding service." In the 1950s, while a resident of Washington, D.C., Jervis happily joined the Army & Navy Club, and "he loved that group." Generally, Jervis found life in the U.S. Army Air Corps satisfactory and the bureaucracy not too burdensome. Differing from his previous railroad experiences, once a decision was made, implementation followed, and that pleased him; after all, he was decidedly goal-oriented. Likely

With his commanding officer not available, Colonel Jervis Langdon Jr. had the pleasant duty of informing troops in the Pacific theater that Victory in Europe (VE Day) had officially occurred. In the words of General Dwight D. Eisenhower, Supreme Allied Commander in Europe, "The crusade on which we embarked in the early summer of 1944 has reached its glorious conclusion." (Irene Langdon)

because of the war, Jervis became a lifelong admirer of Winston Churchill, Franklin Roosevelt, and Harry Truman, even though the latter two were Democrats and Jervis considered himself a Republican.

Yet there were negatives associated with Jervis's long tour of military duty. He worried about his family while he was away and feared that he might not return home. He made certain that Jean and the three children enjoyed life as much as possible. This involved purchasing a house in Ithaca and making arrangements for a live-in nanny and housekeeper. The location made sense; this is where Jean's family lived. Jervis also arranged for an Elmira pediatrician, a personal friend and fellow pilot, to attend to the children's medical needs. And he was delighted that his parents became actively involved. "A comfort to Jerv as he was going off to war was that his mother and father were nearby and anxious to be part of their grandchildren's lives and of help to Jean." There would be frequent visits and gatherings in Ithaca and at Quarry Farm.

Although Jervis said little about what happened, he and Jean had grown apart during their long separation. After Jervis's return, the marriage disintegrated, and divorce followed in 1949. But he continued to be a supportive father, and his family remained financially secure and comfortable.[38]

Railroad Lawyer Once More

With discharge papers in hand and a commission as a colonel in the U.S. Army Air Corps Reserves, Jervis arrived home in late fall 1945 to consider his future. He could return to Cleveland and resume his job as assistant vice president for traffic for the C&O. But during his absence the flamboyant financier Robert R. Young, "the populist of Wall Street," had consolidated his control and had fired C&O president George Brooke, "to whom I was devoted." Jervis's friend Robert Tunstall, the general counsel, also had been terminated. Then he discovered that several other associates had left the railroad, prompted by the personnel and policies of the new regime. "There was a different ball game out here," Jervis was told, "and you won't like it." So he resigned. He probably could not have worked with the feisty Young, who was variously described as "brilliant, contentious, litigious, egotistical, messianic, and publicity-hungry."[39]

Jervis did not join the ranks of the postwar unemployed. Yet his returning job was that of a part-time consultant, including a rate arbitration case for the Lehigh. Still uncertain about his career plans, Jervis soon agreed to take a six-month trial with the Bankers Trust Company in New York City, likely in a general law capacity. But just days before he was to join the bank, he received a telephone call at Quarry Farm. He was needed in the traffic department at Capital-PCA Airlines. In September 1946 he became general traffic manager for this airline, one of the country's best-managed midsized carriers. Based in Washington, the company served Chicago, Detroit, New York City, and Pittsburgh. Jervis's World War II involvement in air logistics transferred nicely to the private sector. In fact, some of his closest friends in the Army Air Corps, who had left positions in commercial aviation at the start of the war, returned to their previous firms. "Jerv was urged to come to either Pan Am or American where there was promise of a successful career in an industry that was expanding, but Jerv's interest was railroads," related his wife Irene. He would remain at Capital for less than a year.[40]

Wishing to return to railroading, Jervis's professional connections led to a job with the NYC, specifically to represent the company before the ICC in the never-ending parade of rate cases and related issues. The fact that

Robert Young's Alleghany Corporation was actively acquiring an important stake in the NYC troubled Jervis not at all; he expected his tenure to be of short duration. As the result of personal contacts with several lawyers with the Southern Railway (SR) in Washington, D.C., Jervis learned of an attractive employment possibility. The Southern Freight Association, a regional organization of Class 1 roads based in the nation's capital, needed legal assistance. Its leaders soon decided that Jervis would be the ideal person to serve as a special counsel for a complicated and potentially lengthy rate-division dispute. The major southern railroads, including the SR, considered the matter to be far more than their own law departments could manage.[41]

Jervis became a resident of Washington, D.C., while his former wife and children remained in Ithaca. His new home made it easy to maintain contact with key railroad and government personnel. While the rate cases that involved the NYC had gone smoothly, the issue of the North-South rate divisions unfolded as predicted—difficult and drawn out, beginning in 1947 and lasting until 1953. Jervis was hardly a novice in such actions before the ICC, and he readily realized that there is nothing like a divisions controversy "to open our eyes to the pathetic condition of the railroad industry in its continuing inability to resolve its own internal disputes." As he explained, carriers traditionally went before the Commission "with their dirty linen rather than set up machinery for arbitrating these purely industry problems." For years Jervis rightly and cogently railed against the unwillingness of most railroad executives to cooperate on various issues of mutual importance and not just matters of rates.[42]

The determination of a "fair" division of the freight rates charged for movement of interline traffic had long been a subject of shipper, carrier, and regulatory interest. After all, the loaded freight car typically moved far beyond the originating road's rails. A boxcar of watermelons might begin its journey on the Georgia & Florida Railroad (G&F) in the Wiregrass Region of south Georgia and then be turned over to the Piedmont & Northern Railroad in Greenwood, South Carolina, and handled by this strategic former interurban to its interchange with the Clinchfield Railroad at Spartanburg, South Carolina. Next a Clinchfield freight would move the melons to the C&O connection at Elkhorn City, Kentucky, for delivery either on-line in the Midwest, perhaps Cincinnati or Chicago, or to some other connecting carrier, for instance, the NKP, for final delivery to a Cleveland or Buffalo consignee. But how would the revenue generated by this shipment be divided between four or more companies? For decades auditors for the respective roads consulted "division sheets," a tariff schedule that had been approved by the ICC, to learn the exact amount of income that the participating roads had earned on this carload of melons.

If controversy erupted about the rates to be received for the transit of Georgia watermelons to a midwestern or northeastern destination, it generally fell into two types. An individual carrier, such as the G&F, might be dissatisfied with the division it received. And there might be disagreements that centered on so-called rate territories. Carriers that generally operated north of the Ohio River, including the NKP, might fuss that northern roads' share was grossly unfair when compared to what their southern counterparts received. This discord involved more than shipments of melons. Such complaints likely involved *all* carriers in the respective freight-rate territory and divisions of revenues on nearly *all* traffic moving on an interterritorial basis.

When Jervis became special counsel for the southern roads, he immediately became involved in the growing conflict between rate territories, specifically North and South. (The boundary line for the two regions ran largely along the Ohio River from the confluence with the Mississippi River to Kenova, West Virginia, and then extended through southern West Virginia and Virginia to Hampton Roads. The western territory, with certain exceptions, consisted of the vast region beyond the Mississippi River.) Over time, with ICC approval, there developed a substantial revenue differential between northern and southern roads, largely prompted by the generally weaker condition of Dixie's carriers and their mostly less remunerative traffic of agricultural and lumber products. There existed greater revenue needs as the ICC explained. "Therefore they [southern railroads] should get inflated divisions of the rates," related Jervis. "A 100-mile haul in the South and a 100-mile haul in the East [North], the cost per mile in the South, . . . before the war was a lot higher than they were in the East because their density was so low as compared with the density in the East." And he elaborated, "That for one mile of transportation in the East you could pay for only about a half a mile of transportation in the South. There was kind of a complicated formula, but the point was that they [southern railroads] were getting reimbursed much higher than a mileage pro-rate . . . and this was what the eastern [northern] roads were contesting." Indeed, in 1924 the U.S. Supreme Court had ruled in *U.S. v. Abilene & Southern Railway* that "in determining what the divisions should be, the Commission may, in the public interest, take into consideration the financial needs of a weaker road." A weaker railroad "may be given a division larger than justice merely as between the parties would suggest in order to maintain it in effective operation as part of an adequate transportation system, provided the share left to its connections was adequate to avoid a confiscatory result."[43]

But big changes were occurring. The wartime boom in the South that created new or enlarged military bases and increased manufacturing and distribution activities had altered the economic picture, and despite the brief recession of 1949, the uptick continued. The "Sunbelt South" was rapidly evolving; more firms were either expanding or coming into the region, and the process of urbanization accelerated.[44]

The Southern Freight Association understood that member roads benefited from the status quo on revenue divisions, realizing that northern carriers could hurt income if they succeeded in ending the revenue subsidy. Yet the Association correctly sensed that if there were a mile-for-mile division formula, most Class I carriers in the South could compete effectively with their northern counterparts. Such a policy would likely produce the same revenues that the existing agreements generated, especially for longer hauls. Still, a fair division had to take into consideration that roads in the North "have been less efficiently operated than Southern ones." Therefore, Jervis's clients challenged the opposition's contention that present divisions were "grossly unfair." And the Association sought harmony with roads in the West. Jervis also needed to work with related regional organizations, including the Southeast Association of Railroad and Utilities Commissioners, the Southern Governors Conference, and the Southern Traffic League.[45]

Jervis labored diligently in defending the interests of the Southern Freight Association. He prepared briefs, organized witnesses, and kept participants informed. Dealing with Association members was tricky at times, since strong rivalries existed between some of the largest roads; for example, there was little love lost between the top managements of the SR and the Atlantic Coast Line.

Ultimately, the ICC reached a decision that both parties found acceptable, but as Jervis observed, "No division case is satisfactory to anybody." The northern roads no longer underwrote the revenues of their southern partners, which was important because carriers, especially in the Northeast, were in decline. These companies were particularly vulnerable to highway competition for high revenue goods and were adversely affected by cost problems, including labor and taxes, that increasingly plagued the region. And those historic haulers of anthracite coal experienced a sharp reduction in this once profitable traffic. Yet members of the Association got acceptable divisions, based in part on mileage, protecting themselves against the potential loss of $40 million in annual freight revenues. Based on the Transportation Act of 1920, the ICC had to consider that income generated from divisions was needed to pay a carrier's "respective operating expenses, taxes, and a fair return on their railway property held for and used in the service of transportation."

When not working directly on the North/South division case, Jervis conducted other matters for the Association. After all, there were breaks after briefs had been submitted and before hearings occurred and decisions were rendered. Jervis spent most of this time on general revenue cases before the ICC, for carriers constantly needed to seek rate hikes as postwar inflation, higher material costs, and increased wages eroded profits.[46]

On May 1, 1953, Jervis became the full-time chair of the newly launched Association of Southeastern Railroads (ASER). This trade group was the result of a recent restructuring of the Southeastern Presidents' Conference (SEPC) and had as its purpose the continued promotion and protection of affiliated carriers. "The new association will deal with matters in which the southeastern railroads have a common interest," noted Harry DeButts, president of the SR and chair of the SPEC. "Member roads will be all Class 1 railroads operating in the area generally south of the Potomac and east of the Mississippi rivers." Yet Jervis hardly considered this assignment the pinnacle of his career. As he told DeButts, "It's o.k. for the time being, but I'm on the lookout for another job. But I'll do this until I'm successful." Much later Jervis confided that "one of my secrets of my life has been to have another job in the ready."[47]

As with Jervis's involvement with the Southern Freight Association, his duties at the ASER varied. In the spring of 1956, Jervis developed a strategy to counteract a publicity and lobbying campaign being waged by the Mason-Dixon Line, a trucking company based in Kingsport, Tennessee. The firm's attack, "Watch Out, Boys . . . You're Being Railroaded," opposed any meaningful changes to ICC rate-making practices. This was one of a number of trucking industry assaults on a recent study, officially titled *The Cabinet Committee Report on Transport Policy and Organization of 1956*, prepared by Sinclair Weeks, secretary of commerce in the Dwight D. Eisenhower administration, which called for limited price competition between trucks and railroads, a process Weeks labeled "dynamic competition." Indeed, Jervis and the ASER "strongly endorsed" this early attempt to assist the rail industry through greater rate-making freedom. The concept of a "zone of reasonableness," in which markets would determine shipping costs, had real appeal. However, opposition from truckers and the traditional anti-railroad feelings in Congress doomed the creative work that Weeks and his advisors had overseen.[48]

It would be during his affiliation with the ASER that Jervis began to contribute pieces to professional publications. His journalistic experiences at

Cornell, authorship of legal briefs, and driving ambition likely explain this activity. This was somewhat unusual for a nontechnical railroader to pursue. The most important of these early writings was a carefully argued and documented article, "Criteria in the Establishment of Freight Rate Divisions," which appeared in the winter 1954 issue of the *Cornell Law Quarterly*. And Jervis made contributions to trade journals, including the influential *Railway Age*. Getting into print contributed to his enhanced standing in railroad legal and regulatory circles. Moreover, in 1953 he assumed a three-year term as editor-in-chief of the *ICC Practitioners' Journal* that further spread his name.

Jervis was emerging as a highly visible railroader. He did more than write and edit; he spoke before an array of groups. In the legal and railroad fields these ranged from the Public Utility Law Section of the American Bar Association to the New England Transportation Council. At times Jervis dutifully represented the ASER or the Association of American Railroads at congressional hearings, usually subcommittees of the House of Representatives Committee on Interstate and Foreign Commerce. He also contributed to the industry response to the Weeks Report both before lawmakers and at public meetings. Not only did Jervis prepare his presentations carefully, but he was skilled at being able to think on his feet. He could field a variety of listener questions with exactness and clarity. "Mr. Langdon has achieved national prominence as a spokesman for the railroad industry," noted an official of the B&O in a 1956 press release.

While a hired gun for the Southern carriers, Jervis became interested in arguing for a more level playing field in transportation matters. He knew that the railroad enterprise was excessively controlled and that competitors exploited these restraints. It was not merely the Interstate Commerce Act of 1887 but subsequent pieces of legislation that came mostly during the progressive era when reformers believed that the public interest could best be protected through intense federal regulation of an unpopular and politically vulnerable monopoly. Although the Transportation Act of 1940 (Wheeler-Lea Act) allowed the ICC to decide corporate mergers on a case-by-case basis and brought about a modest amount of supervision of inland water carriers, a growing hauler of low-grade, heavy-volume bulk commodities, the ICC continued to impede most nontechnological innovations, and this included rate-making.

Jervis used a variety of venues to express his concerns about rate policies. In an address on December 10, 1954, to the Third New England Institute of Transportation in Boston, he went to the heart of the matter. Each form of transportation—air, barge, motor carrier, and rail—should be free to publish rates that could meet competition, and these rates needed to be subject only to the condition that they be "compensatory." As Jervis explained, compensatory rates "should fully cover out-of-pocket expenses of handling the traffic and make a contribution to overhead or constant expenses," so the carrier would be "better off by moving the traffic than by not moving it." The ICC often disallowed competitive rates based on a railroad's own costs. "On the contrary, railroad rates are held up by the full costs of using [competitive] water service plus a stiff differential which is added whether railroad service is more valuable or not." As a result, railroads suffered. Jervis thought that this was wrong. Lower rates to customers were unquestionably in the public interest and supported the long-held notion by most Americans that competition benefited the national economy. Why then should the ICC seek a distribution of traffic among the possible competing forms? In the mid-1950s some railroaders and others began to worry about the long-term fate of the industry, just as they had during the Great Depression. There had been those wartime profits, a relatively strong postwar national economy, and handsome savings derived from dieselization of motive power, but increasing modal competition, directly or indirectly subsidized by government, hardly augured well for the future. Most worrisome was the rapid increase in total truck ton miles and market share. "The railroad industry cannot be permitted to slide quickly into government ownership and control without having been given the chance to save itself through competition, subject to a floor of costs," Jervis told his Boston audience. The hope involved remedial legislation, and carriers and important rail users needed to press hard for change in the rate-making process.

As Jervis was building his professional career, his personal life had changed. On August 26, 1949, he married the attractive and vivacious Irene Fortner, who also was an accomplished artist. A native of Brentwood, California, Irene came from a family of six, and one of her three brothers, a marine, had been killed on Iwo Jima. After high school and during the war she worked in a brokerage house in Oakland, California, and then became excited about the possibilities of a career in the expanding airline industry. Although she contemplated becoming a stewardess, "I had too many freckles." So she got a job in the reservation operations of Capital Airlines. It was during this time when Jervis worked for Capital that they met. But as Irene explained, "We who worked in reservations were a far stretch from the executive offices and with a supervisor to whom we were accountable." She added, "I did meet him sometime during this period at the Red Cross office where I was volunteering and where he had come to confer with the director." After a quick courtship, the couple married in Chicago in a simple ceremony, far from the fancy affair that was Jervis's first wedding 18 years earlier. And the Langdons warmly received Irene into the family, with Jervis's mother giving her a letter that Uncle Sam Clements had written to her at the time of her marriage to Jervis's father. This treasured document closed with these words: "Enter into our tribe and enrich it with the graces of your youth and of your heart; be you welcome, and let us love you."[49]

Jervis's B&O

The newlyweds made Washington their home, but in 1956 Jervis and Irene moved to Baltimore. That better job Jervis had hoped for finally materialized. He accepted an offer from the B&O to become a general counsel, and on December 1, 1956, he officially began his new position in the company's stately 13-story general office building located at the corner of Baltimore and Charles streets. Jervis would receive handsome paychecks, based on an annual salary of $45,000 (approximately $327,000 in 2006 dollars). Moreover, in computing his allowances at retirement, the B&O would consider his previous years of railroad service as time with the company.[50]

The B&O's vice president and general counsel Edwin Burgess was the individual most responsible for the hire. Burgess and Jervis had known each other for decades; Burgess had been the assistant general solicitor at the Lehigh when Jervis joined his uncle Edward Loomis's road, and the two had worked together on various tax and rate cases. Clearly Burgess and other officers at the B&O recognized Jervis's talents, and they thought that he would likely be the replacement when the 68-year-old Burgess stepped down, knowing that the company had a mandatory retirement age of 70. And that is exactly what happened. On October 1, 1958, Jervis succeeded Burgess.[51]

Although Jervis developed a deep affection for the Lehigh and to a lesser degree for the Erie and Lackawanna, his other hometown railroads, he had a strong, positive feeling about the B&O. As early as Jervis's days at Cornell, when he established a friendship with Samuel Shriver, son of a high-ranking B&O official, he casually discussed with the senior Shriver the possibility of employment with the company. Then in 1927 Jervis and his father attended the lavish Centenary Exhibition and Pageant of the Baltimore & Ohio Railroad, better known as "The Fair of the Iron Horse." This B&O public relations extravaganza, which cost approximately $1 million and attracted more than 1.25 million visitors, was held immediately south of Baltimore on the road's main line to Washington. At the fair the Langdons took in the exhibits and entertainment, and they met the charismatic president of the B&O, Daniel Willard. These became cherished memories. "I'd seen the B&O over the years, too," as Jervis later related. "And they always seemed like a superior railroad in the sense that the people who were running it were a little bit different level than some of the others that I'd seen in the industry. They were real people and I had gotten to know a lot of them."[52]

The B&O that Jervis joined was not the most stellar of carriers, yet the company possessed a long, proud heritage. On July 4, 1828, with great celebration, dignitaries including Charles Carroll, director, stockholder, and last surviving signer of the Declaration of Independence, broke ground for this projected railroad between the Baltimore harbor and the Ohio River that was designed to protect the economic livelihood of its home city. While not the first railroad in the United States, the B&O was the first common carrier that offered regularly scheduled freight and passenger service.

The B&O became the prototypical American railroad. Indeed, it was the quintessential company during the "demonstration period" of the 1830s and 1840s. For one thing, the B&O, resembling some other pioneering roads, initially followed the British precedent and constructed masonry bridges, but then opted for wooden trestles that were cheaper, easier to erect, and avoided the need for costly earthen and rock fills. And the railroad briefly (and unsuccessfully) installed iron strap rail on wood stringers on top of regularly spaced cubical stone blocks and even tried longitudinal granite stringers laid end-to-end in a trough with strap rails attached directly to the stones. Wisely, the company subsequently opted for the practical iron "T" rail laid on wooden crossties. Still, like comparable contemporary carriers, the B&O responded to economic conditions, making as its primary objective serving an expanding service territory.[53]

The process of building to the West went slowly for the B&O. By December 1, 1831, its rails extended only to Frederick, Maryland, 60 miles from Baltimore. Then in the early 1850s the road sported a line to Washington. It finally reached Wheeling, Virginia (later West Virginia), on the south bank of the Ohio River, nearly 400 miles from its original starting point on Pratt Street in downtown Baltimore. After the painful years of the Civil War, when the company lost or had severely damaged sizable amounts of rolling stock, structures, and track, a renewed optimism took hold. Under the leadership of John W. Garrett, the B&O increased efficiency, reduced costs and avoided unnecessary expenditures, and undertook large-scale expansion, reaching Pittsburgh, Columbus, and America's railroad Mecca, Chicago. Even following Garrett's death in 1884, the B&O continued to grow, and by the end of the 1880s, the greatest boom decade in American rail-line construction, the company had gained entrance to Cincinnati, New York City, and St. Louis. And the road had engineered a better and more direct route to Chicago, closing the gap between Pittsburgh and Chicago Junction, Ohio (later Willard). On the eve of the Civil War, mileage stood at 515, but by 1890 it had reached 1,845. The B&O served a number of important freight and passenger gateways. Still, main routes were somewhat circuitous and in places hampered by heavy mountain grades.

Operating a railroad network that truly went from somewhere to somewhere did not create financial security. The Panic of May 1893, which triggered the worst depression in the nation's history and one that would not fully lift until 1897, placed the B&O and scores of other railroads in dire financial straits. In 1896 the company tumbled into receivership. Yet the B&O rebounded. Three years later, the road emerged from court control and would take advantage of a growing national prosperity.

Between 1899 and 1901 the giant PRR took a keen interest in the B&O, acquiring a sizable block of stock. It then placed into the presidency Leonor Loree, a capable and aggressive executive. The Loree administration (1901–1904) embarked on a host of betterments, including modern motive power, and secured for the company a large stake in the Reading that in turn controlled the Jersey Central. Until 1913 the PRR remained a powerful albeit progressive force on the B&O. When the U.S. Supreme Court decision in 1912 forced the "unmerger" of the Union Pacific from the Southern Pacific, the UP subsequently traded a substantial block of SP stock that UP's subsidiary Oregon Short Line owned to the PRR for its B&O shares.

Before direct PRR influence vanished, an important personality arrived in the executive suite in Baltimore. In 1910 Daniel Willard assumed the presidency, having earlier served as assistant general manager of the road, and he remained in charge until 1941. During his exceptionally long tenure at the company, Willard expanded the property by acquiring control of such carriers as the Buffalo, Rochester & Pittsburgh and the Cincinnati, Indianapolis & Western (by the 1930s mileage reached 6,351). "Uncle Dan" held an enlightened position on labor-management issues, enhanced the quality of passenger service, and developed a well-deserved reputation for his fairness, honesty, and sincerity. It was his belief that the railroad's employees and customers all shared essentially the same long-term interests. Moreover, he demonstrated considerable financial skill, keeping the company out of bankruptcy during the Great Depression.[54]

Following the Willard presidency, the B&O would not have another prominent leader until Jervis assumed the office. Colonel Roy B. White, who took the throttle on the eve of World War II and remained until 1953, and his successor Howard E. Simpson, who occupied the executive suite until 1961, confronted a host of nagging problems, mostly stemming from increased modal competition and labor and material costs. But these executives offered neither inspiring nor imaginative leadership. Moreover, White and Simpson were not generally recognized for their grasp of industry matters, except for Simpson in the area of passenger operations.[55]

Port Differential Case

When Jervis arrived at B&O headquarters during the Simpson presidency, he immediately confronted a major issue, the "port differential case." As Jervis recalled, "I remember that I spent a substantial part of my time on that case for the first three years. Not all of my time, but practically all of my time."

This was not a small matter for the B&O, the City of Baltimore, and the State of Maryland. At first the conflict arose between the port authorities of Maryland and New York over existing import-export freight rates. Rail charges through the Baltimore facility were three cents per 100 pounds of general cargo *less* than New York. The justification was that rail distances between interior points, specifically Central Freight Association territory, and New York were longer. Baltimore representatives also contended that their harbor enjoyed greater efficiency in dockside performance by both management and labor. But executives from such railroads as the Erie, Lackawanna and NYC and New York City port officials wanted to end the lower Baltimore charges, hoping to capture additional traffic that flowed from the Midwest over B&O rails and in lesser volume via the Western Maryland to Baltimore. The nine protesting railroads claimed that they were being "bled white" by the lower rates that incidentally stemmed from an agreement signed by the principal carriers in 1877. By the mid-1950s, business interests in port cities throughout the region were fighting to boost revenues through their harbors, and Gotham-related interests were losing the battle for waterborne exports, due to dock congestion, labor problems, and economic growth in the South and West. Then there was the impending opening of the St. Lawrence Seaway. New York was not pleased either that Newport News and Norfolk, Virginia, also had the three-cent differential. Philadelphia, on the other hand, charged a lower rate of two cents. The issue went to the ICC, and on January 3, 1961, after extensive hearings regulators decided in favor of Baltimore and the "southern tier" ports. The Commission likewise upheld the Philadelphia differential. These locations could continue to hold an advantage over New York in rail rates on commodities in foreign trade. Jervis, the railroad, city, and state were delighted: "We all felt great."[56]

The battle for the B&O and its supporters continued when Boston and other "northern tier" ports intervened, including Albany, New York, and Portland, Maine. Since Boston and its partner ports shared New York rates, largely because of their distance from inland points, local officials wanted to end any economic advantages that Baltimore and the southern tier ports received. The matter went to a Boston federal court where a special three-judge panel ruled to overturn the ICC order. "The court," recalled Jervis, "was so offended by the fact that anybody should have a lower rate than Boston." In time the case reached the U.S. Supreme Court, and Jervis argued on behalf of Baltimore and also for Newport News, Norfolk, and Philadelphia. Yet the parties represented by Jervis lost when the high court in May 1963 divided four to four, thus allowing the lower court decision to stand.

Jervis did not accept defeat, however. In December 1965, the ICC sanctioned reduced carload commodity rates on paper and paper products for export through the Port of Baltimore, a case that Jervis had initiated immediately after the adverse Supreme Court ruling. He correctly sensed that to start the differential battle anew, the strategy needed to be on a commodity rather than a general basis. By the time of the ICC victory, Jervis had left the B&O, yet he still cared deeply about this matter.[57]

As the port differential case progressed, Jervis took the initiative to reorganize the legal department. With Burgess retired, Jervis had the opportunity to make the day-to-day work more efficient, a hallmark of his subsequent presidency. The B&O long had attorneys in offices in Chicago, Cincinnati, and New York City. "I thought that was unnecessary, that we could cover the situation by bringing these fellows to Baltimore." At Jervis's request, local counsel would be retained to handle accident cases. As head of the legal department, Jervis also made it clear that colleagues should never show any extravagance. One day as Jervis left a passenger coach and was walking down the platform at Camden Station in Baltimore, he received greetings from several of his lawyers, who were leaving the first-class parlor car. Quipped Jervis: "If the VP can ride coach, so can the assistant attorneys." Recalled an associate: "After that encounter, they did!"[58]

In his newfound position Jervis revealed additional aspects of his executive style. He did not shun performing small details, particularly if they would assist others, yet he realized that he could not be overburdened with too many tasks. As a reporter put it, "His natural ability guides him as to where to draw the line." Significantly, too, there must be delegation of authority to competent individuals and open, honest dialogue was critical to the success of any endeavor.[59]

Even though deeply involved in the port differential case, Jervis continued to use public presentations and publications as bully pulpits to promote awareness of the necessity of rate-making reform. And he kept fellow executives at the B&O properly informed. "During the past five years the railroads of the country have been trying to obtain a competitive rate rule in the Interstate Commerce Act which would give them the unquestioned right to make rates based on railroad conditions and without regard to truck or water carrier conditions," he told President Simpson in early 1959. "Shipping interests throughout the country have been generally sympathetic to the railroads and given them valuable support. Motor and water carriers have been strongly opposed." Explained Jervis, "If railroads have the right to make rates based on their condition (subject of course to a prohibition against practices which are 'unfair' or 'destructive' in fact), their objective in each instance should be a rate level that maximizes *their* net revenues." How is such a rate level set? According to Jervis, "It is arrived at by measuring the probable effect of varying rate levels on traffic volume and then (after some trial and error perhaps) selecting that particular level which will produce the most revenues *after* deducting the costs which attend the movement of traffic. In most cases, such costs should be those that vary over the long term, including return on investment." He urged Simpson to take the rate matter before the Eastern Railroad Presidents Conference and to underscore that the established albeit amateurish practice conducted by "the old-time rate men" had to end. "While the objectives of rate-making are today the same as in the pre-competition era," Jervis reminded Simpson, "the complexity of the factual situations which must be unraveled has increased 100 times, and the help of technical people including economists, cost people, and trained investigators is indispensable in my judgment."[60]

By the late 1950s, though, Jervis was not overly pessimistic about the fate of the railroad industry. He recognized challenges, particularly in the area of rate-making and public subsidies for competing forms of transport. Yet he had hopes that the regulatory environment would improve. After all, the ICC recently had sped up the administrative machinery, and indications signaled that inequalities in regulation might be reduced. Specifically, Congress had passed the Transportation Act of 1958 (Smathers Act), which brought about a promise that the regulatory stranglehold might be loosened. In fact, in a single remarkable sentence, the statute commanded the ICC not to keep any railroad's rates high to protect another mode of transportation, including motor carriers. This is exactly what Jervis had long advocated.[61]

Other matters required attention. Jervis remained convinced that something must be done about "the inclination to dump in the Commission's lap controversies which the railroads are completely free to settle themselves." Reminiscent of Herbert Hoover's rhetoric as secretary of commerce during the early 1920s, Jervis believed that *private* corporations and expertise could perform public functions but without the drawbacks associated with government bureaucracies. This maturing railroad executive realized that his industry needed better, stronger guidance, for carriers operated in a highly regulated environment that left little room for the entrepreneurial spirit. Soon he would contribute that much-needed leadership at the B&O and become widely recognized for his accomplishments.[62]

3 B&O President

The Urge to Merge

As Jervis dealt with the port differential case and a host of often mundane legal matters, first as a commerce lawyer and later as vice president and general counsel for the Baltimore & Ohio Railroad (B&O), he became aware of a force that appeared to be on the verge of buffeting, even engulfing, the national railroad industry: corporate mergers. The 1960s became the time of "merger madness," particularly in the East. A variety of consolidations occurred, ranging from parent companies adding subsidiaries to the formation of wholly new corporations.

Railroad unification was hardly a new issue. Virtually every existing carrier reflected this process. System building, which in the latter part of the nineteenth century had swept the industry, involved various legal arrangements, typically corporate stock purchases and long-term leases. Examples abound. In 1893 J. P. Morgan, who sought to bring order and stability to the railroad enterprise, spearheaded the welding together of an assortment of roads into the mighty Southern Railway, thereby enhancing the quality and profitability of rail service in the Southeast. Other companies were reorganized or created between 1893 and the early 1900s. Following federal control of most carriers during World War I, Congress passed and President Woodrow Wilson signed the Transportation Act of 1920 (Esch-Cummins Act). A key provision of the law called for the Interstate Commerce Commission (ICC) to prepare a set of consolidation plans whereby strong and weak roads would be merged. The notion of enforced competition as a panacea for perceived railroad abuses was rejected; instead, the idea prevailed that the public interest would be better served by encouraging financially healthy carriers to take over their less fortunate brethren. For the next decade the ICC toyed with two basic plans that would produce a dozen or so robust albeit largely competing systems. Under the initial consolidation scheme, which the ICC unveiled in 1921, the B&O became the core component of "System No. 3–Baltimore & Ohio." The company would be joined by six smaller carriers, the most significant being the New York, New Haven & Hartford (New Haven) and the Reading. Then, in late 1929, the ICC announced its revised or "final" plan. This time the B&O became the principal unit in "System No. 5–Baltimore & Ohio." Although the New Haven was dropped, the much larger System No. 5 still included the Reading, but also contained the Central Railroad Company of New Jersey (Jersey Central), Chicago & Alton, and a variety of shortlines and terminal roads. Strong resistance from the wealthiest carriers and the numerous bankruptcies triggered by the Great Depression of the 1930s led federal officials to abandon their dreams of a limited number of railroads. While the ICC approved a few corporate unions during the 1920s and 1930s, they were largely of modest import. More significantly, the urge to merge before the Crash of 1929 was achieved through holding companies and stock strategies, most effectively executed by the remarkable Van Sweringen brothers of Cleveland. The outbreak of World War II and the ensuing conflict in which railroads contributed so much to an allied victory ended, with a few exceptions, any serious discussion of corporate unifications. In fact, in the years between the Transportation Act of 1940 (Wheeler-Lea Act) and the Transportation Act of 1958 (Smathers Act), a Senate subcommittee on antitrust and monopoly concluded that "the impact of these merger and control transactions upon competition and concentration of economic power was not extensive."[1]

In time, however, striking changes came. In the immediate postwar period, most railroad leaders thought that the future looked promising. Profits earned from the crush of wartime business and income produced by a peacetime boom boded well, indeed. But soon there developed a widespread feeling that the massive savings derived from technology replacements, most of all expensive steam locomotives with more economical diesel-electric motive power, offered exciting prospects. But vanquishing the venerable iron horse could generate only finite savings. That economic reality needed to be recognized, as well as the increasing and often intense competition from private automobiles and commercial trucks, which operated on an ever-improving network of public highways. That fact became paramount with the interstate system that took shape after 1956. There was also the negative impact of aggressive barge operators who used federally subsidized waterways. Moreover, a thriving air transport industry, which all levels of government promoted, adversely affected long-distance passenger ridership. These factors collectively stimulated a renewed interest in railroad unification with a goal of economy of scale. The consensus grew that if carriers were to remain economically viable, mergers were the practical solution. Enlightened observers realized that mergers could save money, especially by consolidating duplicate operations, and that a strong company might save a weaker road. Yet uniting two languishing carriers would likely produce only a larger anemic railroad. And after passage of the Transportation Act of 1958, few railroaders anticipated a radical lessening or even a weakening of regulatory control that might offer meaningful economic assistance.[2]

The industry generated speculation, and several companies announced plans for actual unification. On August 31, 1957, the first merger of what became a rash of corporate marriages took place when the 1,043-mile Nashville, Chattanooga & St. Louis Railway (NC&StL) united with the 4,785-mile Louisville & Nashville Railroad (L&N), the latter having had stock control of the former since the 1880s. Designed to save nearly $4 million annually, the combined NC&StL–L&N claimed to be the initial merger designed for retrenchment. Line abandonments and elimination of duplicate support facilities and personnel would create the expected economies. Although the NC&StL–L&N combination, which was mostly a paper transaction, performed well, the industry paid closer attention to the union of two competing roads, the 611-mile Virginian Railway (VGN) and the 2,132-mile Norfolk & Western Railway (N&W). These Pocahontas coal carriers already enjoyed robust health, but consolidation of their business and operational activities would further enhance profitability. This merger, which the ICC speedily endorsed, became effective on December 1, 1959, and helped to intensify unification talks among major railroads in the East.[3]

The merger proposal that caught the immediate attention and deep concern of Jervis and his colleagues came on November 1, 1957. On that day Robert R. Young, the power at the New York Central (NYC), and James Symes, president of the Pennsylvania (PRR), surprisingly announced their "mutual intent" to explore the possibility of unification. At this time these carriers were superpowers in railroading, yet they had long been intense rivals. The NYC and PRR, if united, would be the tenth-largest corporation in the nation, with assets of $5 billion and nearly 185,000 employees. Symes boasted that the combination could generate savings of $100 million annually and perhaps even more. Observed historian Richard Saunders Jr., "The Penn Central proposal threw all other merger talk in the East into a state of panic." And that is exactly what happened at B&O headquarters in Baltimore. Jervis recalled, "I was called into the president's office and Howard Simpson . . . was white. He was so upset. Here were the two principal competitors of the B&O, which was the smallest of the three, getting together." Jervis calmed Simpson by pointing out that the U.S. Department of Justice would surely intervene and "that there would be enough antitrust problems in the case so that the Commission [ICC] wouldn't approve it." Jervis astutely commented that if the government cleared the tracks for merger, the NYC–PRR would be "screwed up for years" and that the B&O would probably benefit.[4]

The B&O dared not ignore what could happen in the East. Not long after the NYC–PRR announcement, Simpson mentioned to Walter Tuohy, his counterpart at the Chesapeake & Ohio (C&O), that they should consider unification. Feelers were also extended to the strategic and profitable New York, Chicago & St. Louis Railroad, better known as the Nickel Plate Road (NKP). There was real concern among those roads most likely to be damaged by an NYC–PRR union. Indeed, in November 1958, William White, the gifted leader of the Delaware & Hudson Railroad (D&H) and former head of the Delaware, Lackawanna & Western (Lackawanna) and NYC, brought together high-ranking representatives from the B&O, C&O, D&H, Erie, Lackawanna, and Reading to discuss the evolving merger situation. "No commitments were made, but channels of communication were opened."[5]

But for the B&O and the other major carriers in the East, the "heat was off," at least momentarily, as relations between the NYC and PRR cooled. NYC president Alfred Perlman said that "the merger was the PRR's idea in the first place, that James Symes was its only real proponent, and that the PRR people had badgered him about it ever since." The story, however, was more complicated. The PRR had given approval for its subsidiary, N&W, to take over the VGN, and this angered Perlman because the VGN was the friendly connection for his road to tap lucrative coal traffic in West Virginia. An N&W–VGN marriage would ultimately strengthen the PRR but weaken the NYC. Moreover, union of these roads would diminish the bargaining position of the NYC as a merger partner. Another factor in the collapse of this proposed merger was the suicide of Robert Young on January 25, 1958.

This put Perlman in charge of the NYC, and he had "no love for the PRR Neanderthals."[6]

Still the possibility of a union between the two giants in the East made a number of railroads proactive on the merger front, the most notable being consolidation of the faltering Erie and the Lackawanna, creating the Erie-Lackawanna Railroad on October 1, 1960. Simpson and Tuohy had not forgotten their earlier conversations. At an informal meeting in March 1960, Tuohy indicated that the C&O was interested in the B&O, but as a "consolidation" rather than as a merger. (Simpson preferred to call the arrangement an "affiliation.") If this were to happen, the C&O would need to obtain 80 percent of the B&O's stock; the Internal Revenue Service required that amount before the C&O could reduce its federal taxes by taking advantage of B&O's sizable tax loss carry-forwards. Tuohy shunned actual merger because of the B&O's considerable debt, recent poor earnings, and growing maintenance and rolling stock needs. The debt matter was extremely important to Tuohy and his associates. "At the time, the C&O was paranoid about its dividend and credit rating and wanted no part of B&O's debt," explained a junior officer. The C&O, too, was not anxious to lose the handsome Maryland state property tax exemptions that would disappear if the B&O were dissolved. Yet Tuohy knew that based on operating revenues the B&O was "no small potatoes." The Baltimore-based company ranked as the nation's sixth-largest railroad and the C&O as its seventh. If a union occurred, the C&O and B&O would be the biggest transporter of coal in the world. More discussions followed, and on May 18, 1960, the B&O board of directors accepted the C&O offer.[7]

Yet all was not well for corporate coupling. Perlman and the NYC wanted into this arrangement, believing that an NYC–C&O–B&O merger would create a healthy property and certainly one that could fend off an expanded PRR or any other mega-merger in the region. This union, Perlman thought, would produce an ideally balanced rail structure in the Northeast, resulting in a system of about 21,000 miles with approximately $1.5 billion in annual gross revenues. In fact, it was widely acknowledged in industry circles that the PRR should go in with one group of eastern roads and the NYC with another. Tuohy appeared ready to discuss a three-way arrangement, and the B&O concurred. On August 15, 1960, Simpson, with authorization from the B&O board and the board's executive committee, met with Tuohy and Perlman. Although the gathering adjourned without an agreement, Simpson informed them that the B&O "stands ready to propose to our stockholders a merger of the three companies that would result in a new corporation." In a subsequent pronouncement Simpson restated the position of the B&O,

namely, that "a merger between the C&O, NYC and the B&O is in the interest of the security holders of the three companies and, imperatively, in the interest of the general public."[8]

While B&O forces were willing to accept a three-way union, by that summer the C&O had changed its mind. One explanation involves the role played by Cyrus Eaton, the iconoclastic chairman of the C&O board of directors. The crusty Eaton did not like Perlman, whom he considered "gruff and undiplomatic" and likely to dominate. And Eaton worried about the financial condition of the NYC, including its debt load, unprofitable commuter operations, and declining freight traffic. In a similar vein, Tuohy explained to Hays Watkins, C&O general auditor, that he had told Perlman that the C&O could not afford a three-way merger. "C&O's financial strength is not enough to carry both New York Central and B&O, so we're going to stick with the B&O, [and] there's more compatibility." Both men knew that the consolidation strategy with the B&O was a way for the C&O to hedge its bet. If the B&O turned out to be a disaster, the C&O could cut the financial strings. Yet Tuohy had stressed to Simpson that "the plan for B&O–C&O affiliation now, followed by merger, is a unique means by which to realize early benefits to both properties." And Tuohy told Perlman to be patient "and let our two roads get together" and that he would consider "the New York Central's inclusion at a later date."[9]

Nevertheless, the NYC wanted in, and so in June 1960 the company made a direct bid for the B&O. Specifically, the package involved $9.00 cash and 1.5 shares of NYC common for each B&O share until the NYC had control of 60 percent of B&O's voting stock. At the time of this tender offer, the value of this proposal amounted to about $42.50 a share. Earlier the C&O extended an offer for the B&O that totaled $35.00, but this coal-rich carrier faithfully paid a $4.00 annual dividend while the financially struggling NYC gave only a $1.00 dividend, and that payment was in doubt. One source branded NYC stock as "speculative." Unlike the NYC, the C&O had "enormous resources." Reflected Jervis, "The New York Central didn't have a chance."[10]

A full-blown proxy fight erupted. Investors and financiers took notice of the battered B&O. Soon the C&O and NYC sent high-ranking officials to Switzerland to persuade banking executives, who allegedly held about 40 percent of the 3,146,949 outstanding B&O shares, to tell investors to back their respective positions. *Trains* editor David P. Morgan wrote, "The traceable costs of the 'who gets B&O' affair now include brokerage fees, mimeograph press release stencils, several airline tickets to Switzerland, and some very hard feelings." Although the C&O had much greater success with these financiers than did its rival, only 29 percent of B&O shareholders had committed their certificates to the C&O by September, when the offer expired. B&O leaders did not care for this conflict. Said Simpson, "Neither the interests of our three railroads nor the public interest would be advanced by a struggle for control of the B&O between two of the great railroad systems of the Nation."[11]

In the midst of the battle between the C&O and NYC for B&O shareholder support, Simpson and some fellow executives developed second thoughts about C&O control. If successful, the B&O would not be guaranteed anything except the promise of widespread betterments, and "the C&O could loot it and leave it helpless." Simpson and his colleagues, including Jervis, wanted a specific merger proposal from the C&O, thus allowing the B&O to have a voice in determining a variety of matters, including executive leadership and location of corporate headquarters. That sentiment explains why the B&O board at its September 21, 1960, meeting directed representatives to participate in studies with the NYC to determine what could be saved through outright unification. The C&O made its intentions clear: first control and then merger. Perlman, on the other hand, announced that the NYC wanted immediate union with the B&O and not control as either a first step toward merger or an end in itself. This position pleased some powerful B&O executives and investors. "A control situation," explained Simpson publicly, "would make possible only a minimal portion of the savings that would be possible were a merger accomplished."[12]

Throughout this time of financial Ping-Pong, Jervis preferred alignment with the NYC rather than the C&O; he disliked "the caliber of the [C&O] management" and appreciated the imaginative improvements that had been occurring on the NYC. Unlike the C&O, the NYC was a much more venturesome railroad. Jervis was well aware that Perlman had recruited bright young men and promoted others of talent. These "Perlman boys" were energizing the property, perhaps most visibly with intermodal "Flexi-Vans," a novel concept in truck-train service that particularly captivated Jervis's fancy. He was also impressed with the NYC's interest in developing a program of market research. Moreover, the NYC and the B&O would be a good physical fit, for the NYC paralleled about 1,200 miles of the B&O and the two companies had 81 common interchange points. Even though Jervis was a respected vice president and regularly attended meetings of the B&O board, "I didn't say much about it one way or the other." After all, he was hardly in a position to alter the course of events. Yet it is likely that other officials and board members knew his feelings. Later Jervis revealed that he had preferred a B&O–C&O–NYC union and a PRR–N&W–Wabash affiliation. "Such a merger pattern would have produced two strong competitive systems in the East." He explained his reasoning this way: "Each system would serve the coal fields in southern West Virginia and eastern Kentucky and thus have the assured support of heavy volumes of that most desirable rail traffic: high grade bituminous coal." Only after years of maneuvering did a system that resembled what Jervis endorsed finally appear.[13]

The fight for the B&O continued, and on December 16, 1960, the C&O happily announced that it had 53 percent of the B&O stock tendered. Ultimately that amount climbed to approximately 60 percent, yet that did not stop the NYC. Not long thereafter Perlman's company offered $46 for a large block of B&O shares, a price that was about $10 more than what these securities were trading for on Wall Street. When the dust settled, the C&O had invested $29 million and the NYC and parent Alleghany Corporation had paid $13 million with the latter owning about 20 percent of the stock. While stymied in the proxy battle, the NYC believed that it still might prevent unification at the upcoming hearings before the ICC.[14]

On June 19, 1961, the fate of the B&O went before John Bradford, the ICC's veteran hearing examiner, and into the official jungle of red tape. There was not only the C&O proposal but also an application for joint NYC–C&O control of the B&O. During the summer and fall, 37 days of well-attended hearings were held at the imposing ICC quarters on Independence Avenue in Washington, D.C. The C&O argued that unless a favorable decision was quickly rendered, the B&O would sink into bankruptcy, but, of course, the C&O did not want the NYC to be included. The NYC made much of its contention that if the B&O–C&O combination occurred, 40 percent or more of NYC's traffic would be diverted, causing catastrophic financial results. Then on January 15, 1962, all the principal parties, except the NYC and its supporters, filed their final required briefs. On that day the Perlman road informed the ICC that three days earlier a merger agreement had been reached between the NYC and PRR boards. Symes had been the driving force in reopening NYC–PRR merger talks; in fact, nearly 11 months earlier, Symes and Tuohy had held a secret meeting at the C&O's Greenbrier Resort where Symes agreed to back C&O's bid for the B&O and Tuohy endorsed merger of the PRR and NYC. Perlman and his associates felt somewhat better that their railroad would not be left out in the cold.[15]

The Presidency Begins

A month before the ICC hearings commenced, 56-year-old Jervis Langdon took the presidential reins of the B&O. On May 17, 1961, the board of directors, meeting in New York City, voted him into office, effective June 1. His election, however, surprised many in the company. Some believed that the heir apparent to Howard Simpson would be Lloyd W. Baker, vice president for staff, who had been Simpson's right-hand man since 1956. In fact, there was a celebratory party planned by friends of Baker in Baltimore on the day that the board selected Jervis.[16]

The decision may also have surprised Jervis. In a June 1961 interview with Robert Bedingfield, business reporter for the *New York Times*, Jervis indicated that he had merely an inkling that he would be tapped to become the company's seventeenth president: "He was asked by Mr. Simpson two days before a B&O board meeting last month to redraw the company's by-laws to designate the chairman as chief executive officer." This was an indication that change was about to occur at the highest level of management. Would Simpson soon be vacating his post? If this happened, who would replace him?[17]

Although the exact reasons why B&O board wanted Jervis to succeed Simpson are not precisely known, evidence suggests that the Chase Manhattan Bank, which had loaned the railroad $15 million, was alarmed by a dramatically growing deficit and wanted Simpson out and "fresh blood" in. Simpson, who was 65 and approaching the customary (and mandatory) retirement age of 70, appeared ill-equipped to handle the challenges of the "merger crises" and "a railroad in financial trouble." And Baker seemed to have been cut from the same cloth as Simpson; he shared a similar career path, having risen through the ranks of the freight traffic department after joining the B&O in 1923 following high school. As a confidant put it, "The Board of Directors realized that the company required real leadership." A knowledgeable insider said simply, "Mr. Langdon just overshadowed everybody else." The fact that Jervis had been general counsel had allowed him to gain considerable knowledge of the strengths and weaknesses of the B&O, and board members grew to trust him, "even though [most] . . . didn't have any idea at all of what was going on in the operation of the road."[18]

The decision by the board to retire Simpson—actually to elevate him to the position of chairman of the board and chief executive officer and to send him off on an extended vacation—was surely not easy. There were ample critics of Simpson, of course. Remarked one official later: "The only thing that Simpson knew was when lunch was served," a cutting reference to his love of dining with associates and friends in his elegant executive dining room, which adjoined his suite on the third floor of the headquarters building. "Papa Simpson didn't have a clue about railroading," snorted another B&O officer. And hardly anyone applauded Simpson's fondness for baseball and racehorses.[19]

Jervis frequently addressed audiences, including an unidentified
gathering at the Greenbrier Hotel in White Sulphur Springs,
West Virginia, in the early 1960s. (Irene Langdon)

Perhaps criticism of Simpson and his regime should be tempered by noting
the tenor of the times. After all, most authorities saw the 1950s as a decade of
conformity. Young men were being trained to think and act in unison, to absorb the values of the team, and to suppress any truly innovative ideas in the
interest of harmony. It was the age of "the man in the gray flannel suit."[20]

Howard Edward Simpson unquestionably possessed talents, and they
were easily visible. Everyone could admire his rise to the B&O presidency.

Born into a large family in Jersey City on March 15, 1896, Simpson's child-hood had been difficult. His father, a traveling salesman, and his mother would die prematurely, and so relatives had taken in the lad and his siblings. Being the oldest child, Simpson received only a grade school education be-fore entering the workforce. Yet for years he "supplemented his grammar school training with business courses and planned reading programs." At the age of 16, Simpson accepted an entry-level job as a $20-a-month file clerk in the passenger department of the Jersey Central (a far cry from his $130,000 salary as B&O president) and received several minor advancements. This tall and "stocky" man, who had been raised in a rough-and-tumble neigh-borhood, excelled at playing baseball, including industrial baseball on a team sponsored by the railroad. During World War I Simpson interrupted his career to join the Navy, going to sea as a quartermaster. After his return to civilian life, he rejoined the Jersey Central as a rate clerk and advanced to the position of city passenger agent in Jersey City. He continued to win promotions, becoming assistant general passenger agent in 1926. Five years later, he joined the parent B&O as general eastern passenger agent. By 1952 Simpson had advanced to vice president for traffic, and in September 1953 he became president. His impressive rise revealed an atypical path to the presidency of a major railroad, for he was not an accountant, engineer, or lawyer. Simpson understandably was enormously proud of his accomplish-ments.[21]

The gregarious Simpson learned "all sides of railroad operations." But his foremost skills involved the passenger sector. It was Simpson who originated the concept of reserved coach seating. Surely, though, his most remembered triumph involved introduction of one of the most acclaimed passenger trains of the interwar period, the *Blue Comet,* which on February 21, 1929, made its inaugural run between Jersey City and Atlantic City. "The Seashore's Finest Train" sported an eye-catching cream-colored band that extended the length of each richly painted dark-blue car and reminded trackside observers of a comet streaking through space. But Simpson knew more than how to attract revenue riders; he realized early on that the "passenger train was on life sup-port." The automobile, he argued, "offered convenience, and people did not have to take the 7:09." Yet, until the advent of the interstate highway system, Simpson thought that long-distance passenger trains that were clean, com-fortable, and dependable had a future, particularly the flagship trains of the B&O, the *Capitol Limited* (Baltimore–Washington–Chicago) and the *National Limited* (Baltimore–Washington–St. Louis). For years these popular trains remained star performers and provided considerable marquee or ad-vertising value for the company.

Simpson also exhibited personal qualities that Jervis and others could readily admire. Simpson was kind and generous—"he showed great charity to all people"—and he revealed no ethnic or racial prejudices, unusual among railroaders. Simpson was a doting family man with a wife and son. He attended a Presbyterian church and walked two to three miles daily around the running track at Johns Hopkins University. He smoked cigars but drank in moderation. People often were drawn to him because he possessed all those stereotypical traits of the crackerjack salesman.[22]

In the final assessment, Howard Simpson represented the traditional railroad executive of the regulation era, an individual who might show an innovative spark but who largely accepted the status quo. Simpson continually lauded increased carload volumes, "the carload count system," but he never wanted to explore the actual cost of handling the traffic. "The old up-from-the-ranks management had only the objective of increasing freight volume," recalled a highly critical associate. Simpson possessed a salesman's mind, wishing to promote but not to understand the true economics of the situation. Similarly, he believed that the ills of the industry could be largely resolved by confronting "passenger problems," most likely through public subsidies. Simpson avoided the more pressing impact that barges, pipelines, and trucks had on railroad revenues. And the B&O president allowed old habits to prevail, including rampant nepotism at all levels of employment and excessive drinking by some officials. Also, he seemed to share the resentment of some executives, including those in the traffic department, toward employment of college graduates.[23]

Fortunately, Simpson thought highly of Jervis, and he knew him well. The two men had worked closely for nearly six years, especially after Jervis became a vice president. Simpson respected Jervis's legal training, his intellectual and managerial abilities, and his forthrightness. As Simpson said, "The Company is fortunate to have a man with the character, experience, and capabilities of Mr. Langdon to lead and guide it in the days ahead." Jervis was honest and direct with his boss. "I never minced my words with him." No wonder Simpson "felt comfortable turning over the B&O to Langdon."

Simpson was also impressed with Lloyd Baker and may have sought to advance his candidacy. Baker was not bereft of talent, and the day that Jervis received the presidential nod, the board named Baker senior vice president. Yet Baker became "essentially a supernumerary" and dropped out of sight after being named in early 1962 vice president for purchases, properties, and industrial development. "Langdon didn't like Baker," related an underling, "and perhaps that feeling was long-standing."[24]

Jervis was ready for the biggest assignment in his professional career. A man who disliked pomp and shunned attention, his first days in the presidential suite accurately reflected his personality. Al Clements Jr., Jervis's administrative assistant, vividly recalled that, as soon as Jervis took over, he instructed Clements to do three things immediately. First, he was to sell the two Cadillac limousines: one used by Simpson and one reserved for senior executives or visiting VIPs. Next, he was to find jobs in the railroad for the displaced chauffeurs, who were men of color. Third, he was to close the executive dining room. And it would not be long before Jervis made another demand: "Retire Mr. Simpson's office car, the No. 904."[25]

Jervis had both professional and personal reasons for this immediate simplification of presidential life. "I am going to sell those limos," Jervis told his wife. "They are the worst things for morale!" The B&O was in a perilous position financially, and having these trappings of power and wealth certainly conveyed the wrong message. A signal needed to be sent that the new president was concerned about all the employees and the carrier. Frankly, Jervis did not want to ride with anyone; he would either walk or drive himself. He would certainly rather hike the 10 blocks between headquarters and Camden Station; Simpson had usually taken the Cadillac. The new attitude pleased the employees. B&O locomotive specialist Harry Eck recalled "the pleasure of seeing him walk from the Central Building to Camden Station." Jervis often walked from his home on Warrenton Road in suburban Guilford to North Avenue to catch a transit bus to the office. The operation of an executive dining room also wasted company money, and Jervis preferred a light lunch that he ate at his desk or at a nearby cafe. His usual fare included soup, especially cream-based ones, applesauce, and possibly half a sandwich. These favorites reflected his modest, healthy eating habits: for breakfast it was "hot oatmeal from scratch," toast, and coffee, and for dinner it was fish or meat, potato, vegetables, and maybe fruit compote as the dessert. The thought of regularly using an office car also had no appeal. As Jervis once told a journalist, "You can't tell anything about the road hitched onto the tail of a train." If he did take a B&O passenger train, he preferred sleeping in a Pullman or even a less comfortable Slumbercoach and eating in the diner, perhaps with a shipper or politician. On lengthy business trips Jervis flew coach class or piloted his own airplane, which he dearly enjoyed. "On long trips, time is too valuable for any other mode of transport," he opined. Along the way Jervis often used a telephone booth as his office.[26]

If employees at the B&O did not learn of Jervis's immediate office reforms, they knew that he cared for them. In early 1961, prior to his presidency, all salaried employees took a 10 percent reduction in their income, an effort by the Simpson administration to save resources. However, Jervis immediately canceled the salary cut, indicating that families needed to be properly supported. He realized that the B&O was not paying officers and staff excessive wages. "That decision," recalled a rising professional, "was really a morale booster and a shrewd move on the part of Langdon." Jervis, though, did not seek a salary increase for himself, remaining content with his base annual income of $75,000 (approximately $493,000 in 2006 dollars).[27]

Jervis quickly established a daily work routine, paralleling the regime that he had practiced as a lawyer. Jervis was a "morning person," rising early and engaging in a vigorous workout program outlined in the newly popular Royal Canadian Air Force exercise training manual, *The 11-Minute-a-Day Plan for Men*. By 7:00 AM he customarily reached his office and would read the daily railroad report that Al Clements, who had arrived somewhat earlier, had left on his cluttered desk. But unlike his predecessors and most fellow railroad presidents, Jervis "worked without much assistance." He often typed his own letters and reports "on a vintage machine," although he might dictate letters to Clements. And he willingly used interoffice "squawk boxes" to communicate with other executives in the building. In late afternoon, Jervis left for an occasional meeting or dinner. His preference, though, was to go home. Not only was there his adoring second wife, Irene, but also on September 1, 1957, their son, Halsey Warren, arrived, and later, on April 20, 1962, another son, Charles Jervis, was born. Jervis told office employees not to work on Saturdays or Sundays so they could enjoy their own families and "recharge their batteries." On weekends he, with his high energy level, would contact operating personnel and others to check on the general status of the railroad or to deal with specific problems or emergencies.

This office style reflected Jervis's personality and appealed to most others, high and low. "A few people did not care for his informality," however. Since Jervis liked to work in shirtsleeves, but always wearing a tie, he never complained about an individual's dress. This "casual person" shunned hats; in fact, he ended that tradition at headquarters. Jervis annoyed some executives when he made it clear that expensive Christmas presents from suppliers and others, and to each other, would not be tolerated. He did indicate, though, that "you can have a gift as long as you can eat or drink it in one day." This had not been the policy during previous administrations when Simpson especially reveled in the "considerable spoils of his office." Jervis gave few if any gifts to colleagues. His secretary vividly remembered a "gift" that he once received before Christmas. "I found on my desk a note that was on a piece of torn scrap paper that read, 'Al, You have a lot of talents and you do them well. Jervis.'"

To observant employees, the boss appeared to be a boat-rocker in a tradition-bound company. As might be expected, "the old types were scared to death of Langdon." On the other hand, "young Turks" showed excitement about his emerging presidency. "These young men wanted to build a railroad. . . . Langdon appeared to be their man. They liked his style and his willingness to try novel ways to save the B&O and make it a solid component in any future system, whether part of the C&O or not."[28]

Crisis

Being the newly elected president of the B&O should have given Jervis an acid stomach or some other health problems, for the railroad faced a final crisis of massive proportions. In 1961, the B&O's net income deficit soared to a staggering $31,347,341, the poorest performance for any railroad that year and the worst showing in the 135-year history of the road. Insolvency loomed. "I thought to myself that this company is headed for bankruptcy," Jervis later confessed. "Can't avoid it."

The B&O's troubling financial condition had not developed overnight; problems had been mounting for years. Although during the early and mid-1950s the railroad had experienced relative prosperity, conditions worsened after 1956. A variety of factors contributed to these difficulties. Since the B&O had avoided receivership during the Great Depression and had not benefited from a streamlined debt structure as a result of reorganization, a high level of bonded debt plagued the company. This drained income for interest, and payments had to be made regularly regardless of cash flow. The B&O also suffered from increasing equipment and joint-facility rental debits. Annual obligations to banks and insurance companies for loans for diesel locomotives and freight cars coupled with higher per diem rates on freight equipment inflicted additional financial pain. Moreover, losses mounted on passenger operations. Based on "fully distributed costs," they exceeded $10 million in 1962, even though the company had won regulatory approval to discontinue 138 passenger trains between 1949 and 1959. This accomplishment had produced an annual net savings of more than $15 million. The most celebrated and cost-effective passenger train removal, which saved about $5 million annually, had come in 1958 with elimination of service along the "Royal Blue Line" between Baltimore and New York City. It was Howard Simpson who helped to make this substantial contribution to the bottom line. He employed his exceptional salesman's skills, convincing community leaders and others along the route that the "takeoff" was in the public interest. "Declining patronage, heavy deficits, and lack of public need for the service made this action necessary." The B&O was battered further by the opening of the St. Lawrence Seaway, which shifted some bulk commodities from the rails to barges and cargo vessels and forced a downward adjustment in freight rates. Then there was that steady erosion of traffic as motor carriers increased their market share. And steam coal shipments to power plants in the Northeast were being lost as residual oil was more commonly used. There was also the very real threat of nuclear power stations replacing conventional electric-generating units.[29]

Yet there was still another cause for the B&O's failing financial health: the national recession of 1958. The railroad was heavily dependent on cyclical heavy industry, though historically having weaker market penetration than either the NYC or PRR. When automobile makers, coal operators, steel manufacturers, and other shippers cut production, freight revenues fell 17 percent. Car loadings, which started to slide in early September 1957, dropped from roughly 10,000 a month to about 8,000 a month and remained at that depressed level for more than a year. Then in 1959 the company felt the sting of a costly 116-day steel strike. Adding to the financial woes were the unusually harsh winters of 1959–60 and 1960–61, the latter costing the railroad nearly $1.4 million in extra expenditures.[30]

The Simpson administration had attempted to cope, but some forces were beyond anyone's control. Although involved in several major and much-needed capital improvement projects, the company had no choice but to retrench. The partially completed yard and terminal improvements at Cumberland, Maryland, for example, were placed on hold. Also troubling was the railroad's inability to push ahead with the program to raise clearances of 18 tunnels on an 80-mile stretch of the main line to Cincinnati and St. Louis between Clarksburg and Parkersburg, West Virginia. These obstructions, which prevented handling modern (13-foot 6-inch) piggyback trailers and the new high or wide boxcars, had to be enlarged, bypassed, or "day-lighted" (removing the tunnel top). "Here we were, the shortest route between Baltimore and St. Louis," noted Jervis, "and we were not competitive because we couldn't handle the equipment." Similarly, the B&O suffered from a plethora of "bad order" equipment. Sidings became clogged, as nearly a quarter of the road's cars were stored awaiting major repairs or the scrapper's torch. The locomotive situation, too, was not good, as deferred maintenance had taken its toll and more powerful, modern units were badly needed. And throughout this 13-state network, poor track conditions caused costly derailments and spawned a blizzard of "slow orders," making service less reliable.[31]

Simpson had thrown himself into efforts to keep the B&O afloat. This consummate salesman opted for repeated pep talks: "Your management retains its same, firm faith in the future of the industry and the company." He shared these thoughts directly with the rank and file: "Employees can help by getting on with the job, by curbing needless worry and speculation, and by accentuating the positive at work and when discussing our business with others." Perhaps these directives were reasonable, but moral suasion usually has little positive impact on a financial crisis.[32]

Irrespective of Simpson's relentless cheerleading, an unbiased examination of management the day that Jervis took charge would reveal numerous shortcomings. Considerable ossification had taken place, dating back to the time of Daniel Willard. "People just did the things the way that they had always done them," observed an official. "There was really the feeling among certain department heads that they did not need to change anything." Commented another, "There really were a lot of old school railroad types." One of Jervis's lieutenants was more blunt: "The whole B&O leadership was dead above the neck."

Even if top management were not brain-dead, department heads frequently lacked the necessary information to perform properly. Managers needed to know the facts if they were to respond effectively. "If you had money, you couldn't spend it if you did not know that you had these resources," remembered one officer. "I know that a lot of key personnel at the B&O did not understand the dire financial situation as of 1961." These systemic weaknesses made it difficult to cope with a host of pressing problems.[33]

Jervis Responds

Jervis realized that an immediate thoughtful and direct response to the financial woes of the B&O was mandatory. Selling the Cadillacs, closing the executive dining room, and taking related actions were hardly enough, although admittedly they sent an immediate message to the corporate family about the priorities and expectations of the new boss. Cutbacks, especially among personnel, were mandatory. Within a year the number of employees had dropped to slightly below 30,000, or about 10 percent less than in 1960. And in late 1961 Jervis and the board agreed that the company would have to skip the next interest payment on its 4.5 percent convertible income bonds, forestalling an outlay of nearly $1 million. Since the indenture provisions on these bonds prevented dividends from being paid on either preferred or common stock, additional funds were saved. He hoped, even expected, that the company could turn around its financial affairs and pay both interest and dividends, and that is what happened. Jervis also decided to liquidate the B&O Insurance Fund, which dated from 1901, and to continue the protection of company property through self-insurance, supplemented by commercial carriers as needed, thus saving several hundred thousand dollars annually.[34]

Jervis sensed that the path to corporate success depended on the efforts of enlightened personnel who had the "competitive instinct." Opined a close associate, "Having the right people in the right places was what Langdon believed would turn around the railroad, and you know, he was 100 percent correct." The trait that helped to make Jervis an unusually capable railroad executive was his remarkable ability to size up individuals, for they were the critical components in making any bureaucracy function properly. In a sense, Jervis would begin to energize the faltering B&O on a one-to-one basis. Coupled to Jervis's people skills was another talent: according to David P. Morgan, "He knows which jobs have to be done and he does them."[35]

During the early months of his presidency, Jervis worked to replace those individuals who contributed little or nothing to overall performance. He benefited from the prompt retirements of senior officers in finance, marketing, and operations. With board approval Jervis announced that the retirement age would be lowered from 70 to 67, and then it would be lowered again annually until the age of 65 was reached, a policy in line with most major American businesses. Additional retirements followed. "So that really redid the top managerial positions almost overnight," remembered an associate. Moreover, he willingly dismissed unqualified or unneeded executives. For instance, Jervis got rid of Douglas Turnbull, who served as vice president for research and development under Simpson and whom President White in the early 1940s had hired for his local contacts. Turnbull came from a prominent Maryland family and was "well connected socially and politically," yet he was an inept administrator. Also during Jervis's tenure some "nonprogressive people were interchanged," meaning that these individuals, who were not devoid of skills, were moved to less important jobs at affiliated properties, for example, the Terminal Railroad Association of St. Louis and the Washington Terminal Company.[36]

Jervis then turned to identifying talent from within the B&O organization "at which he excelled" and subsequently sought outstanding individuals from beyond the company and even the railroad industry. "I was awfully lucky with the young talent that I found," he later admitted. Jervis wanted creative, aggressive, and dedicated employees who could "do things a different way," and he would succeed spectacularly.

Arguably the most valuable person that Jervis found within B&O ranks was William J. Dixon, a research engineer who had been with the company since 1948. Discovery of Dixon, who "was as smart as hell and had a high degree of integrity," came about through Jervis's contact with Aaron Gellman, a planning professional at the North American Car Corporation and then director of the transportation center at Northwestern University. Gellman had recognized Dixon's talents and told Jervis at a private dinner in Chicago that Dixon "was buried in the mechanical department so he wouldn't cause trouble."

Bill Dixon, who would become Jervis's unofficial chief-of-staff "and a sounding board" at the B&O and later at the Chicago, Rock Island & Pacific, was something of an "egghead." Born into a middle-class family in Pittsburgh on December 6, 1918, Dixon won financial aid for his college education at the hometown Carnegie Institute of Technology, where he graduated in 1940 with a degree in chemical engineering. The following year he completed a special transportation program at Yale University. Then came war, and Dixon, who had loved trains since childhood, entered the U.S. Army Military Railway Service. Commissioned an officer in the 711th Railway Operating Battalion, he participated in the construction of the 50-mile Claiborne-Polk Military Railroad in Louisiana and subsequently traveled with that army unit to the Middle East to assist in the operations of the Trans-Iranian Railroad, which served as a supply link to the Soviet Union. After the war, Dixon aided the Republic of South Korea in rebuilding its railroad infrastructure following the Japanese occupation. Before joining the B&O in 1948, he served as assistant transportation inspector for the New Haven, expanding his knowledge of the workaday world of railroading. During the Korean Conflict, Dixon, now a captain in the Army Reserves, interrupted his tenure at the B&O to serve for several years with the Army's Transportation and Development Station.[37]

Bright, hardworking, superbly trained, and experienced, Dixon had not flourished under the Simpson regime. This had happened largely because of Dixon's independence and demeanor. "Bill Dixon knew what needed to be done, but his various superiors often ignored his recommendations or gave him unimportant assignments," noted an associate. Moreover, "Bill was not an impressive guy. He didn't talk much and was shy and never developed much self-confidence."[38]

Even though his skills were not appreciated by the Simpson administration, he made important contributions. One involved computers. Not until the late 1950s did a few railroads take notice of the dawning computer age. But Dixon was convinced that the B&O needed to utilize this developing technology and carefully considered the options. Believing that DATAmatic Corporation, jointly owned by Raytheon and Honeywell, produced the best product, he used personal vacation time to explore details at DATAmatic's headquarters outside Boston. Dixon then recommended that the B&O invest $1.5 million in this giant first-generation computer, "the last of the broad-gauge computers with its three-inch tapes." Although IBM complained to B&O officials, disparaging Dixon's judgment, the DATAmatic-1000 was superior to the comparable IBM 705, in part due to its ability to read tapes backwards. It would not be until 1970, more than a decade after installation of this equipment on the tenth floor of company headquarters, that this machine was retired. The DATAmatic-1000 would do yeoman's service with such tasks as interline and freight-car accounting and payroll processing.[39]

Once Jervis plucked Dixon out of the ranks, he placed him in charge of the industrial engineering group (IE), a unit of the finance department. This think tank, which came into being in early 1962, was an entirely new concept as applied to railroad management and the first of Jervis's innovations at the B&O. Dixon was elated at becoming general manager of IE, and the bonds of commitment between Dixon and Jervis grew. "Working with Jervis was so pleasurable that I would have gone to the Podunk & Northern Railroad to be on his team," Dixon recalled. He particularly liked Jervis's style. "I had the independence to do what needed to be done, and I liked that control a great deal." Jervis never micromanaged. "There were weekly meetings and reports made to Jervis, and he would ask questions, and so could the staff. There was always an openness in communications." Dixon and others quickly realized that their boss was a superb motivator. In Dixon's words, "People wanted to work for him, and that allowed change to happen in the workplace."[40]

As IE evolved, Dixon assembled an able team of more than a dozen experts, "a very special group of mavericks," who studied an array of matters. Some were recruited from colleges and other railroads by Dixon himself, but most came from within the B&O organization, where they had often participated in the Technical Graduate Training Program (TGTP). This was the name the company gave to its management training operation, which dated from the White regime, officially beginning in 1950. These young TGTP men, who held an engineering degree or "comparable education," were exposed during a two-year program to all of the operating and nonoperating departments, including "lots of unnecessary stuff." In the second year, however, a trainee received an assignment in a single department and likely the one of his choice. "The instructors were carefully selected that were good teachers and good mentors and had good records," recalled one participant. Annually there were usually 12–15 trainees, but during the later part of the Simpson era many left the B&O after completing the program. In fact, Simpson rightly worried about this brain drain, but he was unable to stem the exodus. Resignations largely stopped after Jervis became president, and understandably he strongly supported TGTP. Yet Jervis made his position clear to potential TGTP participants: "If your one goal is security, you should look elsewhere. If on the other hand you seek challenge, and if your ambition is to build, I suggest that your place is with us."[41]

A star member of Dixon's emerging brain trust was Kent Shoemaker, an engineering graduate of the University of Michigan and son of Perry Shoemaker, a distinguished railroad executive at the Lackawanna who hailed from Jervis's hometown. "I was a difficult recruit," remembered Shoemaker, who earlier had participated in the TGTP but was then a 26-year-old trainmaster on the Baltimore Division. Years later he recalled the details:

One morning in the fall of 1961, upon arriving for work at Camden Station [in Baltimore], I found a note from my boss, Bill Johnston, Superintendent of the Baltimore Division. The note directed me to proceed immediately to his office down the hall. Bill had received instructions to have me report the next morning to Bill Dixon, who was forming a newly created Industrial Engineering group. . . . I told Bill [Johnston] I had no interest in an "uptown staff job," and Bill said, "no problem," just decline if offered a job. The next day Bill Dixon gave me a sales pitch on a position with the new group. I declined the job.

The following morning I found another note on my desk from Bill Johnston, again demanding my immediate presence. Bill greeted me with the question, "Don't you know how to say no?" He went on to say he had just received instructions to have me in Fred Baukhages's office [the newly appointed vice president for finance] the next morning. I arrived at Fred's office with considerable trepidation. His was a corner office with a brightly burning fire in a coal-burning fireplace. Fred wasted no time turning up the "heat." He told me I had a wonderful opportunity to join a group where I could directly impact the company's direction and results. He said the company would fail if drastic positive change was not achieved. He continued by telling me that, if I remained as a trainmaster and the company went bankrupt, my job would essentially remain unchanged, but what an opportunity I would miss. . . . Our meeting concluded with my agreeing to call him the next morning with my decision. I didn't know what to do, but after talking to my boss I decided to turn it down. The next morning I called Fred, thanked him for the offer, and declined. He replied with these words: "OK, the best of luck to you." I then left Fred's office and walked back to my own in Camden Station.

Word of my action had already reached my boss, Bill Johnston. Bill said he already had received instructions to have me in Mr. Langdon's office the next morning.

When I entered Jervis's office he looked over the top of his glasses and said, "I know how you young guys like to be out with the trains, but some time in the General Office with Bill Dixon will be good for you." He then looked back down to his papers and I knew the conversation was over.[42]

Just as Kent Shoemaker discovered that he could not ignore Jervis's wishes, Jervis found additional ways to add to the talent pool. In 1962 he and his associates still wrestled with an inadequate freight-car fleet, particularly hopper cars. "Coal shippers were complaining they couldn't get cars, and if they did get cars, they weren't serviceable," noted Jervis. Frank Rykoskey, the chief mechanical officer, although possessing considerable administrative talents, needed to be replaced. It was believed that he was taking kickbacks from suppliers and using that money to finance his children's college education. Moreover, Rykoskey was accused of showing preferences to fellow Roman Catholics. "If you were a Catholic, you got special treatment," somewhat ironic on a railroad that most observers considered to be dominated by Protestants and Masons. With the need to replace Rykoskey, Jervis learned of the skills possessed by George Beischer, who was then chief mechanical officer for the affiliated Western Maryland Railway. One day Beischer received word that Jervis wanted to see him at his office about the matter of coal cars. Since traffic was expected to soar before an announced miners' strike in the fall of 1962, Jervis asked whether the Western Maryland could handle the large number of straw cars that were on the B&O. In order to make serviceable hundreds of hoppers that had been damaged by rusting caused by the acid in coal, employees had used straw to plug the holes. Jervis may have wanted information that Beischer could supply, but the conversation had another purpose. "Langdon just listened," remembered Beischer. "He was sizing me up. I didn't realize that Langdon was interviewing me. But I did wonder why the president of the railroad was directly involved in the discussion." Soon Beischer became assistant chief mechanical officer, and a year later he replaced Rykoskey.[43]

Jervis did not ignore talent from outside the railroad industry. When the B&O revamped its piggyback operations (trailers on flatcars, TOFC or, as the B&O called it, TOFCEE), a glaring weakness appeared. In common with most large railroads, there was no one in charge. In this case Jervis learned from a friend at the American Trucking Association about a highly capable, even "brilliant" motor-carrier specialist, Ernest W. Wright, who served as president and general manager of Southern Plaza Express, a subsidiary of Ryder System, in Dallas, and he was quickly hired. As general manager for trailer services, Wright and an assistant, Stanley Christovich, who possessed a similar background, soon produced impressive results, largely because of their intimate knowledge of the trucking business. "Wright was a trained trucker who knew how to do it," remembered Jervis, "how to coordinate the services, how to handle the truck end of it."[44]

One roadblock that Jervis discovered in his efforts to keep the B&O solvent involved his lack of full executive control. At the time the board named him president, Simpson became chief executive officer, and this "technically put him in a position to overrule anything that I did." Getting rid of several top officials who had close ties to Simpson would be difficult. But fortunately for Jervis's objective of revitalizing the organization, the board on December 20, 1961, stripped all executive powers from Simpson and gave them to Jervis. Simpson also no longer served as either chairman of the board or chairman of the board's executive committee; he became just one of 12 company directors. With Simpson's power diminished, Jervis got the retirements that he wanted and made the necessary replacements. "What a difference it made." Young college-educated executives contributed to the renewal process.[45]

Even with Simpson looking over Jervis's shoulder, the Langdon administration pushed forward with the policy of streamlining operations to produce greater efficiency and economy. An early response came on August 1, 1961, when the real estate and tax department was dissolved. Jervis endorsed moving the tax section to the accounting department and real estate to the finance department. All tax work became part of a single unit. "The need for combination was dictated by the mushrooming growth of tax laws that has taken place in recent years," proclaimed a company spokesman. "Today, many taxes formerly handled separately are found to be interrelated under the new laws prevailing. With the new setup, closer control and marked economies are expected to result." Renamed the department of properties management, the real estate section focused exclusively on real estate issues, including leases, purchases, and sales of railroad property, and its head reported directly to the vice president for finance. And two months later, changes took place in the operating department, where the company reduced the number of general managers from five to three. Consolidation in the engineering section also occurred. This reshuffling created annual savings of approximately $188,000.[46]

About the same time, Jervis took pleasure in abolishing the traffic department as a single entity, splitting it into three units: freight sales, marketing, and passenger. Jervis had a low opinion of the way that the traffic department functioned, being a traditional commercial organization with a single vice president in charge. Now each activity reported directly to him. Daily operations in freight sales were headed by Walter Haensell, who had been regional sales manager in Cincinnati, and his principal assistant became William Ollerhead, the former director of trade for the Maryland Port Authority. The coal traffic operation also reported to Haensell, although after the C&O assumed control, the coal function would be split off into its own department. The marketing section conducted pricing, tariff publication, and industrial development. It also formed a nascent marketing research body that embarked on a much-heralded nationwide traffic survey. Jervis named Charles Henry, a B&O commerce lawyer, to head marketing, and Henry "knew what Langdon was after." The passenger department came under the supervision of Edward Riecks, but "he was not really a Langdon man." Within a few years Riecks would be replaced by Paul Reistrup, who understood what Jervis wanted done with the passenger sector.[47]

As part of this reshuffling, Raymond Holter, an experienced passenger department rate person, became the point man in executing the Langdon-Henry pricing policies, which stressed highly innovative "incentive rates." Under the new staffing arrangement, a major breakthrough occurred with pricing. The time-honored industry approach to rate-setting involved only specified minimum weights for a given shipment, and there was no encouragement to load a car beyond that amount. However, with incentive rates, the B&O built business by offering progressively reduced rates for heavier loadings along with multiple cars and full trainloads. Thus incentive rates tied reduced rates to increased equipment utilization whether it involved a single carload or a unit train. Jervis and "his boys" could not claim to be the true inventors of this concept, but they were modern pioneers. After all, early in the century Union Pacific's E. H. Harriman, as historian Maury Klein has noted, "dragged the railroad industry into the new era of high-volume traffic carried at low rates." Added Klein, "What he did was implement the strategy on a grand scale from which other rail managers shrank because they lacked the vision or the backbone."[48]

While shuffling bureaucratic functions made sense and contributed to the "Langdon revolution," the management team knew that fact gathering would be even more crucial in efforts to end the financial hemorrhaging. For these reasons the IE group took on a variety of critical assignments, especially the pressing matter of the excessive number of unserviceable freight cars. Shippers had been complaining loudly to the ICC's Car Service Bureau about the inadequacies of the B&O's car fleet, and action needed to be taken. It did not take long before Dixon's team determined what equipment should be repaired, where the work should be performed, and what it would cost. "You don't want to waste money!" asserted Jervis, and he concurred with Dixon that repair and rebuilding activities should fit marketing or customers' needs rather than the convenience of shopmen. The latter had been the long-established policy throughout the industry.[49]

Soon repair facilities throughout the system hummed with activity. By August 1961, shopmen in Keyser, West Virginia, processed about 60 repaired coal hopper cars daily, although they faced enormous challenges in the volume of jobs that needed to be performed. In Glenwood (Pittsburgh), Pennsylvania, coil steel gondola cars were being repaired at the rate of seven per day. And at the new diesel shop in Cumberland, Maryland, the mechanical department added a third shift, providing 24-hour-a-day, seven-day-a-week work on the road's motive power. Efficiency at Cumberland improved dramatically. By August diesels moved into and out of the shop in 16 hours in contrast to the old average of 32 hours. Out-of-service time for locomotives dropped by 50 percent. Although much more work was required, especially with freight cars, the railroad had begun to address these shortcomings.[50]

The new B&O administration also willingly innovated with equipment. Trade publications lauded the introduction of "Auto-Porter" service, "the greatest thing to come down the pike in years." The company extensively tested this novel piece of rolling stock, a low-slung, double-decked auto-rack car that was an Americanized version of an auto-carrying car widely used in Europe. On September 19, 1961, the first car, which contained 16 French-built Renault Dauphines, left the Locust Point Marine Terminal in Baltimore for St. Louis. Later, the B&O experimented with the use of these rack cars to haul the personal cars of passengers. It was a "VERY successful experiment," and the concept inspired the creation of the Auto-Train Corporation in 1969.[51]

With development of auto-rack cars, piggyback units, and other pieces of larger rolling stock, the B&O needed to accommodate such equipment. Unlike competitor Erie, whose main line had been constructed extensively to a six-foot track gauge and hence benefited from wide clearances, the B&O had numerous bottlenecks that stretched the length of its system. There were 54 clearance restrictions that needed be removed, nearly all bridges and tunnels, and these obstacles were duly overcome. Similar problems confronted the affiliated Reading and Jersey Central properties (the B&O held a substantial position in the Reading, and in turn the Reading controlled the Jersey Central), and they were dealt with accordingly, including the lowering of track beneath the Broad Street bridge in Elizabeth, New Jersey.[52]

By the time these betterments were completed in fall 1963, the B&O had spent about $12 million with $8 million of this amount being concentrated on the line between Clarksburg and Parkersburg, West Virginia. The company was so proud of these changes that on October 29, 1963, it celebrated with an inspection trip for guests and a press conference and luncheon in Parkersburg. Simultaneously the B&O took out eye-catching advertisements in the *Journal of Commerce, Wall Street Journal,* and a host of daily newspapers and later in *Railway Age* and other trade publications heralding the success of the clearance triumphs. Jervis was elated. "We expect that the improvements will pay for themselves in two years." To the more than 100 newspaper, radio, and television representatives who joined the "Press Special" either at Washington Union Station or in Clarksburg, he offered ongoing commentary through the train's public address system. At Jervis's insistence, the railroad thoughtfully provided these opinion-makers access to two glass-topped stratadome cars so that they could better sense the much-improved line through the Allegheny Mountains. Soon, too, the B&O distributed an attractive promotional brochure, *Now! Room at the TOP,* which explained this "major railroad engineering feat . . . to open its main lines for the high-speed movement of all traffic." Not only did the B&O score a public relations victory, but it also benefited from the improved operations. "The long-term result [was] a sharp increase in traffic over what had become the short route between the East and the Southwest for piggyback business and high and wide box cars," as Jervis later observed. "Total volume over this long-haul route doubled in a relatively short time."[53]

Clearance improvements could be big attention-getters, especially in the mountains of West Virginia. But basic yet absolutely vital track improvements attracted little interest from journalists or others. Although the Simpson administration proclaimed that "the mechanization of track forces was completed in 1959," the quality of the right-of-way nevertheless deteriorated, due largely to the developing economic crisis. Ballast was often thin and fouled, millions of ties had rotted, tie plates and spikes were missing, and rails had worn badly, especially on curves. "We didn't have T-rail," joked a mechanical officer. "We had I-rail instead," meaning that part of the rail head had worn away. It was an easy decision for Jervis to agree that money should be poured into track betterments. In 1962 the company decided to invest approximately $3.2 million in 400 pieces of machinery and equipment, and this allowed an accelerated program of installing state-of-the-art continuous welded rail (CWR). In time, management succeeded in getting concessions from the Brotherhood of Maintenance-of-Way Workers that allowed for creation of interdivisional track gangs. There would also be regional seniority for these employees, permitting greater flexibility in assignments. The mechanization that Simpson glorified continued. For example, the old "speeders," small self-propelled track cars that maintenance personnel had used for decades, disappeared, replaced by fleets of heavy-duty trucks that featured retractable flanged wheels so that they could travel over both roads and rails. When Dixon and his IE associates, including two outside industrial engineers, studied yard facilities, they advocated flat-switching configurations rather than traditional manual hump operations and more practical switches and leads. Jervis agreed. Costs dropped, and efficiency rose. By the end of 1963, John Ward, business writer for the *Baltimore Sun*, who showed a keen interest in the B&O, reported these impressive improvements: "Engineering forces have accomplished laying of 25,000 tons of new rail, 650,000 ties, and 700,000 tons of ballast—all of this at $6,000,000 less than in 1957 despite the fact that labor and materials costs have risen substantially."[54]

This October 1963 photograph reveals the huge cut, carved through the Allegheny Mountains in West Virginia, that was part of a massive $12-million project designed to enhance clearances for freight equipment on the Baltimore & Ohio, including piggyback movements. This particular improvement helped to make the railroad the shortest high-car route to and from the Southwest. (Irene Langdon)

During and after the Langdon years at the B&O, trackside observers often saw unit coal trains, including this eastbound movement, pulled by locomotive No. 4498, which in April 1964 was coming off the Old Main line at Relay, Maryland. (Herbert H. Harwood Jr.)

With an ever-improving physical plant, the B&O could dispatch faster trains. Even before completion of the clearance and track improvements, *Railway Age* took notice of the better freight service being offered. Part of the speedup in freight service came from nontrack betterments. Reduced times became possible, according to Jervis, "by a complete revamping of freight scheduling and operating procedures to eliminate costly delays in terminal and switching and to provide uninterrupted service from origin to destination." The acquisition of 77 GP-30 locomotives from the Electro-Motive Division of General Motors contributed to the revving up of service. "These were the locomotives that introduced the nose 'Sunburst' paint scheme," noted an employee. "They were the pride of the road!" There were now five named trains—freight hotshots—that held the main tracks between eastern and midwestern points. The *New Yorker,* for one, which operated between

Chicago, Philadelphia, and Jersey City, cut 75 minutes from the service time formerly provided. Again, as Jervis explained, the revamped freight operation was "part of our program for making competition, instead of merely meeting it."[55]

Coal

With an improving physical plant that allowed for better train performances, Jervis and his newly assembled team focused on the traffic that long had been the B&O's bread and butter. In the early 1960s, bituminous coal accounted for about 45 percent of total freight tonnage and more than a quarter of freight revenues. As with the dominant coal-carrying roads in the East, much of these "black diamonds" originated along the property, totaling about three-quarters of all coal handled. Quality was good, and customers were plentiful, although the threat existed that electric-utility generating plants might burn more residual oil, mostly from Venezuela. As of 1962, about a third of the coal transported by the company was destined for electric utilities, a fifth to steel and coke-making facilities, and the rest for export and miscellaneous consumption.[56]

How could the B&O maximize profits from its vital coal business? Jervis and the IE group concluded that much of this traffic should move from large shippers to principal destinations in unit trains. Such movements were just in their infancy, with the Southern Railway leading the way. In 1960 this progressive company started such service with a string of 100-ton-capacity hopper cars from on-line mines in the central Appalachian fields going to a power plant in Alabama. But unit or "unitized" trains were unknown in B&O territory. The C&O, for one, did not run unit coal trains, nor was the company interested. Crews regularly stopped at sidings and picked up cars and then repeated the process until they had assembled their trains. If a unit coal train could travel from mine to destination and back to mine in five or six days rather than the traditional turnaround time of 20 to 25 days, reasoned Jervis, Dixon, and others, the railroad could dramatically increase hopper-fleet capacity, perhaps by 300 percent, and could share these savings with the shipper. A unit train would be faster because classification and other terminal delays would be avoided and the movement could operate on predetermined schedules. And crews would be more efficiently employed; there would be none of the traditional train makeup and breakup procedures. An added dividend would be that the productivity of unit coal trains would help to keep these shippers loyal to the B&O. In a cutting-edge fashion,

Jervis, the veteran commerce attorney, argued that rates needed to be linked to the release of equipment. If mine operators wished to receive the full advantages of this coal delivery service, they would be required to load cars within a 24-hour period.[57]

Jervis and his associates also worried that unless the B&O acted creatively, mine operators might push for coal conveyor belts that could easily supply proposed "mine-mouth" power plants. Or perhaps a consortium of mine and power plant owners might install coal-slurry pipelines, an emerging technology. In fact, Jervis told the *Wall Street Journal* that a slurry scheme operated by the Consolidated Coal Company between West Virginia and the East Coast was a "live subject." In "Baltimore in particular and Philadelphia and other places a pipeline was a practical, or at least alleged to be a practical solution for the problem of high railroad rates and poor service." He grasped the vital concept that unit trains simulated pipeline technology.[58]

What Jervis and his colleagues did with the coal business would produce considerable rewards and earn them much praise (and some criticism) from both within and outside the industry. Rates, too, continued to decline for B&O shippers, and they did so because the company carefully determined operating costs. After April 1, 1963, unit trains, often with as many as 120 cars and 9,000 tons of steam coal, traveled from major mine and collection sites to such customers as Baltimore Gas & Electric, Consolidated Edison, and Philadelphia Electric. They also included long-distance moves to power plants in New England. Jervis described a typical operation:

> The train would move in on their [utility company's] track and go in a very large circle and go over the unloading point and the cars would be flipped at the unloading point in a regular momentum. The whole train would be unloaded in a period of less than an hour. This was 100 cars or so. Then the train would be kept intact and moved back to the origin point . . . without any switching or any change in the consist of the train at all. This meant that all the cars were returned to the mining district ready for reloading in a matter of 3 days, 4 days, 5 days as compared with sometimes 23 days, 24 days under the preexisting operation.[59]

The statistics were impressive. Between April 1963, when the low-rate trainload rates became effective, and March 1964, the B&O handled 1,440 unit coal trains with a minimum of 70-ton-capacity hoppers assigned to these trips. That meant that the railroad hauled more than 10.1 million net tons of coal. By then the company transported more than half of the originated steam-coal tonnage in these unitized movements.[60]

More creativity was part of this newly inaugurated service. For one thing, the B&O used special markings on hoppers assigned to these runs, a concept conceived by Ted Klauenberg and his colleagues in the transportation department. Shopmen were instructed to add gold stripes to these cars, and they became known appropriately as "Gold Stripers" or occasionally "Yellow Stripes." The marked hoppers would only haul coal; they would not be used for ballast, sand, stone, or any other commodity. What happened was not only an effective marketing concept but also a practical operating idea. Since these Gold Stripers were good cars—the best the railroad possessed—inspectors did not need to provide frequent examinations, and switching crews could easily tell what should be done. "Most were routed to the Western Maryland [Railway] thence to the CNJ," remembered Al Dungan, who was then assistant supervisor of transportation. "When these empties returned to us, the gold stripes would be mixed in with other regular hoppers. We would switch them at Kayser [West Virginia] or send them over the hump at Cumberland." But because of the expense with these marked yet mixed empties, the company wisely decided to keep the Gold Stripers together.[61]

When the Gold Stripers appeared, the B&O had impressively updated its car fleet. A major shot in the arm for unit-train operations came early on with the lease from the C&O of several thousand 70-ton hoppers "of excellent quality." As Jervis explained, "C&O then followed the practice of equipping itself for annual peaks in traffic and the cars leased to B&O at good rates were surplus and not in use." The B&O also bought at a fair price from the C&O a large number of 50-ton unserviceable hoppers, which were then sent to the B&O's car shops at DuBois, Pennsylvania, for rebuilding.[62]

In updating hoppers with greater carrying capacity for coal service, B&O personnel discovered that consists of these cars experienced braking problems. Since unit movements regularly encountered the rugged Allegheny Mountain slopes that included a 17-mile downgrade near Altamont, West Virginia, averaging 2.25 percent for descending loaded coal trains, conventional cast-iron brake shoes pushed the limits of braking requirements. But in late 1963 and early 1964, George Beischer, chief mechanical officer, C. C. Shelleman, supervisor of air brakes, and their associates worked with representatives from the Westinghouse Air Brake Company to develop the "Cobra," a high-friction composition brake shoe. "These shoes require less braking force," reported *Railway Age*. "They brought the braking ratios into line with accepted practice. . . . Cobra shoes need less braking force. Wheels show uniform, smooth wear. No defects have been caused by braking." Soon other coal-hauling roads followed the B&O–Westinghouse lead.[63]

Before the Langdon administration, the B&O regularly loaded short cuts of hopper cars from on-line coal mines. This practice, which lacked efficiency, was the industry standard. (Courtesy of Baltimore & Ohio Railroad Museum)

During the Langdon years, the B&O began operating unit coal trains in marked hopper cars that featured distinctive gold stripes. A string of these "Gold Stripers" rumbles through the mountainous terrain toward an East Coast power plant. (Courtesy of Baltimore & Ohio Railroad Museum)

The process involved much more than locomotives and long strings of specially marked and adequately braked hopper cars. Even though the volume handled rose modestly, from approximately 38 million tons in 1961 to 41.5 million tons for 1963, the B&O reduced rates by $1.25 per ton if the coal moved in a unit train. The efficient utilization of equipment more than compensated for

the lower charges. "A great many of the mines were big enough so that they could load in one loading a solid train of hoppers," noted Jervis. The company, though, did not ignore lesser operators. "The smaller mines that couldn't handle a train load on one loading would load what they could and then we had another system for putting the train together," explained Jervis. "The

"Gold stripe" cars move through a dumper operated by an electric utility customer. Following the rapid unloading process, these cars will return as a unit train to the producing mine or "assembly" site. (Courtesy of Baltimore & Ohio Railroad Museum)

loadings of the smaller mines would be put together in the assembly district into a solid train. The only requirement was that the coal had to go to the same destination, to the same consignee." It did not take long before five concentration points appeared: Cowen, Grafton, Fairmont, and M&K Junction, West Virginia, and Rockwood, Pennsylvania. Later the number of these assembly sites increased to 12, and the railroad launched a central scheduling bureau to control these trainload movements. By not making a pricing distinction between size of operators, the B&O avoided any charge of discrimination among large, medium, or small coal operators.[64]

The PRR fussed the most about these "assembly train runs" on the B&O. Initially the PRR matched the coal rate and then complained to the ICC, but this tactic failed. That, however, was not all. "The Pennsylvania Railroad was so upset and so mad," recalled Jervis, "that they started to try to get me fired." Jervis believed that if Simpson had been president, he would have caved in to the PRR's demands for keeping the status quo. "Howard Simpson would have been scared to death of the Pennsylvania."

Of course, the PRR, which was slipping financially, had reason to complain. "We got the business, a lot of business," noted Jervis. "All that big account of Consolidated Edison in New York; 13 million tons that they take annually and that was brought to New York in the old days by the Pennsylvania Railroad for direct handling, but which we had diverted to the B&O, Reading, Jersey Central. . . . We got the whole thing. And sure, we hurt 'em badly. That was why they were screaming." In time, the PRR embraced the unit coal train, making for a keenly competitive environment.[65]

Unit coal trains on the B&O captured considerable outside attention. In November 1964, *Railway Age* argued that the company's approach, if adopted by more carriers and developed fully, might well "save" the highly regulated railroad industry. The writer smartly began the piece with a description of a typical B&O coal move:

> As dusk settled over Valley Camp Coal's Elm Grove mine, eight GP-30s, humming in unison, eased 95 70-ton hoppers loaded with black gold from the West Virginia hills down the spur. A scant 27 hours later Baltimore & Ohio unit train 824 rolled into Philadelphia Electric's Eddystone generating station with 7,000 tons of coal delivered at passenger-train speed and at rates which promise to usher in a new era for the beleaguered coal industry and the railroads.[66]

Yet coal utopia had hardly been achieved. In March 1964, Jervis told shareholders that the company required better facilities for transferring coal from rail to water at Curtis Bay in Baltimore and at Lake Erie ports. He also saw the need for new hopper cars, additional yard improvements, and "weighing-in-motion" scales. The objective was to outperform competitors by providing the most efficient unit-train operations, again the idea of making competition.[67]

Although the B&O was in the transportation business, the company sought to exploit another asset, its extensive coal properties. The railroad owned more than 300,000 acres of coal lands, mostly in Pennsylvania and West Virginia, with an estimated 775 million tons of recoverable reserves. So in 1962, Jervis energized a subsidiary firm, Mid-Allegheny Corporation, by bringing in S. Dunlap Brady Jr., a West Virginia consulting mining engineer, to assume management as executive vice president. Working out of Mid-Allegheny headquarters in Summersville, West Virginia, Brady joined with mining interests and coal traffic sales personnel to develop and market company-owned coal.[68]

Trailers on Flatcars (TOFC)

Although the B&O could claim to have been a trailblazer in several fields, the company missed being in the vanguard of intermodal (piggyback or trailer-on-flatcar) operations. It would be the spunky and hard-pressed Chicago Great Western and New Haven railroads that in the mid-1930s spearheaded this traffic. Not until the 1950s did railroads begin to offer this service in an expanded way. Industry innovators—most of all Gene Ryan, who launched Rail-Trailer Company in 1952—rectified the technical shortcomings and helped to popularize the concept. It would be Ryan and others, including Jervis, who understood that railroads had the greatest ability to carry heavy loads over long distances and that trucks possessed the speed and flexibility to handle pickup and delivery chores and operated shorter hauls efficiently. TOFC dealt directly with the inherent inflexibility of the rails. Some railroad leaders, though, continued to fret about TOFC drawing business away from boxcars, generating less revenues as a result. At last, in July 1954, the B&O entered the field, at the same time that several other carriers, including the PRR, Union Pacific, and Wabash, launched their own TOFC operations. That year the ICC, which had not been too keen on intermodal operations, finally outlined the conditions under which the service could be provided. Yet the several "plans" approved for joint rail-truck movements were highly controlled. Under "Plan I," for example, the railroad could transport only trailers of a motor carrier that had ICC authority to serve the route of travel. However, it did not take too long before some relaxation of regulations occurred. The Transportation Act of 1958 enabled railroads to set rates without concern for their effect on competition, provided carriers could prove that rates were compensatory. Subsequently, the ICC modified its restrictions, allowing for greater flexibility and profitability. After 1961, that led to the takeoff in TOFC volume and revenues.[69]

When the B&O embraced TOFC, the company did not show any originality in overall management of what proved to be a unique business. Like other roads, the B&O grafted the various TOFC functions, including car and trailer distribution, pricing, sales, and terminal (ramp) operations, onto existing departments. Sales representatives, by way of illustration, simply added TOFC to their list of client calls. There was nobody in the organization who was specifically responsible for TOFC. "A railroad in the early days," observed Jervis, "was shooting in the dark until and unless it obtained services of top truckers who had been through the mill." He cogently added: "You must know something about other forms of transportation." By not having a qualified person in charge, financial problems would likely result. "TOFC was and is a marginal business that demands close, specialized management to make it profitable," noted a former B&O executive. "Service demands are high. Equipment—both flatcars and trailers—is expensive, and high utilization is a must." And the business was inordinately competitive because customers could take their trailers to any railroad ramp, which, of course, was different from boxcar users. If a business was on a B&O siding, the customer was largely tied to the company.[70]

When the talented Ernie Wright, whom Jervis lured away from the Ryder System in January 1963, arrived in Baltimore, he initially worked as a special assistant to the president. In this capacity Wright assessed the strengths and weaknesses of the TOFC operations, noting immediately that the B&O closed most ramps on weekends, the busiest time for commercial truckers. Several months later, the company launched the trailer service department with Wright as its general manager. Some B&O personnel did not care for Wright's presence: "Oh, he's a trucker." Still, Wright did not have complete control over all aspects of TOFC—"that was too hard a step on too many toes"—but he headed an organization that was apart from the general railroad bureaucracy, giving it broader authority and accountability to develop independently. Significantly, the Wright operation was the first step toward true intermodal profit center management, a concept that eventually became an industry practice.[71]

Wright and his colleagues, who enjoyed full backing from Jervis, did wonders for TOFC on the B&O. Not only did the company aggressively market its intermodal service, "Coordinated Rail-Truck Service Coast-to-Coast," but Wright's department functioned smoothly and effectively. The fleet of new GP-30s made tight schedules practical, speeding these "Trailer Jets" between Chicago, St. Louis, and East Coast terminals. Specialized central control of trailers and flatcars generated more productivity from fewer units. And interchange of trailers with trucking firms at through rates brought traffic of a promising type. Revenues rose steadily, from $6.6 million in 1961 to $11.1 million for 1963. In September 1963, for the first time the monthly numbers exceeded $1 million. A year later, TOFC revenues climbed to an impressive $15 million. A significant portion of this intermodal traffic consisted of meat from packing plants in the Midwest that went to supermarkets in the East. Yet no one at the B&O, including Jervis, anticipated that by the early twenty-first century intermodal freight would surpass coal as the largest source of rail revenue.[72]

Passenger Service

When Jervis assumed the presidency, he knew that freight traffic was the B&O's staff of life, but one challenge that he faced for the foreseeable future involved reducing the financial losses incurred by passenger operations. Even though previous administrations had had some success in cutting money-losing service, mostly on secondary and branch lines, the B&O had been swallowing a multimillion-dollar passenger loss seemingly without too much concern. Jervis knew, too, that the railroad had a long tradition of operating high-quality and popular varnish, including the *Capitol Limited,* Nos. 5 and 6, which ran overnight between Baltimore, Washington, and Chicago. (Varnish is a commonly used railroad term to refer to passenger trains. In the era before all-steel equipment, companies employed wooden cars, often with oak exteriors and highly polished mahogany and walnut interiors, hence the expression.) The *Washington Post* rightly called the *Capitol Limited* "the ultimate in civilized travel" and a "pleasure on wheels." Because of the marquee value of the road's premier trains, it would be difficult to seek their immediate discontinuance. "You could not go cold turkey," explained a passenger department official. "Langdon needed to make one more crack at saving passenger service." If he had not responded, "it would have been too much of a cultural shock for the railroad." Also, downgrading service was politically unpalatable.[73]

Jervis and his colleagues took the bull by the horns and sought ways to maintain high-quality passenger service on the core routes, but as economically as possible. The initial response, however, involved a much-needed shake-up of personnel. "The passenger department was full of corrupt people and needed a real housecleaning." Previous administrations had overlooked the disgraceful practice of cash kickbacks to passenger representatives from tour directors. For decades and usually during the spring, the B&O had transported thousands of children and young adults and their chaperones from throughout the system, but especially from Ohio and the Pittsburgh area, to the nation's capital. "They were very popular," commented Jervis. "We had as many as 16 or 17 trains in a weekend." B&O passenger personnel sold "comprehensive packages" to schools that covered the cost of rail travel, hotel rooms, meals, and related services. "A student wouldn't have to spend a dime." While the ICC controlled fares, other charges were unregulated. In the 1950s, B&O passenger representatives commonly received $10 for every $100 package sold. Not only was this immoral, if not illegal, especially if recipients failed to report this income on their taxes, but, as Jervis recalled, "there was great consternation in other sections of the sales and traffic department because the passenger people always seemed to be better dressed than the freight agents and would never accept an assignment or transfer to the freight department."[74]

When Jervis got wind of the "school trip skimming business," he ordered a thorough investigation. With ample evidence of wrongdoing, Jervis ordered the guilty parties dismissed, including the general passenger traffic manager, although a few employees were able to take retirement. A couple fought back, but they did so unsuccessfully. Yet some thought that Jervis was not being wholly fair. Passenger people actually received salaries that were less than their freight counterparts. Moreover, the culture of "skimming" had long existed at the B&O and also took place on several other railroads, including the C&O. Perhaps a written reprimand or a short suspension would have been a more humane approach.[75]

Jervis and associates also concluded that the company should reduce the excursion business and later decided that it should be ended entirely, thus saving on equipment costs while better managing underutilized motive power. Jervis personally saw the need for a reduction, even elimination, of school-excursion trains. Remembering a visit to Washington Union Station, he counted nearly a score of idle locomotives assigned to these specials. "And my God, here they were sitting in the station handling a bunch of kids going to Washington when we needed them badly for the movement of coal." In that examination of the passenger department, Jervis also learned that employees frequently failed to attend to business, a work attitude that he would not tolerate. For one thing, at staff meetings personnel regularly "spread out a green cloth and played poker." Soon the people and the practice were no longer part of life at the B&O.[76]

Although unwilling to push for takeoffs of the flagship trains, Jervis endorsed discontinuances of other varnish. "We continued to withdraw the other less conspicuous passenger trains." In 1961 the B&O won regulatory permission to end connecting service between North Vernon, Indiana, and Louisville, Kentucky, and in 1962 the railroad saved $550,000 annually by exiting the Cleveland market with abandonment of the *Cleveland Night Express*. Soon thereafter the company dropped another money loser, the Baltimore–Pittsburgh Rail Diesel Car–equipped *Daylight Speedliners*. Also in 1963 the ICC allowed the B&O to end passenger operations between Toledo and Detroit. Connecting equipment would be turned over to the C&O. And in 1964 Nos. 23 and 30, which operated at a substantial loss between Cincinnati and Cumberland, Maryland, became only memories. There would also be train consolidations. In the fall of 1961, for example, the *Capitol Limited*, *Columbian*, and *Ambassador* were combined into a single movement between Baltimore and Willard, Ohio, a strategic division point.[77]

In other economy moves, the B&O responded in various ways. The company decided not to provide free passes to personnel of other railroads or industry associations after January 1, 1963. "The practice had been way too generous with 'deadheads' filling up revenue space." Substantial returns were expected, perhaps as much as a whopping $750,000 annually. Ending the serving of its famed bottled spring water and free morning coffee on the *Capitol* and *National Limiteds* produced far less in savings, but "every penny counted." And Jervis willingly ignored an industry taboo by allowing passenger rates to be listed in the monthly *Official Guide,* a practice that airlines had done for years.[78]

While there was much more to accomplish with passenger operations, the B&O had begun to curb the flow of red ink. Later, in 1964, during Jervis's last year as president, he would again focus on the problem and further reduce losses.[79]

The pressures of the B&O presidency were enormous on Jervis, whether involving passenger deficits, rate disputes, or growing modal competition, and they consumed vast amounts of time, thought, and energy. Still, Jervis was able to eke out moments with his family, usually on weekends. He relished the chance to be with Irene and their two young sons. Boating on Chesapeake Bay became a particularly cherished diversion from work. And there might be a few hours devoted to "crabbing" in the Bay when he was not aboard the Boston Whaler, "the old stink pot," a small, virtually unsinkable outboard power boat. These activities were all made easier by the annual rental of a summer cottage on Gibson Island near Baltimore. Later there would be sailing on a small Sunfish boat. Often with Irene, Jervis continued to take long walks and to play the occasional game of tennis. And the couple enjoyed having dinner with friends, listening to classical music, or attending performances of the works of Gilbert and Sullivan.[80]

Especially important to Jervis was the considerable relaxation that he derived from flying, whether for personal or professional trips, although members of the B&O board of directors worried about his solo journeys. It might be a flight to Elmira to visit at Quarry Farm with his widowed mother, who would live to be 94, or to an on-line city to meet shippers. Until he bought a Piper Comanche 250 in April 1965, Jervis rented planes at the nearest airports, and his logs record several flights weekly. The aircraft used revealed his skills: Stinsons, Reliants, Fairchilds, Ercopes, Cessnas, Tri-Pacers, Beechcraft Bonanzas, Fornairds, and Comanches. "Boy, did he love to fly," recalled Irene. And in Jervis's typical financial ways, the costs of these flights always came out of his own pocket.[81]

When in the office, on a business trip, or just thinking about work, Jervis could take enormous satisfaction in the astonishing financial turnaround that had come during his watch. The B&O no longer was that Class 1 railroad "basket case." In 1962, the company's net income was $1.6 million, representing a swing of more than $32 million from the previous year's deficit of $31.3 million. In 1963, net income reached $5.5 million, and a year later it rose to $7.2 million. The figures would get even better. In 1964, B&O freight revenues climbed to $344.3 million, the best in five years, and $10.7 million more than during the previous year. The company's increase of 3.5 percent in car loadings proved to be one of the best showings among eastern carriers. Investors, employees, and journalists were overjoyed or at least impressed. Admittedly, a stronger national economy after 1962 contributed to the improved health of the B&O, but as a financial analyst correctly observed in 1964, "Langdon and his team with their new ways of thinking should get much of the credit."[82]

C&O Control

Part of being in a pressure-cooker job for Jervis centered on the pending purchase of the B&O by the C&O. Then there would be the expected corporate merger of the two carriers. Jervis believed that railroads, including the B&O, must consolidate, modernize, and streamline operations. Early in his presidency, he told the Senate Antitrust and Monopoly Subcommittee, "Instead of suppressing competition, railroad consolidations, including acquisitions or control, have the completely opposite effect of promoting competition by strengthening individual railroad competitors." Of course, C&O involvement in the B&O would enhance both properties: capital for the B&O and creative ideas for the C&O.[83]

A major step toward creating "a new era of railroading in the East" took place one minute after midnight on February 4, 1963, the earliest moment that control of the B&O by the C&O could legally occur. At that bewitching hour, a brief ceremony took place in the B&O boardroom that involved the signing of papers by officers of the two railroads and a transfer of stock certificates. The agreement involved one share of C&O common stock for each share of B&O preferred stock and one share of C&O common stock for each one and three-quarter shares of B&O common. In all, the C&O eventually paid about $100 million for the B&O, and "that was cheap, an incredible bargain for the C&O." The combined 11,000-mile system claimed assets of $2.3 billion and in 1962 had operating revenues of $705 million. The C&O/B&O was approximately the size of the NYC but with slightly better annual income. "If the railroads are to survive as privately owned entities," duly observed the *Baltimore Sun*, "it just may be that the old B&O with its new aggressive attitude and the infusion of strength the C&O can lend will show the way."[84]

The green light, however, had come slowly, taking precisely two years, eight months, and 13 days. Although the consolidation proposal had been instigated in May 1960, it was not until a year later that the ICC examiner gave his approval. Then on December 31, 1962, the 11-member commission approved by a vote of eight to three. "The B&O–C&O partnership," concluded the majority of the regulators, "offers an exceptional opportunity for the major growth and beneficial diversification of the two railroads." Unfortunately, there would be a legal battle, instigated by labor and spearheaded by the Brotherhood of Maintenance-of-Way Employees. Ultimately the U.S. Supreme Court upheld lower court decisions and the ICC order.[85]

Changes came quickly. The two railroads began to share personnel. At the top, three C&O men, Cyrus Eaton, John Kusik, and Walter Tuohy, joined the 12-member B&O board of directors, and they constituted half of the B&O's powerful executive committee, with Jervis also being included. Then on December 16, 1963, Tuohy assumed the chairmanship. A number of officers served both companies while others moved from one to the other. Kusik headed C&O's finance committee and became B&O's vice president for finance. Arrangements were also made for additional acts of coordination, including the merging of common yards and terminals. And something new in the industry took place by early 1964 when the B&O and C&O launched a unified planning department, staffed by key officers in engineering, equipment, and transportation and based in Baltimore. The new unit took in the highly successful IE group. "Given the mission of probing the future without inhibitions and proposing new standards, practices, and facilities to develop the full capabilities of B&O and C&O," wrote Jervis in his annual report, "the planners are free from the burden of supervising day-by-day operations." This arrangement appealed to Jervis and truly reflected his management style. He was happy, too, with the cooperation that developed on maintenance-of-way matters, including replacement rail. In early 1964, the two companies selected a specially designed 122-pound rail that met the needs of both roads. The financial coupling also allowed the B&O to borrow more than $230 million over a five-year period with the C&O pledging its credit, funding essential for debt obligations and an array of betterments.[86]

More visible was how the infusion of capital was spent. Immediately, the C&O made available new maintenance-of-way equipment valued at $3.2 million, helping to accelerate track improvements. And in anticipation of control, the C&O had advanced funding for new and refurbished rolling stock. This is exactly what the B&O needed, as Charles Bertrand, B&O vice president for operations and maintenance, had aptly told the ICC examiner during the control hearings:

Q: Do you assert the B&O is an unsafe railroad?
A: No, we maintain safety.
Q: Do you feel yourself qualified to run it?
A: Yes.
Q: Do you need C&O direction?
A: *No, I need money.* (emphasis added)[87]

In a highly significant aspect of the C&O control arrangement, the B&O would be operated independently of the C&O, at least initially. Jervis continued to wield considerable power, and he discovered that he could usually work effectively with his counterpart at the C&O, Walter Tuohy, a kindly chief executive. Yet Jervis did not consider Tuohy to be in a class with Perlman or Ben W. Heineman of the Chicago & North Western or even D. W. Brosnan of the Southern Railway. "Tuohy was awfully good at public relations, but he really didn't know the first thing about running a railroad." Encouragingly, though, Tuohy repeatedly referred to Jervis as "my dear friend," and that was a heartfelt feeling. Jervis also realized that the 62-year-old Tuohy did not enjoy good health, having suffered a mild heart attack in 1959. His likely successor, Gregory DeVine, "the C&O's coal man," lacked nearly all of the positive personal qualities that Tuohy possessed, although Jervis admitted in an overly understated way that DeVine was "always frank."[88]

Control was bittersweet. Jervis had wanted a full corporate mating. "In a merger, the B&O, as one of the two parties involved, would have had a voice in its terms, including the name of the merged company, its headquarters, the composition of the first board of directors." Yet Jervis knew that the B&O bore a considerable level of debt. As he told Jesse Glasgow, financial editor of the *Baltimore Sun,* at the start of coordination, "There will be no merger until there is a major adjustment in our debt." Somewhat surprisingly, that event would not occur until 1987, long after Jervis had nominally retired from the industry. By then the Chessie and the Seaboard systems had been united for nearly seven years under the control of CSX Corporation, a holding company, a product of the mega-merger impulse of the late twentieth century. Then on April 30, 1987, the B&O, a subsidiary of CSX Corporation, merged into C&O, another subsidiary, and four months later the C&O merged into CSX Transportation. These restructurings brought an end to the historic tax break from the State of Maryland that the B&O had enjoyed since its origins. Thus the B&O vanished under three layers of corporate structures.[89]

Still the financial involvement of the C&O helped Jervis and "the Lang-don team" to make the B&O much stronger, winning for them considerable recognition in the commercial and trade press. Jervis hoped that with ulti-mate merger the B&O corporate culture would dominate B&O–C&O or whatever the moniker would be, and that Baltimore, rather than Cleveland, would be the corporate center.[90]

Mount Royal Station

Jervis had long realized that the B&O, like virtually every railroad, possessed considerable real estate holdings and facilities that by the 1960s often had little or no use to operations. The B&O owned parcels of land, at times of consider-able acreage, that had been acquired for rights-of-way, yards, water supply, and the like and possessed structures that were obsolete, whether small-town depots or remnants of the Age of Steam. Although during the Simpson administration the company started to sell off surplus property, the process became more sys-tematically studied and executed after Jervis took charge. He made clear to real estate personnel that there were three objectives: selling property, leasing prop-erty, and acquiring property for industrial development. "Mr. Langdon wanted to make sense out of the real estate activities," recalled Norman Murphy, a real estate department manager. "While real estate sales were not critical to the rail-road's bottom line, he sought to balance what needed to be done to make real estate serve the best interests of the B&O." During Jervis's tenure the board of directors regularly approved the disposal of surplus land. In July 1963, for ex-ample, the company sold 1.57 acres, which included the abandoned Kenyon Street freight house, to the City of Cincinnati for $159,230.[91]

Yet Jervis was not always coldly rational about property. He loved history and had an appreciation for historical preservation. Jervis closely watched over Quarry Farm, realizing its significance to Elmira and to the larger Mark Twain community. As he said of the Langdon family property, "It has to be protected." That feeling was expressed in the rehabilitation of the B&O's Transportation Museum in Baltimore. In an economy move during the late 1950s, the Simpson administration had closed this railroad gem. But Jervis pushed for its reopening, and that would take place on July 2, 1964. "In the first four days after the museum's reopening," noted *Railway Age,* "some 8,000 visitors filed past what B&O claims is the nation's largest collection of historic railroad equipment." The facility would continue to be an important educational asset and tourist attraction.[92]

Then there was Mount Royal Station in Baltimore. On September 1, 1896, the B&O had proudly opened this magnificent Renaissance-Romanesque passenger depot. The structure featured a soaring 150-foot clock tower and granite and limestone exterior, reminiscent of the Vendramini Palace in Venice. A prominent Baltimore architect, E. Francis Baldwin, had designed it. Created to supplement Camden Station and to take advantage of the new Howard Street railroad tunnel, Mount Royal became an important stop for Royal Blue Line trains between New York and Washington and functioned largely as a suburban station. "Mt. Royal was everything that Camden was not," observed historian Herbert H. Harwood Jr., "spacious, supremely fashionable, aesthetic, and well-matched to its genteel surroundings." It was a city jewel.[93]

After the last passenger train departed Mount Royal on June 30, 1961, B&O employees boarded up the station. But later in the year Jervis, who was now in charge, and Eugene Leake Jr., president of the Maryland Institute College of Art, revealed that the art school, whose main building stood nearby, would use the station on a rent-free basis. This was an ideal adaptive use for what was undeniably a white elephant for the railroad. Leake told the press that "painting and drawing classes will be held in three second-floor offices and student sculptors and their instructors will meet in the baggage room." If the building were to be retained, he expected that "the spacious lobby might be used for assembly programs and lectures." The plan was well received, for "Baltimore residents were very possessive of the Mt. Royal Station."[94]

While the arrangement between the B&O and the Maryland Institute worked well, a crisis loomed. By 1964 parent C&O wanted the property sold, for the station occupied nearly four acres of valuable land that might be suited for an office building. Real estate appraisers placed the value at $835,400 for the land, structure, and air rights over the adjoining tracks. This disturbed Jervis and Leake. Even though the art school could not afford the appraised price, Jervis decided to battle to save Mount Royal for its art school occupant. In a July 3, 1964, letter to John Kusik, he explained the situation. "Mr. Leake asked whether we might possibly be in a position to donate this station building. He also suggested that, if this were impossible, a purchase price that could be regarded as realistic by an institution of learning might be an alternative, provided payments were so arranged as to make it possible for this to be absorbed by public subscription." Then Jervis made a powerful argument. "As you know, the B&O is most anxious to dispose of the Mount Royal Station property and to do so in keeping with its environment. In the long run I think it is more important for this building to be in the proper hands at a sacrifice than in the wrong hands at a higher price."[95]

Although Jervis knew that he was "getting himself in hot water with the C&O if he sold the station for below market price," his commitment to historic preservation succeeded. Kusik and the C&O brass agreed to sell Mount Royal at a much lower figure. Subsequently the art school paid what it could afford: $250,000 with no-interest payments spread over three years. The B&O correctly considered the difference between the appraised value and the sale price as a donation and accordingly took a federal tax credit.[96]

Jervis's determination to save Mount Royal resulted in the preservation of much of the building's grandeur and detail. This historic station, structurally sound and painstakingly remodeled, became the southern anchor for the art campus and centerpiece of the Mount Royal cultural district. Appropriately, in 1996, the centennial year of Mount Royal, Fred Lazarus IV, art school president, thanked the former B&O president for his involvement, noting that "Mount Royal's renovation has been heralded throughout the country as a pioneering step in adaptive re-use. . . . Its re-use encouraged the renovation of The Lyric and the construction of the Meyerhoff Symphony Hall. None of this would have happened without your help and support."[97]

A sense of community pride led Jervis in directions other than historic preservation. One example involved the largely closed Mount Clare Shops in the inner city of Baltimore. For some time, vandals, presumably teenagers, had broken windows, painted graffiti, and caused other damage to the facility. But Jervis had an idea other than increasing nightly railroad police patrols. He convinced Delmas Dunn, a passenger engineer for the B&O whom he had met while riding the locomotive between Baltimore and Washington, that he should start a Boy Scout troop for the youth in the neighborhood adjoining the shops. Since Dunn already led a flourishing troop in suburban Baltimore, Jervis knew that he had a capable, experienced person. "Dad told Mr. Langdon that these boys can't afford to buy their own canteens much less cook kits, sleeping bags, knapsacks . . . and pup tents," remembered Dunn's son, Ron. "Mr. Langdon told Dad to let him know how much money he needed and the B&O would provide it." The scheme worked. "The troop was successful and vandalism decreased!"[98]

Completing the Presidency

The quest for progressive change continued under C&O control, and much remained to be done before Jervis left the presidency. One event of importance involved the restructuring of terminal operations in the New York City area. For years, the B&O leased piers on Manhattan Island and provided connecting carfloats and lighters to Staten Island and the company's subsidiary, Staten Island Rapid Transit Railway (SIRT), for this traffic. Traditionally much of this B&O business involved less-than-carload (LCL)

freight that forwarding companies assembled and consolidated into carloads at company piers. Empty boxcars, which rested atop carfloats, were
loaded and then floated to the Staten Island railhead and assembled in outbound trains that operated over the tracks of the SIRT, Jersey Central,
Reading, and B&O. The operation was extremely expensive. The railroad
consulted forwarders, thereby learning that cargoes could be trucked to
Jersey City without a negative impact on service. Such an approach would
allow elimination of more than 1,000 jobs and provide substantial savings
in terminal costs. Moreover, intermodal service could also be employed,
and this became the method of transit once LCL operations ended. The
maritime equipment was then either sold, scrapped, or used for the interchange of freight cars with the New Haven and Long Island railroads and
terminal roads along the Brooklyn side of the harbor. The B&O also abandoned the handling of all LCL shipments, a big money loser and a policy in
line with what some carriers had done or were contemplating. Usually
less-than-truckload (LTL) operations were more efficient and cost-effective.
This business, Jervis correctly believed, might be captured, even expanded,
with TOFC service.[99]

With New York harbor and LCL matters in hand, Jervis returned to the
nagging passenger problem. In a final attempt to save remaining trains or at
least to go down with the flag flying, Jervis turned to an exceptionally talented B&O officer, Paul H. Reistrup, naming him director of passenger services with orders "to get the job done." Unlike a typical railroad passenger
organization, which was really a traffic department with a marketing function, Reistrup would control marketing and sales, rate-making, equipment
utilization, service design, and mail-baggage-express activities, a structure
similar to TOFC operations under Ernie Wright and another effort in
profit-center management. Reistrup would also have a hand in mechanical
decisions, although he would lack control over motive power. Operating
personnel would continue to control that function. On February 1, 1964,
Reistrup officially assumed his duties. This young, creative, and energetic
engineering graduate of the U.S. Military Academy, who had become disenchanted with Army career life, had joined the B&O's TGTP in 1957 and had
become an assistant division engineer, trainmaster, and general superintendent of car utilization and distribution.[100]

When Reistrup took charge, the passenger situation remained grim; deficits had climbed to multimillion-dollar levels. But the new director responded imaginatively, even though it had been apparent to Jervis, Reistrup,
and other knowledgeable observers that the "future of the passenger train on
the B&O was dim if not hopeless."[101]

Even though the Langdon administration at the Baltimore & Ohio realized that the future of the passenger train was dim, a sincere effort was made to maintain high-quality service and to be creative, including the introduction of onboard movies. The advertising message became "Trains are fun!" (Author's collection)

Even though Reistrup originally thought that being in charge of a passenger department might impede his career, "the mission was too intriguing to sidestep." He realized that he would have the necessary authority and the backing of the president. Reistrup became unique among the nation's passenger officials in that he had carte blanche jurisdiction, reporting only to the president. Reistrup would do what he could to reduce deficits, but he would also strive to maintain the company's traditionally high standards for cleanliness, courtesy, safety, and on-time performance.

A high priority for the newly launched department was to assess rolling stock. "The B&O had a lot of ancient equipment, including horse transport cars," recalled Reistrup. "I had the authority to get rid of all passenger rolling stock that was older than 40 years," and he did. Reistrup selected the best remaining equipment from a rather large fleet and wisely assigned the oldest cars to serve "shorts," those passengers that had only limited trips to make, and the newest to accommodate long-distance travelers.[102]

But there was much more to do. Reistrup and his two able assistants worked on improved utilization of equipment and better car maintenance schedules. They also made arrival and departure times as attractive as possible considering distances and population centers. And they creatively tackled the empty seat problem on the "financial strong man of the B&O timetable," the *Capitol Limited*. Although weekend patronage was good, midweek load levels were low because more business travelers were opting for airplanes instead of taking this overnight luxury train. Reistrup responded with "Red Circle Day Fares." Starting April 13, 1964, the railroad charged 31 percent less on one-way fares on Mondays, Tuesdays, and Wednesdays, the slowest times, and slashed by 25 percent the cost of a Pullman accommodation. This pricing strategy for noncommuter trips might coax back some business travelers, granting that these passengers would still fly in one direction. The penny-conscious, too, would surely appreciate a transportation bargain. "Cutting passenger fares to attract business is not a new idea," commented *Railway Age*. "But the Baltimore & Ohio is going after passenger traffic in a relatively new way. . . . The Baltimore & Ohio's new rate reduction is one of the largest ever offered by a U.S. railroad."[103]

The Reistrup group did not overlook additional ways to attract and to retain business on its flagship trains. Beginning in December 1964, the railroad at a minimal cost added complementary current-release movies and cleverly gave viewers free pretzels—"they were double, triple salty," recalled Reistrup. "And beer sales were wonderful." Noted one observer: "Did you ever hear applause on a train? B&O trainmen do every night at the end of the free movies on the *Capitol* . . . and the *National*." The introduction of on-board movies not only generated a great deal of free advertising and may have increased ridership but also "demonstrated that the B&O was serious about upgrading these trains." Diners also continued to serve excellent meals, including the popular "Help Yourself Salad Bowl" that was topped with French dressing and blue cheese. In one 1965 advertisement the company told riders: "Enjoy a delicious meal served on crisp, fresh linen, with gleaming silver," and noted that complete luncheons and dinners cost as little as $1.95. The *Capitol*, too, offered business travelers the use of Dictaphone equipment to dictate letters or reports. "One extra service—if the passenger desires, the B&O will mail the completed dictation free of charge." And everyone could use free self-service luggage carts at the major terminals.[104]

Although the St. Louis *National Limited* received somewhat less attention than the Chicago *Capitol Limited,* Reistrup made certain that service was good and that costs were managed. Since the company owned the Budd-built Slumbercoaches assigned to the *Capitol Limited,* this popular equipment remained in the daily consist, but Slumbercoaches used on the *National Limited* were leased from the manufacturer. When the agreement expired, the B&O returned these high-capacity sleepers and rehabilitated nearly a dozen surplus 16-duplex-roomette, four-double-bedroom Pullmans and imaginatively dubbed them "Slumber-Room Coaches." Fares were slightly more than those charged for Slumbercoach accommodations, compensating for the somewhat reduced passenger capacity. Jervis approved, although he would not authorize expenditures on new passenger rolling stock.

Reistrup and his department made remarkable accomplishments. The sharp downturn in ridership ended, and hence revenues improved. Because of the Red Circle Day Fares, the *Capitol Limited* filled up and on some days sold out completely. At times this train became amazingly long. Opined Reistrup, "There were nights when it was 24 cars, almost too big." Other passenger carriers in the East, though, were not too pleased or impressed with the Reistrup operation. Most industry officials did want to cut rates during the time of the popular New York World's Fair when rail travel was strong. A few thought "that any effort to save the passenger train was sheer lunacy." Indeed, the feeling grew that the unprecedented support marshaled on behalf of interstate highway construction had completed the transformation of the passenger train from a national resource to a relic of the past. Still, naysayers must have been impressed with the B&O covering a substantial percent of its out-of-pocket passenger costs.[105]

Just as the company sought to make passenger operations as profitable as possible, Jervis continued to seek structural adjustments just as he had done with the flurry of personnel changes and reorganizations after assuming the presidency. A notable triumph came with formation of a product development bureau. The idea for much of what took place came from the fertile mind of Bill Bamert, who served as assistant vice president for marketing. A Phi Beta Kappa business graduate of Lehigh University, Bamert began his career in 1937 as a traveling auditor for General Electric, working his way rapidly up the corporate ladder. In time Bamert joined the C&O to help organize several innovative financial functions under the guidance of John Kusik. Eventually Bamert created a marketing research department, located in the finance department. But this tradition-bound railroad gave little

"The competitive instinct of our employees and their great impatience with things as they are will make the emerging C&O-B&O system one of the great railroads of the nation"

As you plan your future, I invite you to look closely at the opportunities offered college graduates by the Baltimore and Ohio Railroad Company. Here, you can pursue a diversified career in an industry that is face to face with the necessity for adjustment to the changes of a competitive and complex era. You will be confronted with a wide variety of interesting and challenging problems. Our training program can help you develop your capacity for managerial responsibilities and afford you the chance for personal growth and recognition according to your abilities.

If your one goal is security, you should look elsewhere. If on the other hand you seek challenge, and if your ambition is to build, I suggest that your place is with us.

Jervis Langdon Jr.

JERVIS LANGDON, JR.
President

Mr. Langdon received his law degree from Cornell University in 1930 and, after completing studies at Dijon University in France, began his career as a railroad lawyer. In World War II, he served in the United States Army Air Force, becoming chief of staff of the Air Transport Command in the southwest Pacific. He is a licensed pilot and still flies his own plane. Mr. Langdon became president of the B&O on June 1, 1961, after serving as the railroad's vice president and general counsel.

Jervis continually sought out the best talent for his railroads. In 1964 he wrote an introduction to a brochure designed to attract recent college graduates to the Baltimore & Ohio, *For Those Who Think Ahead!* (Author's collection)

support to the creative Bamert. Recognizing his genius for planning, Charles Henry brought Bamert to the B&O, with Jervis's blessings, and gave him special powers in the marketing-research wing. The assignment allowed this "true maverick" to surround himself with other imaginative people, including Peter Hart, "a car guy," who came to the B&O from the American Car and Foundry Company, and Walter Cramer, a specialist in auto transport, who had been director of traffic research for the St. Louis–San Francisco Railway (Frisco).[106]

The Bamert group, which was under the general direction of Charles Henry, vice president for marketing, quickly tackled a host of tasks. These individuals focused on car types and service designs, matters that had historically been the domain of the mechanical and transportation departments. They questioned shippers about their transportation requirements. "What are your products, and what are your needs?" After learning the commercial specifications, they could suggest equipment. In the case of grain movements, the B&O decided to employ 100-ton covered hoppers and to retire conventional 40-foot box cars with their cumbersome grain doors. Bamert and his associates worked with shippers on freight schedules and considered such data as how long it took equipment to travel between points, patterns of yard switching, and the true cost of adding a car to a train. With this knowledge, the B&O introduced the incremental costing system, benefiting both railroad and customer. This particular concept, the brainchild of Walter Wright, who had been a Bamert associate at the C&O, broke new ground in the industry. If a railroad used cost measurements at all, an ICC formula was consulted that was "almost universally judged inaccurate." But the Bamert team could now figure more precisely a proper rate and decide which business should be solicited. The unit also developed merchandise traffic-flow analyses "so that we could tell what traffic was moving where, what revenue it was producing, and, ultimately, what its incremental contribution was." Additionally, the bureau made continuing checks on freight service performance, seeing how it compared to what marketing representatives sold and what the railroad actually provided. What was so special about the Bamert operation was that marketing people worked with equipment people, and "this was a revolution," both at B&O and in the industry.[107]

Jervis was delighted with the melding of operations and marketing. As always, he wanted imaginative, interdepartmental cooperation. Jervis knew from his tenure in the traffic department at the C&O that traditional traffic personnel, with their glad smiles and warm handshakes, spent most of their time dining, playing golf, and chatting with customers. "They weren't getting to problems at all," he said, adding that "there's a science of marketing." Bill Dixon concurred: "This was just the ticket. All of this was a pronounced change from the way railroad people had always worked. Operating people didn't have much to do with sales people nor did sales people with operating people."[108]

Although the C&O cooperated with the B&O for the Bamert appointment ("the C&O was happy to be rid of him"), tensions mounted between the administrations of the two railroads. With undisputed control of the B&O, C&O management began to interfere. In 1964, the C&O moved in, recalled Jervis, "and in the meantime they were checking the figures over in the accounting department and all that sort of stuff." Snooping through records was just the tip of the proverbial iceberg.[109]

A major annoyance involved the C&O's view of the relationship between the B&O and the Reading. The B&O had long had a financial position in the 2,349-mile Reading, which was based in Philadelphia, with main stems extending from its headquarters city to Harrisburg, Reading, Allentown, and New York City, via the Jersey Central connection at Bound Brook, New

Jersey. As of 1963, the B&O owned 600,800 shares of common stock, 235,065 shares of first preferred stock, and 345,600 shares of second preferred stock, representing 42 percent of the voting stock. The NYC held the second-largest interest, albeit far less than the B&O.[110]

Jervis wished to improve the Reading, seeking to protect and develop a valuable freight connection. "The Reading took our coal to New York." The Reading also gave the B&O friendly access to major markets in the Northeast, including Philadelphia, "where the B&O was very weak." In October 1963, he sought to strengthen the Reading by sending Charles Bertrand to serve as executive vice president. Within a year Bertrand became president, thanks to Jervis's role as a member of the Reading board, and Bertrand bolstered the property. But Jervis wanted to do more. In 1964 a large block of securities became available from a Reading bank that could increase the B&O position to about 75 percent. He urged the C&O to obtain the stock and to apply to the ICC for authority to control the Reading and thus ensure an efficient and secure route to the Northeast. He even suggested an outright merger between the B&O and Reading. The C&O refused, being "terrified" by the high terminal costs at New York. In fact, in September 1964 the C&O forced the B&O to sell 300,000 shares of Reading common "from among the company's present holdings." Eventually the Reading slipped into bankruptcy and became part of Conrail. Yet portions of the former Reading developed into high-density freight lines under Conrail ownership, a testimony to Jervis's sense of the strategic importance of this connecting carrier.[111]

While Jervis perhaps could excuse the C&O for avoiding the Reading, he was highly displeased with the attitude that officials in Cleveland took toward further efforts by the B&O to enhance its profitable coal business. B&O personnel conceived of novel ways of conducting export coal operations at Curtis Bay in Baltimore Harbor. Inspired by a coal scheme employed by the Bessemer & Lake Erie Railroad at Conneaut, Ohio, the concept involved unloading unit coal trains independent of ship arrivals. Much of this metallurgical and steam coal would be "blended" and stored on the ground or in silos, a process replacing sequence loading of coal by grades. If adopted, the B&O could substantially reduce operations at both the Curtis Bay and Brunswick, Maryland, switching yards and garner better use of rolling stock. "The number of coal cars released would have been in the thousands." Even though the B&O had developed engineering plans and arranged financing for these betterments, which featured a new ship loader, pier extension, thawing shed, and supporting facilities including dumpers, the C&O rejected this coal storage/distribution scheme. The parent company feared that the operation would lower coal rates. Moreover, the C&O wanted export coal to move through its facilities at Newport News, Virginia, and had no desire to make Baltimore the center for coal exports. Then there was C&O rejection of the B&O plan to improve its Lake Erie coal facilities at Fairport and Lorain, Ohio. The C&O believed that Toledo should be the principal point of contact with lake freighters for shipments that were destined principally for Canadian markets. Yet the Toledo dump site was overtaxed; there existed a repeated backup of cars, and equipment costs eroded profits. "Rail equipment," explained Jervis, "would be tied up for days, even weeks or months." Not surprisingly, the C&O position on coal troubled, even angered, Jervis and his colleagues. "They [C&O] vetoed a large part of the program that was designed to advance the competitive status of the B&O because of its adverse effect on the C&O," reflected Jervis, "namely, a new and modern coal unloading facility at Baltimore . . . and a similar coal unloading facility at Lorain, Ohio . . . , because it would be in competition and hurt their facilities at Toledo."[112]

Issues such as Reading ownership and coal handling caused Jervis to seek employment elsewhere. But there was also the culture of the C&O, which Jervis saw as arrogant. C&O officers bragged about flying first-class, staying at the exclusive Greenbrier Resort and other upscale facilities, and taking advantage of every possible perk, practices that Jervis never condoned at the B&O. These negative feelings toward the C&O resulted in "Langdon not playing the political game with Cleveland." Specifically, he avoided dinners and business retreats at the Greenbrier, in Cleveland, and elsewhere that he thought wasted time and money. An increasing number of C&O officials sensed that Jervis refused to accept the way that the C&O conducted its affairs. "They considered him to be an excellent railroad man but not always a good team player."[113]

Jervis shocked those individuals who did not realize that he had become "bitter about the C&O relationship" when in September 1964 he announced his resignation. No one, though, seemed surprised when Walter Tuohy, chief executive officer of the C&O and chairman of the B&O board, immediately replaced Jervis. As Tuohy told the press in early October about his election to the presidency: "It's a welcomed opportunity to work more closely with its fine men and women whose talents and dedication are helping assure the long-term future of the combined B&O–C&O system." B&O people seemed to be mostly pleased with Tuohy at the throttle.[114]

Without question, Jervis had given his resignation letter considerable thought. He "had deep affection for the B&O," and he was justly proud of his accomplishments. Yet Jervis found the developing C&O relationship troubling. Still, he was a practical business executive. Since he was 59, he took advantage of the B&O's early retirement plan. At a special meeting held on October 8, 1964, the board of directors granted Jervis a leave of absence until

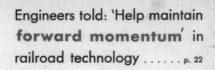

Engineers told: 'Help maintain **forward momentum**' in railroad technology ...... p. 22

March 16, 1964

RAILWAY AGE WEEKLY

B&O's Langdon: How to recapture traffic p. 17

Although a modest individual, Jervis surely took pride in the attention that *Railway Age,* the premier industry trade publication, paid him with a cover photograph and in-depth interview on freight rates in the March 16, 1964, issue. (Author's collection)

February 1, 1965, at which time his retirement became official. Jervis had lined up a top position with the Chicago, Rock Island & Pacific Railroad. Therefore, an exit made sense. He had been an outstanding and nationally recognized B&O executive; he would be free of the Cleveland decision making and the larger self-satisfied C&O corporate culture; he would have his retirement money; and he would have challenging opportunities with another Class 1 carrier. Of course, he did not know that Tuohy, whom he liked, would die suddenly on May 12, 1966. This elevated Gregory DeVine, whom a Baltimore journalist candidly (and accurately) described as that "big, obnoxious, pompous guy." DeVine had been a B&O director since April 1964.[115]

Virtually no one, including the often ultracritical Cyrus Eaton, whom Jervis described as a "terribly difficult person," denied that Jervis had made a positive mark at the B&O. The infusion of capital from the C&O had hardly "saved" the B&O from bankruptcy. Yet having access to capital helped considerably, as Jervis readily acknowledged. The Langdon administrative team had made great strides in creating a stronger, more competitive railroad. In fact, the B&O performance in 1964 was comparable to that of its well-to-do parent. The transportation ratio and operating ratio for the B&O stood at 39.7 and 76.4, respectively; the comparable figures for the C&O were 38.8 and 78.6. In reality, these figures may have been much better, because the C&O, in Jervis's opinion, "juggled the numbers." With enhanced revenues from unit coal trains and other operating initiatives and corporate restructuring, the B&O demonstrated the ability to make competition rather than to meet it. In previous years that had not been the experience.[116]

There would also be a long-term impact. In time, certain Langdon-inspired policies and practices, for example, with coal and TOFC, were largely accepted by the Cleveland hierarchy. In fact, a few C&O executives had applauded progressive measures at the B&O, hoping that success there would be emulated on their own property. Moreover, Jerv's boys mostly prospered at the C&O–B&O and later the Chessie System and CSX as well as elsewhere in the industry. This would be a fondly remembered corporate legacy of Jervis Langdon and his hardworking and imaginative associates. But Baltimore would suffer. "We lost a friend when Langdon left town," remembered former *Sun* journalist and U.S. representative Helen Delich Bentley. The future corporate units either downgraded or abandoned their presence in the city. The old adage that there were three great institutions in Baltimore, the *Sun,* Johns Hopkins University, and the B&O, eventually had to be modified.[117]

4 Running the Rock

"A Mighty Good Road"?

In the fall of 1964, the Langdon family moved to the pleasant western Chicago suburb of Geneva, Illinois, so that Jervis could commute by rail to the Chicago, Rock Island & Pacific Railroad (Rock Island or the Rock) headquarters in the La Salle Street Station located at 139 West Van Buren Street in the "Loop" district. As chairman of the board, he joined a company that had a long and difficult past. By the mid-1960s, the nearly 8,000-mile Rock Island was a less-than-stellar property that teetered on the brink of bankruptcy, a financial condition that resembled the Baltimore & Ohio (B&O) a few years earlier. Much of the track structure had deteriorated, motive power needed to be upgraded, and some freight equipment was either outmoded, in poor repair, or in short supply. The company's several long-distance passenger trains, too, hardly suggested prosperity. Although not yet a transportation slum, the Rock Island was the weakest of the several once-mighty Chicago-based "granger roads." That had not always been the case.[1]

Before the Civil War, the Rock Island had emerged as a promising venture. In 1847, Illinois promoters won a state charter for construction of the Rock Island & La Salle Rail Road (RI&LS) between the communities of its corporate name, planning to connect the newly opened 96-mile Illinois & Michigan Canal (Chicago to La Salle) with the commercially active Mississippi River at Rock Island. On April 8, 1851, the RI&LS became the Chicago & Rock Island Rail Road (C&RI) with Chicago as its eastern terminus. This trans-Illinois road also operated a strategic branch between Bureau and Peoria, a developing manufacturing and trading center situated on the navigable Illinois River. In 1856, the C&RI won fame for becoming the first railroad to bridge the Mississippi River, positioning this infant road to push into rapidly developing Iowa and perhaps deeper into the largely unsettled West. Indeed, Rock Island investors launched the Mississippi & Missouri Railroad (M&M) for that very purpose. Immediately after the Civil War, the C&RI and M&M consolidated to create the Chicago, Rock Island & Pacific Railroad, and under that banner, the main line reached Council Bluffs, Iowa, starting point of the Union Pacific (UP). The completion date was May 11, 1869, a day after the historic wedding of the iron rails between the Central Pacific and Union Pacific railroads at Promontory, Utah Territory. Yet forging a direct interchange connection with the newly opened transcontinental route did not mean a monopoly for the Rock Island to Chicago and eastern connections. More than two years earlier, the Cedar Rapids & Missouri Railroad, an affiliate of the Chicago & North Western Railway (C&NW), had arrived at Council Bluffs, and in January 1870 the Burlington & Missouri River Railroad of Iowa, a surrogate of the Chicago, Burlington & Quincy Railroad (Burlington), would become the third carrier to establish a connecting link. These events revealed a long-standing feature of the Rock Island story: the company repeatedly found itself in a highly competitive environment.[2]

During the heyday of railroad construction, which occurred between the end of the depression of the 1870s and the panic of 1893, the Rock Island expanded enormously. Led by its energetic and somewhat unpredictable president and general manager, Ransome Cable, the company built or acquired properties in several midwestern and Great Plains states. By the 1890s the Rock Island controlled a web of rails that stretched from Illinois to South Dakota, Colorado, and Texas. Of the 3,568 miles operated, the Rock Island owned only 2,877. At times the Cable administration preferred leases and trackage-rights agreements to line building, a policy that later haunted the carrier by escalating fixed costs, especially in terminals. Generally, though, the Cable regime generated profits, allowing for bond payments and regular dividends to stockholders.[3]

Unlike other railroads that had employed Jervis, honest-to-goodness "robber barons" had been part of the Rock Island past. In 1901 the worst chapter began when the property fell into the hands of the infamous Reid-Moore syndicate. Stock speculators and trust makers Daniel "Czar" Reid, brothers James and William Moore, and William Leeds sought to turn their new possession into a personal money-making machine, with little concern for serving the investor, let alone protecting the public interest.

The syndicate's years in power marked a time of intense expansion. Within eight years, mileage of the Rock Island soared to more than 8,000 and its level of debt skyrocketed. The company had entered such cities as Dallas, Memphis, and St. Louis and had claimed the Choctaw Route, which stretched along the 35th parallel between Memphis, Little Rock, Oklahoma City, Amarillo, Texas, and Tucumcari, New Mexico. Also a long feeder extended from Little Rock to Eunice, Louisiana. In conjunction with the Colorado & Southern Railroad, the Rock Island in 1906 acquired half interest in the Trinity & Brazos Valley Railway, later reconstituted as the Burlington–Rock Island Railroad, a subsidiary that provided access to both Houston and Galveston, Texas. But as usual, the Rock Island had to play second fiddle to carriers that already served these new gateways. Moreover, the syndicate acquired controlling interest in several other railroads, most notably the Chicago & Alton (Alton), the Chicago & Eastern Illinois, and the St. Louis–San Francisco (Frisco). In 1909, the house of cards collapsed, and several years later these economic reversals forced the Rock Island into bankruptcy. The plungers, though, did not suffer, as did most investors. "Fully aware of what they would do to the railroad," observed William Edwards Hayes, who wrote a centennial history of the Rock Island, they "unloaded their stock at the top market price—a farewell grab at profits as the dream of empire broke and faded."[4]

Admittedly the syndicate was not wholly evil. There was the expansion that made the Rock Island into a truly interregional system; it was a railroad that "went somewhere." Furthermore, lines were operated in favorable terrains; there were no steep mountain grades or long, expensive tunnels. Although the company never achieved the objective of "& Pacific," early in the twentieth century the road linked up with the Southern Pacific Railroad (SP) in New Mexico to forge the strategic "Golden State Route" between Chicago and Los Angeles, which ultimately became the most valuable part of the Rock Island's freight and passenger operations.[5]

Although the Rock Island emerged from receivership in 1917 after only two years and then from federal wartime control in 1920, the years following World War I were difficult. Since grain accounted for the greatest volume of carloadings, the agricultural recession of the early 1920s adversely affected revenues. Moreover, the "good roads movement," especially strong in the Midwest because of the region's infamous brand of vicious and viscous mud, led to rising modal competition. Farmers and villagers made shopping trips to county-seat towns and other nearby destinations in their "tin lizzies," and local truck owners hauled livestock and other farm goods to neighboring market centers. And management of the Rock Island itself continued to cause concerns. Even with soaring debt and pressing physical requirements, the railroad paid handsome stock dividends rather than reducing financial obligations and investing in needed improvements. In 1927 the company declared a 5 percent dividend; the following year the payout rose to 6 percent and in 1929 reached 7 percent.[6]

Soon conditions worsened. In the aftermath of the stock market crash of October 1929, the Great Depression steadily took hold. For the Rock Island, this economic malaise was exacerbated by the drought of the mid-1930s, which was inordinately severe along the company's lines throughout the Great Plains and sections of the Midwest. As the adage went, "If there's no rain in the plains, there's no grain in the trains." Notwithstanding New Deal relief and recovery programs, the territory suffered greatly. Carloadings plummeted, and passenger volume diminished. If "Okies" fled Oklahoma and the dust bowl by rail, they likely opted to "ride the rods," boarding freight trains "as guests of the Rock Island" to Tucumcari and then the SP to California. It was hardly shocking that in June 1933 Rock Island joined a growing number of roads in bankruptcy, its second receivership in only 18 years.[7]

Luckily for the Rock Island, a talented railroader arrived in May 1936 to assume leadership of the operating department, John Dow Farrington, who had been general superintendent of the Burlington's Missouri and Iowa districts and general manager of the Fort Worth & Denver City Railway, a Burlington affiliate. His background made him aware of the particular problems that a granger road confronted. Farrington would be to the Rock Island what Daniel Willard had been earlier to the B&O. Farrington did much to improve the troubled road physically and bolstered the spirit of employees. Morale was at a low ebb because of the bankruptcy and rumors that this "broken-down" railroad might be dismembered. It would be Farrington who embarked on a modest effort to dieselize yard operations, adding to the first box cab switcher that had arrived in 1930, and he brought about introduction of six diesel-powered *Rocket* streamliners for service on five primary passenger routes. These actions enhanced both revenues and employee pride. Less splashy were line relocations between Davenport, Iowa, and Kansas City, Missouri, and the Akalon Cut-off in Kansas where a new bridge, "the Sampson of the Cimarron," was built over the treacherous Cimarron River near Liberal. Both projects improved operating efficiencies. Farrington also began to push for abandonment of money-losing branch lines, and within a decade about 650 miles, largely in Iowa, would be retired. In 1941, the Rock Island turned a modest profit, and the following year Farrington assumed duties as chief executive officer. Yet because of legal difficulties with bondholders and the destructive antics of a self-centered co-trustee, the company did not emerge from receivership until January 1, 1948. At that time Farrington became president and finally could run his own show.[8]

The Farrington administration did not rest on past accomplishments. After 1948, a variety of improvements took place. Modern freight classification yards appeared at Armourdale, Kansas, near Kansas City, and at Silvis in the Rock Island vicinity. The company became the first large railroad to experiment with microwave transmissions and improved track signaling, albeit in a more traditional fashion. The flagship passenger train, the *Golden State,* was updated and placed on a faster, more competitive schedule. About the same time the Rock Island took pride in inaugurating the first diesel-powered and all-streamlined air-conditioned suburban passenger service in greater Chicago. Farrington wisely did not overlook the need to move away from a heavy reliance on transporting agricultural products to more profitable and less seasonal manufactured goods. In 1950, the Rock Island acquired the 13-mile Pullman Railroad, an important switching road on the south side of Chicago and a company that owned property that was suited for industrial development. And by the end of 1952, the road's dieselization program was substantially completed, and within a year the last scattered steam operations ended.[9]

The Farrington forces made the Rock Island into a respectable granger road, "the razzle-dazzle operator of the prairies." Its financial situation remained at a decent level, although after 1954 operating income took a disappointing and somewhat steady decline. Yet the company's network of lines, which were mostly designed to handle the traditional 40-foot boxcar at modest speeds, continued to meet the needs of shippers, most of all grain customers.[10]

In 1956, a leadership change occurred. Rock Island watchers derived comfort from the new president, Downing Bland Jenks. "The privilege of possessing great leadership such as Mr. Farrington gave the Rock Island carried its special problems of succession," observed John W. Barriger III, who at the time served as a Rock Island vice president. "Genius is seldom a replaceable asset. Fortunately for this company, in its executive vice president, Downing B. Jenks, there was available within its own official family an executive of exceptional talent, capacity for leadership, and experience in railway administration." Although Farrington, who had reached retirement age, remained chairman of the board until his death in 1961, the young and able Jenks took command. In some ways cut from the same piece of cloth as Jervis, the straitlaced, disciplined Jenks loved trains, possessed an Ivy League degree, compiled a distinguished military record during World War II, understood the physical and business dimensions of the industry, and had a vision for the future. Jenks knew that the Rock Island required a major rebuilding of its principal lines, abandonment of deteriorated, low-volume, grain-gathering appendages, and continued efforts to generate high-revenue, nonagricultural traffic since, as he said, the company "had no real industrial base at all." The Rock Island also needed to reduce its unproductive workforce. Although Jenks did not confront "featherbedding" locomotive firemen, he pushed hard for closure of small-town depots, shutting down 60 in Iowa alone in 1959 and prompting the reassignment or retirement of scores of agents.[11]

But if the Rock Island were to survive, Jenks believed, finding a merger partner was paramount. In August 1958, Farrington, who remained a power and was interested in the fate of "his Rock Island," proposed a merger with the Chicago, Milwaukee, St. Paul & Pacific (Milwaukee Road), another struggling granger road, and this pleased Jenks. Informal talks progressed to the point where both boards approved a $350,000 joint study for unification. Farrington and Jenks were encouraged, but on November 19, 1960, the Rock Island board abruptly abandoned the project. About the same time Jenks, on his own initiative, contacted officials at the Missouri Pacific (MOP) about a merger, but again nothing happened. The reason was that Colonel Henry Crown, a powerful board member who chaired the finance committee, derailed these consolidation proposals. This billionaire Chicago businessman, who co-founded the Material Service Corporation, the largest building-supply concern in the world, had an investment in the Rock Island that exceeded $10 million, and he appeared to want union with neither the Milwaukee Road nor the MOP. Said Jenks sarcastically, "Crown seemed to be in favor of all the merger proposals except the one we were working on." Unfortunately for the Rock Island, Jenks's impressive ways led the powers at the long-troubled MOP to court him for the presidency. When the Rock Island board showed no enthusiasm for merger with the MOP or any other carrier, Jenks accepted the MOP offer. After January 1961, he turned this fan-shaped 12,000-mile southwestern carrier, headquartered in St. Louis, into one of the nation's most respected railroads.[12]

After Downing Jenks departed, the Rock Island slipped noticeably. The Farrington mystique faded, motor carrier competition increased with the opening of large sections of the interstate highway network, traffic was lost to the St. Lawrence Seaway, labor "featherbedding" continued, regulation hampered creativity, and the physical plant and rolling stock received minimal attention. "There were slow orders galore." Employees may have smiled when a trainman on the neighboring Milwaukee Road commented that during cold weather "the Milwaukee runs steam through its passenger trains but the Rock Island runs trains through steam," a reference to steam leaks that plagued Rock Island equipment. Fixed costs remained high, and an usually large number of long-distance passenger trains and Chicago-area commuter service further sapped the financial strength of the company. Troubling indeed was the fact that only 3 percent of the Rock Island's track miles, primarily between Chicago and Iowa, were considered "heavily used." Jenks's successor, R. Ellis Johnson, who had been vice president of operations, provided poor leadership. "He was just a caretaker president, an old-time railroader who liked to cuss a lot." By 1964, as Jervis recalled, the Rock Island "was living on borrowed time."[13]

Union Pacific Merger?

Since the opening of the Union Pacific, the company had not expanded farther east than Council Bluffs, the starting point of its historic main line. There the UP interchanged freight and passengers with the initial three carriers that stretched from America's railroad Mecca, Chicago, westward to connect with the first transcontinental. With the spurt in latter-day construction, the UP added more interchange partners for corridor traffic: Milwaukee Road, Illinois Central (IC), and Chicago Great Western (CGW). And under the generalship of Jay Gould, the Wabash in the 1880s connected with the UP by cobbling together the shortest line to St. Louis, although this Gould property offered a less direct route to Chicago. The Burlington and MOP would also provide the UP with access to the St. Louis gateway. And UP affiliate Kansas Pacific, which stretched between Denver and Kansas City, made possible additional connections to St. Louis.[14]

After the railroad map of the nation's midsection had jelled, the UP seemed content to be an interchange partner with a number of Chicago gateway railroads. Even though the UP had a financial stake in the IC, a close relationship developed between UP and C&NW. These two roads created the famed "Overland Route" for passenger service between Chicago and the Pacific Coast with the SP providing the western leg between Ogden, Utah, and San Francisco. The three carriers took great pride in their luxurious *Overland Limited,* which made its debut in 1896, a train as revered in the West as its counterparts, the *Broadway Limited* and *Twentieth Century Limited,* were in the East. Moreover, a sizable amount of through freight traffic, particularly merchandise and perishables, passed directly between the UP and C&NW at Fremont, Nebraska, avoiding delays at Omaha and Council Bluffs. Unlike other Chicago–Omaha roads, the C&NW by the time of World War I operated a fully double-track main line that an advanced signaling system protected, becoming a "raceway" between Lake Michigan and the Missouri River.

In the early 1950s, the longtime positive relationship between the UP and C&NW soured. A combination of bad management, deferred maintenance, and apparent indifference about passenger service on the part of the C&NW prompted the UP in 1955 to divert its *Cities* streamliners between Chicago and Omaha to the parallel Milwaukee Road. In anticipation of this historic switch, the Milwaukee Road upgraded its mostly single-track line across Iowa and improved its double-track artery in Illinois to handle these trains at speeds of 79 mph.[15]

In some ways deterioration of the best route between Chicago and Omaha encouraged UP officialdom to contemplate reversing its policy of remaining on the east bank of the Missouri River and seeking access to Chicago and St. Louis. But there were other considerations. UP brass worried about the future of freight rate divisions. Eastern and midwestern carriers had launched a vigorous fight to increase their share of these splits. If successful before the Interstate Commerce Commission (ICC), and in 1960 that appeared likely, the decision would penalize transcontinentals like UP, diminishing earnings significantly. Then there was concern about possible corporate marriages. Perhaps other carriers would expand either to or beyond Chicago, and the number of friendly interchange partners would decline. As an operation that depended heavily on bridge traffic, the UP wanted access to the busiest gateways. If the UP operated its own line to Chicago, unfavorable merger maneuvers would have less impact. There the UP could forge connections with 20 major roads and directly participate in the city where roughly 60 percent of the nation's rail traffic was interchanged. If trackage to St. Louis could be obtained, there would be additional options, including ties to the Louisville & Nashville and Southern railroads and the growing markets of the "Sunbelt" southeast. UP also recognized that the bulk of the increasing transcontinental business gravitated to the single-line Atchison, Topeka & Santa Fe (Santa Fe) between California and Chicago.[16]

In 1961, the UP started to prepare for expansion. Management hired Wyer, Dick & Company, the railroad consulting firm, to explore the possibility of acquisitions. Wyer, Dick concluded that the best combination would be with the Burlington and the Denver & Rio Grande Western (D&RGW) railroads. The Burlington operated a first-class line between Denver, Omaha, and Chicago, and a circuitous route to St. Louis from Omaha and Kansas City. The D&RGW would provide UP with excellent passage through the Rocky Mountains and direct connections with the SP at Ogden, Utah, and Western Pacific at Salt Lake City for destinations in California.

The Wyer report appeared to satisfy UP officials. In fact, the company had just inaugurated a "secret interchange with the Burlington to get faster schedules than other connections could provide [for Chicago]," related historian Maury Klein, "and it pleased both sides." Soon the UP acquired about 10 percent of the D&RGW's common stock "for purely defense reasons."

Yet these two initial responses to expansion did not provide what the UP wanted most of all: its *own* direct lines to the Chicago and St. Louis gateways. More studies followed, including another one by Wyer, Dick, although it was "done very hurriedly." The UP knew that the Burlington would be impossible to acquire since the Great Northern (GN) and Northern Pacific (NP) had included this granger road in their unification plans and the Burlington was already owned in equal portions by GN and NP. In February 1961, these roads had filed with the ICC a petition for merger, which, after a major setback at the hands of the ICC five years later, led in 1970 to the creation of the gigantic Burlington Northern. Although top officials of the GN, NP, and UP had discussed the possibility of the UP sharing certain Burlington routes, this option appeared less attractive than outright ownership. After sifting through mountains of data, UP officials concluded that the Rock Island was the best candidate for expansion eastward. Still, the UP understood that the Rock Island had limitations. Even though Jenks had spearheaded a modest renaissance on the Rock Island, management estimated that it would require more than $250 million to upgrade the physical plant and equipment. Unfortunately, the St. Louis line from Kansas City through eastern Missouri was hill-and-dale trackage, a legacy of a cheaply built predecessor company. There was also concern about taking over a property that handled only 6 percent of the UP's interchange business, prompting connecting roads surely to divert traffic.[17]

UP leadership remained cautious about acquiring the Rock Island. Some officials, including Edd Bailey, vice president of operations, who would shortly become president, thought that the IC was a better choice, largely because of the superior condition of the road and rolling stock. But the IC connected Council Bluffs with Chicago on a long, largely single-track line whose link between the Missouri River and Fort Dodge (Tara, Iowa) snaked across the rolling hills of western Iowa. Moreover, the IC provided access to St. Louis only by way of Chicago. The price of the Rock Island might be too high, especially since Henry Crown, the largest owner of company securities, was known as a "tough, restless bargainer." There was also the possibility that Crown preferred union with the C&NW.[18]

At last, some action on the Rock Island matter occurred. When word reached UP officials in Omaha and New York City in June 1962 that the SP was eyeing the property, there was much consternation. After UP president Arthur Stoddard learned of SP's interest in the Rock Island, he told his counterpart at the D&RGW, G. B. "Gus" Aydelott, "Those SOBs are going all over the Rock Island with the idea of buying it. By God, that's our baby." Since the forced "unmerger" of UP and SP in 1913 by the federal government, bad blood existed between these two western giants. Yet in a demonstration of cooperation, high-level discussions ensued about merger strategies, resulting in an agreement that the two roads would *jointly* carve up the Rock Island. The SP would take most trackage south of Kansas City, amounting to approximately 3,600 miles. With ownership of the Tucumcari line, the SP could divert traffic from its much longer and in places poorly engineered Cotton Belt route that stretched between northeastern Texas and St. Louis. The UP would receive those coveted lines to Chicago and St. Louis and also trackage to the Twin Cities. Nearly 4,300 miles of the Rock Island would become UP property.[19]

With the UP–SP partnership established, negotiations began in February 1963 with Henry Crown and the Rock Island. Initially the process was rocky, for Crown, based on bad advice, had an inflated notion of the value of his railroad. Yet Crown held firm with his belief that the stock exchange ratio should be 1.5 to 1.8 for each UP share for Rock Island common, although later he reduced the ratio to 1.25. While Crown was unquestionably in a position of power, Roy Ingersoll, former head of Borg-Warner Corporation, and Bruce Norris, president of Norris Grain Company, two other large investors in the Rock Island and fellow board members, wanted Crown to relent, fearing that the deal might fall through and leave them with an ever-weakening property. Finally, Frank Barnett, general counsel for the UP and the field general for the merger negotiations, suggested to Crown a ratio of .718 of dividend-paying UP stock for each Rock Island share. Crown grudgingly accepted, although "he didn't think much of Barnett." With the exchange ratio set, the boards of directors speedily endorsed the merger. The Rock Island body bestowed its blessing on June 27, 1963.[20]

Those involved in spearheading the Rock Island–UP union could barely breathe a sigh of relief. Led by the brilliant and hard-driving Ben W. Heineman, the C&NW was not about to lose its most profitable connection, for the company annually interchanged with the UP between 150,000 to 175,000 cars of mostly long-haul traffic. "The North Western," noted Jervis, "was absolutely dependent on the Union Pacific." On July 5, 1963, the C&NW filed with the ICC an application for authority to control the Rock Island by stock ownership. On September 10, 1964, the ICC officially received the UP–Rock Island merger request. These actions set the stage for what would become the most protracted merger debate in American history.[21]

Jervis Joins the Rock

While president of the B&O, Jervis had received overtures from the Rock Island to take command. "The Rock Island had been in touch with me for a couple of years trying to induce me to come out there to run their property, and I had declined." Because of growing meddling by the Chesapeake & Ohio (C&O) into B&O operations, and qualifying for the B&O retirement plan and wishing to stay active in the railroad industry, he reconsidered the possibility of joining the Rock Island. In summer 1964, knowing the connection between the UP and the Rock Island and being politically astute, he contacted Robert Lovett, chairman of the executive committee of the UP, who worked out of the company's New York City office at 59 Wall Street. "I went to see him [Lovett] in New York and asked him whether that Rock Island job was still open and, if so, whether or not he would suggest that I pursue it, and would it be agreeable from a Union Pacific point of view to have me running the Rock Island." Lovett responded positively. Jervis quickly received telephone calls from Crown and Ingersoll, and these influential Rock Island board members asked to meet with him in New York City. They did, and Jervis was offered the position of "chairman and chief operating officer," since the company already had Ellis Johnson in the president's chair. (Johnson became vice chairman, but soon retired, permitting Jervis to become chairman *and* president on May 17, 1965.) "We brought Langdon in," Crown said flatly, "because Rock Island had been managed badly."[22]

The unfolding of events pleased Jervis. Yet there was a modest sticking point, and that involved salary. He never believed that high-ranking officers should be paid excessively. "You can't have too great of a spread." At the B&O, his annual salary as president was relatively modest for the industry, $75,000 (about $450,000 in 2006 dollars). "I remember that when the C&O was in the process of gaining control, they came to me and said your salary is so low it is an embarrassment to us. Won't you allow it to be increased?" Jervis replied that his salary was satisfactory. "We were living comfortably, my God, [$]75[,000], our needs weren't extreme and we were doing everything we wanted to do." The C&O persisted, and he took a $25,000 annual increase. When he was negotiating for the Rock Island presidency, Crown thought that Jervis should be paid more than he was earning at the B&O. He refused and asked for $90,000, although in time his annual salary reached $100,000.[23]

When word reached Rock Island employees that the board of directors on October 8, 1964, had named Jervis as their new boss, there was great rejoicing. Most employees soon learned about his accomplishments at the B&O, and they liked what they read or heard. "When Langdon arrived at the Rock Island, he brought about a spirit of hope for an extremely troubled railroad," remarked a former clerk. "Morale had been so low that you could pick it up."[24]

Jervis held no illusions about the job when, on November 1, 1964, he entered the executive suite on the tenth floor of La Salle Street Station. He wanted the Rock Island–UP merger, knowing full well that the faltering Rock Island required a prosperous corporate partner, because "the Rock Island was a very highly marginal operation." As Jervis explained: "Physically it was a relatively slow railroad. With the exception of the line to Tucumcari, it was probably a 40-mile-an-hour railroad and in certain cases on the tangent track it was a 50-mile-an-hour railroad. But the line to Denver was marginal and relatively slow . . . and the branch lines [which comprised one-fifth of the trackage] were in marginal condition, so marginal that we had to use boxcars for the origination of grain and corn with most of the elevator operators and the big shippers all wanting the [100-ton] covered hoppers." Even though there had been needed line relocations during the Farrington regime, bottlenecks continued to plague most main stems. The line between Chicago and Council Bluffs, for example, meandered 10 miles through the alleys and side streets of East Moline, Rock Island, and Davenport and 7 miles through Des Moines. Still, Jervis gladly accepted his new responsibilities. "The fun in this job," he told *Business Week,* "is to see the Rock Island getting up a head of steam over very difficult challenges."[25]

When Jervis arrived in Chicago, he found ample evidence that the 7,792-mile Rock Island was struggling to survive. In his first annual report, which appeared in early 1965, the new chief executive told shareholders: "The past year, from the point of view of net earnings, was far from satisfactory. Net income was $3.8 millions. . . . This was $1.1 million less than the preceding year of 1963 and the lowest net income for any year since the Company was reorganized in 1948." He added, "Even more disturbing is the outlook for 1965. There is a distinct possibility, particularly if there is any downward trend in the present economy, that the Company can do no better than to break even." About the same time Jervis received unanimous board approval

About 1965, Jervis and Henry Crown, the largest investor in the Chicago, Rock Island & Pacific Railroad and a powerful board member, pose in the railroad's Chicago yards. (Irene Langdon)

to omit the declaration of any forthcoming dividends on stock. "This money is urgently needed for rebuilding the Rock Island property."[26]

Jervis grasped the varied reasons why the Rock Island faced financial difficulties. The railroad continued to operate in a highly competitive environment that lacked the economic vitality of some other regions. "In the 14 states served by Rock Island are found almost 42 percent of the country's rail mileage, but only 23–27 percent of its economic life, measured by the usual indicators." The company's branch and secondary lines were often lightly used, with some appendages receiving only tri-weekly service supplied by a slow-moving way-freight with its five-man crew. "Our traffic density is 22% less than that of the average western road," Jervis informed *Forbes*. "It's half that of the most prosperous roads." The track structure, including core routes, required attention; rail and tie renewals were woefully inadequate and good, clean ballast was often lacking. Rolling stock was also a concern. "The number of serviceable freight cars is at the lowest point since 1948,"

Jervis informed members of the executive committee, "and the loss of revenue and the recent unfavorable trends in this connection are directly traceable to lack of equipment." The freight car fleet was 4,000 to 5,000 below acceptable levels, and nearly 2,000 of the 26,000 existing units required heavy repairs or faced scrapping. The company especially needed specialized freight equipment, including auto-rack cars and center-flow covered hoppers. Furthermore, the Rock Island had too few yard and road locomotives and so, as Jervis observed, "utilization of diesel power is necessarily so high that proper standards of maintenance are not easy to enforce." The railroad also suffered from a motive power fleet that consisted of too many different types of engines. "Apparently Rock Island never met a diesel locomotive it didn't buy," observed a Rock Island watcher. "As late as 1965 . . . the road stabled power by eight builders . . . in more than 50 models." The company was handicapped, too, by its less-than-carload (LCL) business that resulted in an estimated annual out-of-pocket loss of between $2 million and $3 million. And most of the remaining passenger trains drained resources. Then there were accelerating wage costs and the problem of unproductive labor, most notably from locomotive firemen.[27]

But at the heart of the problems that afflicted the Rock Island was its subnormal level of freight revenues. Although the railroad enjoyed long-haul routes from Chicago, St. Louis, and Memphis to Denver and Tucumcari, it had to fight for interchange cars, especially for eastbound traffic. "These . . . connections have choices and play the field with several connecting railroads (including those they control through stock ownership)." Even with the largely north-to-south grain traffic that flowed from the Twin Cities, Des Moines, and Kansas City to terminals in Texas, the Rock Island was too closely tied to the ups and downs of agricultural production and sales. When all was considered, the company needed to ally itself with a railroad like the UP that had longer hauls and bigger markets.[28]

Getting Started

Immediately Jervis rolled up his sleeves and went to work. "Rock Island's problems cannot be postponed," he emphasized. "They are here now and must be dealt with." One of his first actions was a whirlwind tour of the system in order to conduct a series of meetings with officers and other employees "from clerks on up." He told these audiences that it would likely take years to effect a merger with the UP but that "we will run the Rock Island as if there were no merger in prospect and take every possible step to improve its competitive position and increase its earning power." Jervis wanted to end the belief, held by some Rock Island personnel, that "the Union Pacific merger will solve all our problems." Those who attended were impressed with his directness and his willingness to listen, and they realized that he cared about them and their railroad. "Langdon was really passionate about the men and women who worked for the Rock Island." Still, "there was about six months of trepidation," remembered a ranking operating official, "not knowing what the new head would do."[29]

Then Jervis examined top personnel, but he did not do this in a reckless manner. Observed Ted Desch, a lawyer and later board member and chief executive officer, "He took some time to assess the capabilities of people. There were no snap judgments." But changes occurred. "Among . . . disadvantages on the Rock Island was they had a very, very poor management," Jervis later commented. "They didn't have anybody who was worth a damn except a few fellows in an intermediate state. . . . [T]op people were just no good at all." Soon there was a repeat of what had happened when he took charge of the B&O: retirements (and some early) in key positions. "I encouraged their getting out of the picture." Just as Jervis had learned at the B&O, capable people were to be found within Rock Island ranks, some of whom had participated in an industrial training program that had been launched by Downing Jenks. And Jervis backed the aggressive recruitment of college graduates in various fields. As he told the Railway Supply Association in September 1965, "we have had literally hundreds of applications from boys, well qualified, who want to come to work with us, despite the uncertainties, despite the merger in the background, and despite the condition of the property." There would also be promotions and transfers from within the company; in fact, 40 top officials were reassigned, often to newly created or restructured posts. As on the B&O, Jervis cared about an individual's personality. He remained committed to his belief, aptly expressed by a colleague, that "Jervis always liked to have people around him who liked people."[30]

Yet not all slots could be filled by the rank and file. By necessity there would be outside hires. In July 1965, a major addition to the talent pool came when Jervis brought Bill Dixon from the B&O to serve as director of industrial engineering. "I was particularly happy when he asked me to come to Chicago, even though I knew that the Rock Island was in a precarious condition," remarked Dixon. Two years later, Dixon assumed the post as assistant to the president. Eventually he became senior vice president and Jervis's replacement in the presidential suite. Jervis would have liked to have had more personnel move from Baltimore to Chicago, but he had earlier agreed to limit any brain drain from the C&O/B&O.[31]

Jervis fortunately hired G. W. Kelly, a capable railroad manager, to oversee the operational side of the Rock Island. A former operating executive on the Southern Pacific, Kelly became "the eyes and ears for Mr. Langdon." Kelly stands beside a piggyback train in Chicago. (Irene Langdon)

Jervis discovered that attracting qualified railroaders to the Rock Island was not easy. "We had quite a lot of trouble getting the right people . . . because in a merger case . . . am I going to have a job? How long am I going to have a job?" Fortunately, several veteran railroaders would be attracted from the Southern Pacific. Since he needed to replace the vice president of operations, Jervis learned that the talented G. W. Kelly might be available to take this key post. Kelly served as general manager of the Texas & New Orleans Railroad (T&NO), an SP affiliate, in Houston, and in 1962 he had studied the Rock Island carefully when Donald Russell, SP president, seemed favorably disposed to acquiring the property. Happily for Jervis, Kelly qualified for his SP pension, minimizing any financial risk by leaving the T&NO. Moreover, Kelly and some other SP officers did not care for the leadership of Benjamin Biaggini, the new SP president. Kelly accepted the Rock Island offer and later became senior vice president of operations, serving faithfully in that capacity until he suffered a fatal heart attack on October 7, 1968.[32]

Luckily for the developing Langdon administration, Kelly brought with him some excellent junior SP people, including chief mechanical officer Herbert Bowyer and general superintendent of the car department Eugene Duren. These hires, however, produced unhappiness at UP headquarters, a harbinger of further tensions that developed between the two companies. Edd Bailey, whom Jervis considered to be "a joke as a railroad president," objected to having *any* former SP employee on the Rock Island, seeing these appointments as "permitting the enemy to enter from within." He remembered Bailey being especially upset with the Kelly hire. "How could you do that?" Bailey asked. "They're [SP] in competition with us." But Jervis was not about to back down in light of Bailey's objections to Kelly or anyone else. By 1966 Jervis had hired 18 executives from outside the Rock Island, and these men accepted the challenge to breathe life, action, and profit back into a tattered railroad.[33]

In the case of Kelly, this former SP operating executive proved to be an outstanding addition. "Kelly hit the ground running and knew what needed to be done," recalled a colleague. This "creative thinker," who "brought a lot of good operating practices to the Rock Island," spent much of his time on the road and became "the eyes and ears for Mr. Langdon." Kelly also knew how to motivate employees. Most memorably, he launched his "red knife club," handing out highly prized red pocket knives, emblazoned with his initials, as rewards for those "who deserved some kind of recognition.[34]

From the start of his tenure at the Rock Island, Kelly made solid contributions. He grasped the host of problems that confronted the property and set about making improvements in operations. Ironically, one of the earliest responses caused some uninformed employees to believe that "Kelly and Langdon were up to no real good." Kelly embarked on a program to lift "safety" rails on bridges and remove scores of sidings. These actions caused rumors to spread (at least on the Des Moines Division) that the new management lacked concern about track conditions and that Kelly had a sweetheart deal with a brother in Houston who planned to sell "at a big profit" this rail back to the Rock Island. There was talk about carloads of rails mysteriously moving through Fort Worth without waybills. "This was crazy roundhouse talk," explained a minor Rock Island official. "Kelly didn't have a brother, and taking up bridge safety rail didn't make the railroad any less safe. The Southern Pacific had done the same thing and with no negative consequences. It was a good policy since the SP had additional rail to use elsewhere or to sell for scrap, and that's exactly what happened under Kelly on the Rock Island."

Moreover, the Kelly policy was to remove *obsolete* sidings, ones that usually had a capacity of 10 cars or less, and soon much longer passing sidings, some exceeding two miles, were installed. Reusable track materials were placed where needed, commonly in yards and on branch lines.[35]

Whether personnel were long-term employees, new hires, or transfers from other railroads or businesses, Jervis sought to improve their overall condition. He bolstered commitment in a variety of ways. Jervis never ignored blue-collar workers. He spent time chatting with train, shop, and maintenance men and anxiously sought their feedback about the strengths and weaknesses of management. "Langdon could talk to a lowly trackman and make that person feel comfortable and in the process extract a lot of useful information." Early on he hired an outside firm to meet with workers to discuss minor yet annoying matters, such as the need to replace broken soap dispensers in washrooms. "These face-to-face encounters that led to fixing problems calmed down lots of employees and bolstered general morale," remarked an officer. Operating and nonoperating personnel applauded a much-publicized settlement in 1964 that increased monthly and hourly pay, expanded medical insurance, and provided additional paid vacation time. And there was a severance package for unneeded firemen, trainmen, and switchmen, ultimately saving nearly $3 million annually for the company. Employees, too, liked the cash bonus program that Jervis introduced that paid up to $1,000 for suggestions to improve operations and profitability and to reward outstanding performance.[36]

White-collar concerns were likewise considered. Jervis endorsed a number of changes that improved the morale of these employees, including raising salaries for the noncontractual staff, increasing the number of days off per month from two to three for operating supervisors, and even making hats optional in company headquarters. When it came to executive personnel, he made it clear that they should have time away from the office to be with their families. "They need a breather," he said. "People perform better if they get some time off the job."[37]

As at the B&O, Jervis did not take too much time off from work. Yet he squeezed into his active business schedule time for Irene and their two growing boys. In reflection Irene believed that some of their happiest days were spent at their home in Geneva. They liked their neighbors, their life in the community, and convenient access to an airport near Elgin. Halsey, the older son, became fascinated with flying, and his father encouraged that interest. About the age of 10, Halsey began to take flying lessons; he later graduated from the aviation program at Emery-Riddle Aeronautical University and became a commercial pilot. Irene also took flying lessons and made one solo flight.[38]

But in 1967 the Langdons experienced great sadness. Bancroft, Jervis's third-oldest child and the youngest by his first wife, Jean, committed suicide at age 26. Having graduated from Cornell University, as did his sister, Lee, and brother, Jerry, Bancroft entered the Cornell law program. Perhaps fearing that he would fail his final year of law school, he ended his life. "Jerv was stunned, and the tragedy weighed heavily on him," recalled Irene. "It was a exceedingly difficult time for all of us. But Jerv braced up and went on."[39]

Reorganization

Related to company personnel matters was the need to establish a more productive bureaucracy. Here Jervis enjoyed free rein as he did with other policy matters. Henry Crown "did not interfere with anything," and the two men became good friends. They met several times a week at Crown's downtown office and discussed railroad and other business matters. Resembling actions that had worked so well at the B&O, Jervis, a master of corporate management, streamlined the Rock Island. Within a relatively short time, significant changes occurred in Chicago headquarters and throughout the system.[40]

In what had been a traditional railroad, Jervis concluded that operations required restructuring. By mid-1965 the Rock Island created an office for a system general manager and staff in Kansas City. Located in an extensively remodeled freight house, this facility replaced a two-operating-district arrangement that had been centered in Des Moines and El Reno, Oklahoma. There was also a reshuffling of personnel; 73 employees were transferred from Chicago to Kansas City as were a smaller number from Des Moines and El Reno. Jervis, too, endorsed a reduction in the number of operating divisions. Instead of the Arkansas, Des Moines, Illinois, Missouri–Kansas, Southern, and Western divisions, the new structuring led to the Des Moines, Chicago, Illinois, Missouri–Kansas, and Southern divisions. This revamping consolidated employees, reduced the number of supervisory personnel, and closed buildings. When the Arkansas and Southern divisions were fused in the multistoried office structure in El Reno, the former headquarters for the Arkansas division in Little Rock became surplus. Yet this contraction may have had a downside. "There really was too much railroad for some of the existing divisions to manage," reflected an employee. But no one disagreed about the need to consolidate dispatching in Des Moines and El Reno.[41]

Another action, which resembled the reorganization that had occurred on the B&O, was the creation in early 1965 of the Economic and Cost Research Department. This group evaluated management actions and expenditure of funds on a "before-the-fact basis." During its first year of operation, the center

conducted profit studies of such matters as train operations, equipment purchases, and the restructuring or elimination of facilities. "Things were really
looked at with an analytical eye," noted George Durbala, an employee at corporate headquarters. However, "limited staffing, caused by budget constraints,
reduced the potential of this important unit."[42]

Accounting functions were improved as well. Just as B&O personnel complained about being in the dark about financial matters, a similar situation
plagued the Rock Island. It was difficult for supervisors to know about avail-
ability of resources. But during Jervis's tenure there would be much better
budgeting and goal setting. Reflected a senior operations official, "There was
less of a seat-of-your-pants approach to money matters. I really liked the
greater professionalization."[43]

In an accompanying move, Jervis pressed for an overhaul of data processing using a task force organization approach. Top priority was given to
providing much-needed information of train movements for advanced planning of yard operations and better car tracing for customers. As part of this
operation a passenger coach was converted into a training car that contained
a classroom and tele-processing equipment. In his report to shareholders for
1965, he announced that because of this unit, "a marked improvement in the
accuracy and control of advance train makeup, local car information, and
car detention data has been achieved." Improvements continued as the company's two IBM 360 computer systems were expanded, and John Burnett,
director of purchases and stores and a hire from the Bessemer & Lake Erie
Railroad, added a computer-assisted "instant ordering" system known as
Data-Phone.[44]

In 1966, the Rock Island benefited from unification of industrial development and real estate functions. "New managerial techniques," noted Jervis,
"were adopted to improve efficiency and to better serve customers' industrial
development needs." This energized unit stepped up outside contacts and
took out carefully selected print advertisements, including a double-page
promotion of industrial developments in the Quad Cities (Davenport, East
Moline, Moline, and Rock Island) that ran in *Forbes*. As part of activities of
the combined departments, the company aggressively pushed sales of surplus
land that had neither industrial nor operational value. Within a year, more
than 800 acres had been sold, creating one-time income and reducing recur-
ring property taxes. Additional real estate sales followed.[45]

While additional reorganization of the bureaucracy took place, including
merger on June 1, 1965, of the engineering and maintenance-of-way departments under the direction of the chief engineer, and establishment in 1967 of
a centralized car distribution office, Jervis took particular pride in revamping

what became a comprehensive piggyback (TOFC) business. The model of the B&O was again employed. After all, Jervis, the pragmatist, knew the benefits that could be derived from creating an intermodal profit center.[46]

By the mid-1960s, major Class I railroads were experiencing a steady increase in TOFC traffic, and the Rock Island was no exception. By offering expanded piggyback options, including new service plans, and providing faster (especially on eastbound schedules) and more dependable service, the company opened new markets. At the time Jervis took charge, the Rock Island had seen a modest rise of 6.4 percent in TOFC business over the previous year, and growth appeared likely. Indeed, that is what happened and to a degree more than anyone expected. In 1965 piggyback revenues exceeded $13 million, an increase of 25.1 percent over 1964. Then they soared: $15.2 million in 1966, $19.4 million in 1967, $27.5 million in 1968, and $31 million in 1969, representing expansion of over 100 percent in only three years.[47]

Part of the explanation for the healthy growth came from restructuring. In October 1965, the Rock Island launched its trailer service department that coordinated *all* piggyback operations and development. Headed by a general manager, the unit had two primary sections: operations and equipment control and sales and service. And additional refinements occurred. In 1966, for example, the position of manager of perishable sales was created, and three years later an assistant general manager's post in Chicago was opened along with establishment of three new division managers. Eight regional managers and 11 trailer sales representatives provided support. (Previously, the general manager supervised two general sales managers and six regional managers.)[48]

Just as Jervis had done at the B&O, he found a seasoned trucking executive to oversee operations. The individual was Frank Sutherland, who had been vice president for national sales for Ryder System in Miami. Jervis not only made Sutherland general manager of Rock Island's piggyback services but also installed him as president of Rock Island Motor Transit, the venerable, wholly owned trucking subsidiary. Although Sutherland later resigned, he was replaced by the equally qualified Paul Kluding, an official from the Detroit-based Middle Atlantic Transportation Company.[49]

But more happened with TOFC operations than simply restructuring the corporate flow chart and picking a dynamic head. The Rock Island expanded or updated TOFC facilities in several prime locations, including Chicago, Denver, Memphis, and St. Louis, and removed some of the obsolete "circus ramps" from smaller terminals. In 1969 the largest single expenditure took place when a new $1-million piggyback terminal opened in Houston. The company also skillfully employed leases to replace practically all of its fleet of

Jervis was not about to have the Rock Island become a transportation slum, pushing hard to acquire much-needed rolling stock. New company-owned truck trailers, flatcars, and high-capacity boxcars became part of the Langdon administration's program of equipment upgrading. (Irene Langdon)

900 truck trailers and reduced by 20 percent monthly trailer charges. That replacement strategy continued into the 1970s. Improved TOFC services also occurred by having Rock Island Motor Transit better coordinate its operations. In early 1967 Jervis explained this robust sector of freight operations: "Many innovations and improvements, such as new trailers, more attractive rates and services, better ramp facilities, and an intensified sales effort were responsible for the revenue increase."[50]

Marketing, too, received careful attention. Early in 1967 the railroad named a manager of market analysis who received assistance from a small staff. A year later the marketing department was expanded. Specifically the reorganization led to creation of six marketing manager positions, namely, grain and grain products, forest products, chemicals and petroleum, automotive and farm implements, food products, and ores and metals. Again the overall concept had worked on the B&O and Jervis wholeheartedly endorsed these changes. The marketing specialists along with market analysts, pricing experts, and operating personnel sought to design the best-suited transportation package for the shipper, taking into account equipment, rates, routes, and schedules.[51]

The Langdon administration did not ignore other ways to enhance income. Just as the railroad sold surplus real estate, the board of directors decided to liquidate the company's 50 percent ownership in the Waterloo Railroad, a diesel-operated shortline and terminal company that had been a former electric interurban, which it had owned since 1956. As Jervis told members of the board's executive committee, "The benefits which the Company would derive from the improvement in working capital would outweigh any benefits it might realize from holding the stock as a long-term investment." Fortunately, the Illinois Central, which owned the other half interest, agreed to buy out the Rock Island.[52]

Jervis remained a problem solver. The hands-on, innovative streak that had become his hallmark at the B&O was apparent at the Rock Island. There would be various "special studies." An early example involved assigning lawyer Ted Desch to work with marketing people to determine whether farm machinery manufacturers, who were located in the Moline area, might change their seasonal shipments of equipment, spreading them throughout the year. The railroad faced a chronic shortage of flatcars and wanted better car utilization, since these movements came all at once. "No cigar," remarked Desch. "It was not practical to change the shipping policy, because local implement dealers needed to pay 50 percent of the price and their sales took place in the late winter and early spring. These dealers would face acquisitions costs, storage problems, and related expenses if these tractors and other pieces of farm equipment flowed in month after month after month." The point, though, was that Jervis sought out this information and hoped that benefits would follow.

Jervis continued to stay abreast of events in the field. He regularly used his new Piper Aztec to reach operation centers, problem areas, and other destinations where he might visit shippers, politicians, and regulators. Jervis recalled that elevator operators in Kansas and Oklahoma "were really impressed that I flew in and landed on one of their municipal or private airstrips." Flying gave him great speed and flexibility. As before, he usually traveled alone or with only a few associates. Unlike most railroad presidents, Jervis was not accompanied by a retinue of private secretaries and executives.[53]

Ending Passenger Train Pain

When Jervis arrived in Chicago, he immediately realized that, as with the B&O and virtually every other carrier, passenger service on the Rock Island was on a long and slow downward spiral. He decided not to retain much of the long-distance passenger service that historically had been part of the company's operations. Unlike the B&O, however, there would not be a Paul Reistrup or a profit center. Frankly, the future of virtually all Rock Island varnish was grim, although his endorsement of creative responses would be reflected in company policies toward a shrinking number of trains. Early on, Jervis explained that "the cold fact is that business travel is now using the airplane, almost exclusively, and personal travel, if not by private automobile, is also by air." He also noted that "cheap public transportation is available by bus on the ever-expanding and improving interstate highway system built by Uncle Sam."[54]

The passenger sector could not be ignored. The Rock Island was losing approximately $14 million annually on a passenger gross that generated only 15 cents out of every dollar that flowed into corporate coffers. Passenger trains sadly made up nearly 30 percent of total train miles.[55]

Jervis wisely decided that the company should look before it lopped. After consideration of the situation, the company determined that some passenger trains must be withdrawn but that an aggressive pricing scheme might reduce losses on remaining runs. Although influenced by an existing "Family Fare Tickets" plan that paralleled other promotional schemes in the industry and among airlines after 1961, the successful "Red Circle Fares" on the B&O inspired the new approach. In December 1964 Jervis embraced what was ballyhooed as the "MTT Plan," a similar scheme of off-peak charges. On

Mondays through Thursdays, the railroad reduced coach and first-class fares by 25 percent. The only exception involved the *Golden State,* Nos. 3 and 4, because earlier the Rock Island and SP had jointly cut rates by about 20 percent. If the MTT Plan failed, the Rock Island could tell regulators that a genuine effort had been made to attract riders.[56]

With the aid of cost analysts, Jervis and associates concluded by early 1966 that the flow of red ink from the passenger side of the revenue stream had not been controlled. It was time to seek discontinuances, but there would be a calculated plan. If approved, the Rock Island would exit the long-haul Chicago–Denver (*Rocky Mountain Rocket*) and the Chicago–Los Angeles (*Golden State*) markets and focus on midrange destinations. "The Rock Island proposes a pattern of service specifically designed to serve those cities . . . which are dependent on Rock Island," he wrote. "If successful . . . Rock Island would be ahead by an estimated $2 million a year, based on present-day wage and material costs, and provide a passenger service more in keeping with the demands of the day." This meant that Peoria, the Quad Cities, and Des Moines would continue to see Rock Island streamliners "with improved on-time performance [and] the assignment of the most modern equipment in our possession." These cities had significant populations and the Chicago–Des Moines corridor was dotted with colleges and universities, a good source of traffic. As for the latter constituency, Jervis, however, was not so sanguine about any dependence on collegians. "In my personal experience and observation, the college student is the most ingenious person in the world in getting from A to B without spending a cent. He will hitchhike, bum a ride, or do almost anything to avoid spending the money his father has sent him to get home."[57]

The passenger train "takeoff" process remained somewhat cumbersome, even with a liberalized policy brought about by the Transportation Act of 1958. Still, progress occurred. In October 1967, the Rock Island was especially happy to eliminate Nos. 15 and 16, which traveled between Kansas City and the Twin Cities, an operation that in 1966 produced an out-of-pocket loss of $431,533. The case of the Rock Island with Nos. 15 and 16, along with applications for removal of long-distance and several other trains that all generated substantial losses, was aided by decisions in 1967 of the U.S. Post Office Department to remove railway post office cars, a vital source of income, from virtually all trains and to divert the mail to airplanes and trucks.[58]

There was some shrill local objections to these discontinuances, but the Rock Island won permission to drop the most financially draining trains. The public timetable, which went into effect on March 2, 1969, revealed these successes, listing only two daily trains each way between Chicago and Peoria, a single daily train in each direction between Chicago and Omaha, and a similar arrangement between Kansas City and the Twin Cities. At last passenger train miles had been reduced to an acceptable 3 percent. Of the remaining service the *Peoria Rockets* were the most notable trains, offering a reserved club parlor car at a modest price. "We're doing this in keeping with our policy of providing the type of service which the public had indicated it will support," explained Murl Bonesteel, director of passenger services. By this time the MTT Plan had been canceled, and the company told patrons: "Take advantage of Family Plan or Group fares for BIG savings."[59]

But the last gasp to save Rock Island varnish failed. Shortly before Jervis left the Rock Island, more discontinues occurred. No only did the Kansas City and Twin Cities trains become memories, but on May 31, 1970, the ICC granted permission to end passenger operations in Iowa. Trains Nos. 7 and 10, which ran between Chicago and Omaha, made their final runs. This skeleton operation had lost over $1.2 million in 1969, and the red ink in 1970 was expected to exceed that amount. Observed the *Des Moines Register*, "The trains have been averaging only a station wagon load (nine passengers) eastward from Des Moines, and a motorcycle load (one or two passengers) westward." Long-distance passenger service remained only between Chicago and Peoria.[60]

Jervis and the passenger sector did not overlook its commuter operations in greater Chicago. While the Burlington and the C&NW blazed the way with more practical and economical double-decker or bi-level cars, the Rock Island also modernized. Early in his tenure, 20 Budd-built stainless steel, air-conditioned bi-levels entered service on both the Chicago–Blue Island and Chicago–Joliet lines at a cost of $3.1 million. Control cabs on five of the cars allowed for efficient push-pull operations. By the late 1960s, the commuter sector was breaking even, and Jervis sought more improvements: adding to the bi-level fleet, revising fares to entice off-hour riders, and improving service generally. In early 1970, the fleet of bi-level coaches had increased to 30. Veteran riders, too, appreciated the end to an archaic and unbalanced fare structure with a plan that offered the most economical cost per ride to holders of monthly tickets. And these patrons could now participate in a convenient "ticket-by-mail" program.[61]

Not until after Jervis's departure were Rock Island's commuter problems ultimately solved. On March 19, 1974, voters in the six-county Chicago region approved a ballot issue that created the Regional Transportation Authority (RTA), later reconstituted as the Metropolitan Regional Transportation Authority or Metra. As part of this transit authority, public interests absorbed control of Rock Island operations. Appropriately the route between Joliet and La Salle Street Station became known as the Metra/Rock Island District.[62]

Reflecting Jervis's passion for helping people, he expressed concern about those longtime employees, especially men of color, who had lost jobs because of passenger train retrenchments. What would happen to cooks, waiters, and chair-car attendants? Although these "tub and tray" personnel had a union job-protection agreement, Jervis wanted them to have an opportunity to find other railroad positions, namely, "responsible jobs with some future."

The results satisfied Jervis. He remained true to the Langdon family credo of promoting human equality. Through the diligent efforts of Fred Meyer, director of personnel, about 35 employees, with an average age of 50 plus and 30 years of seniority, found jobs as clerks, brakemen, piggyback dispatcher, and engineering estimator. These dedicated Rock Island employees of color were pleased; many had feared that if they continued to work, they would end up as janitors or in positions not far removed from the dining or parlor car.[63]

Although not directly related to the passenger problem, Jervis and his associates knew that the days of LCL traffic were numbered. The Rock Island and other railroads had lost their comparative advantage to trucks, and their LCL facilities were usually obsolete and heavily taxed. In 1965 the company ended this money-losing service. Still, Rock Island Motor Lines handled less-than-truck (LTL) pickups and deliveries profitably, and other small shipments might well move by intermodal TOFC.[64]

A Better Rock

Under the watchful eye of G. W. Kelly, the Langdon administration undertook an array of betterment projects that improved the physical plant and rolling stock. These improvements enhanced dependability, making shippers more willing to bill cargoes "VIA CRI&P." Jervis's ceaseless support for creativity led to better ways to price and market rail services. No wonder James G. Pate, director of public relations, ceaselessly promoted the new slogan for the Rock Island: "Same Name—New Railroad."[65]

Since overall track conditions, even on main stems, had generally worsened since the early 1960s, maintenance-of-way work needed to be a high priority if the railroad were to remain viable. An early response involved the adoption of a three-year program for track revitalization. To implement this schedule, the Rock Island in mid-1965 committed a modest $1.5 million for modern track power tools, work equipment, and vehicles. The company leased some of the heaviest, most expensive equipment, maximizing the dollar impact. "You had to have decent equipment if you expected to get a better plant at a decent price," reflected Bill Dixon, and he was right. Although some improvements were made to branches, the company concentrated track rehabilitation efforts on the primary arteries, especially the Tucumcari line. Large, mobile gangs descended on various sections of track, strikingly different from the three- or four-man crews with their hand tools or "idiot sticks" who had earlier done this work.[66]

As part of these renewal activities, attention was paid to installing long passing tracks. "Basically a single track railroad," observed Jervis, "Rock Island's sidings are too short and improperly spaced to accommodate modern high-speed freight trains." Most of these projects took place between Herington, Kansas, and Tucumcari and between Fairbury, Nebraska, and Limon, Colorado. Some of these strategic sidings were built with track components that a recently opened panel-making plant in Des Moines had fabricated. "Using the new technique, a crew of four or five men can lay a mile of track in about 34 working hours," explained the Des Moines Division engineer. "It used to take a crew of from 15 to 25 men at least twice that time to lay the same amount of track." The railroad also introduced prestressed-concrete bridge decks that were less expensive to install and maintain than traditional structures built with treated timbers.[67]

Even though Rock Island crews replaced hundreds of thousands of crossties, dumped and tamped enormous quantities of rock ballast, replaced hundreds of miles of 112-pound rail with 119- and 131-pound steel that was often continuously welded, much additional track improvements remained. Jervis hardly oversaw creation of speedways between every major terminal. Slow spots plagued the road; for example, the *Slow Order Status Report* for the Illinois Division issued on June 6, 1969, revealed more than 60 locations where train speeds had to be reduced, mostly for "rough track." Fortunately, the majority of these slow orders affected secondary and branch lines.[68]

The vital Tucumcari line, most of all, was significantly upgraded. Heavier rail, new ties, more ballast, and re-spaced signaling made this possible. "We got it back in shape," recalled Jervis. "The volume through Tucumcari that we were able to generate when we got some really good service for the Southern Pacific escalated. And our percent of the ton miles in the West among the railroads after I came there [Rock Island] kept going right up." This, of course, was the Rock Island's best long-haul route. Making these betterments, which resulted in the line becoming a nearly double-track operation, were smart decisions, indeed.[69]

MR. SHIPPER: THE ROCK ISLAND HAS ORDERED

$57 MILLION

IN NEW EQUIPMENT FOR YOU!

The Rock Island is getting $57,000,000 worth of new freight equipment in 1965 alone. We're now in a position to carry more of your products, and carry them further, much faster, and more safely, too! Orders already entered and now being placed represent 3,609 freight cars and 65 locomotives. Shown below is a capsule list of this new equipment. Let your Rock Island sales representative put this versatile fleet to work for you. Call him today. We want your freight in these new cars!

A. F. Hatcher

A. F. Hatcher
General Manager, Freight Sales

LOCOMOTIVES: 48 of the 65 new diesels will be 2500 h.p. road locomotives and 17 will be switchers.

COVERED HOPPERS: 746 of these 100-ton capacity cars will be available. Roller-bearing equipped with sectionalized trough-hatches, these units will carry bulk materials, grain and milled products.

HOPPER CARS: 153, 70-ton capacity for ores, coal, wood chips, sand, stone, and gravel.

AIRSLIDE CARS: 87 airslide hopper cars, both 70- and 90-ton capacities for flour, sugar, and similar products.

"DF" CARS: 251 cushion-underframe 70- and 90-ton box cars with "DF" (damage-free) loaders for transporting miscellaneous manufactured products, glass, and automobile parts.

GONDOLAS: 300 flat-bottom gondola cars equipped with roller bearings for machinery, steel, or sand and gravel loadings.

COVERED GONDOLAS: 50, 100-ton capacity for coiled and sheet steel and steel products.

FLAT CARS: 200 units, 60 feet long, of 70-ton capacity, equipped with cushioning devices, for general service.

SPECIAL BOX CARS: 47 cushion-underframe 70- and 100-ton capacity box cars with roller bearings and special loading devices for packaged goods and various manufactured items.

INSULATED CARS: 275, 50-foot, 70- and 90-ton box cars, fully insulated with cushion underframes and roller bearings for carrying processed and packaged foods and beverages.

AUTO CARRIERS: 55 multi-level automobile and truck carriers for installation on high-speed super-flatcars.

GP CARS: 1,500 general purpose box cars, 50-ton capacity of the latest design for grain, lumber and miscellaneous products.

 ROCK ISLAND LINES

During the Langdon years, the Rock Island told the public, especially shippers, that the company had significantly improved its fleet of motive power and freight cars. (Author's collection)

Rolling stock likewise demanded attention and these equipment needs were hardly ignored. Soon after taking charge, the Langdon team endorsed a $24.4-million equipment renewal program that allocated $3.8 million for 20 road and yard locomotives and the remainder for various types of specialized freight cars. The former would add high-powered and dependable General Electric–built U28Bs, or "U-boats" as employees called these second-generation diesels. The latter included 2,000 high-capacity covered 100-ton hopper cars, equipped with trough hatches, 550 box cars that were either insulated 50-foot cars or giant 86-foot "damage-free" cars, and 42 bi-level and tri-level automobile rack cars. Twenty-five all-steel cabooses were also ordered, allowing the company to retire some ancient outside-braced wooden "crummies." Later on other substantial additions were made to the motive power and car fleet. Noted *Railway Age,* "the re-equipping of the Rock Island continues," and in 1968 the company acquired 10 general-purpose 3,330-horsepower road locomotives and 221 specialized freight cars.[70]

The Langdon administration did not overlook equipment-repair needs. Improved shop facilities at El Reno, Kansas City, and Little Rock contributed to a reduction of out-of-service time for freight equipment that underwent repairs. With centralization of locomotive control activities, inspection and shopping of motive power became organized on a systemwide basis, ending the former district assignments for maintenance. Especially impressive were the implementations of a carefully prepared proposal by G. W. Kelly for El Reno becoming the focal point for major car repairs and car cleaning for the southern half of the railroad. An investment in 1966 of approximately $600,000 in buildings, equipment, and tracks led to a net annual savings of more than $200,000.[71]

And other aspects of the physical plant saw improvements. New structures, including yard offices, were built and old facilities, especially unneeded country depots, were removed. It would be during the late 1960s that most of the elderly, weather-worn, two-story frame depots, a legacy of predecessor Burlington, Cedar Rapids & Northern Railway, disappeared in Iowa, Minnesota, and South Dakota. While there was not much salvageable material in buildings, junk metal was collected and sold for scrap. Communications were also modernized, ranging from replacement of hundreds of miles of carrier telephone lines to an intercity direct-dialing telephone service.[72]

But occasionally mistakes occurred with betterments. One official believed that "if Langdon had a weakness, it was that he spent money too quickly," making some of these expenditures wasteful. "The company started some projects with no real pay back." An example was a new fueling facility at Goodland, Kansas, on the Colorado Springs–Denver line. "There were big, powerful pumps at seven or eight fueling stations. But the pumps could not be managed by a single person, and a second employee was hired. Because the pumps worked so fast, less powerful pumps had to be installed to prevent expensive fuel spills."[73]

Then there were operating improvements. As Jervis knew from his experiences at the B&O, efficient utilization of rolling stock, best achieved in unit consists, would allow the Rock Island to save on additional equipment purchases and to continue the retirement of obsolete cars. And with less yard work required, further cost savings would result. Although the railroad handled only a modest volume of coal and ore, grain traffic, albeit mostly seasonal, was large and well-suited to unit-train moves. With better car utilization, chronic grain car shortages could be reduced, and that, coupled with competitive pricing, would endear shippers. Unit grain trains appeared to be an excellent way to bolster revenues.[74]

It did not take long before the Rock Island created a unit grain train program. "The plan we worked out," Jervis told participants at a transportation conference in September 1966, "called for train consists of 100 jumbo covered hoppers, 100 ton capacity each, with terminal time, both at origin and destination, limited to 24 hours." If rail volume could be more evenly distributed, with a 10,000-ton train operating on a four-day turnaround, reasoned the company's market research group, that would be a vast improvement over the 1.2 loads per car per month that were then being obtained. An attractive rate would be quoted to shippers.

Although a sound concept, this initial proposal fell apart. Explained Jervis: "While the shippers were at first receptive—attracted principally by the low rate—they soon realized that, with an obligation to load 10,000 tons every 4 days, substantial changes in marketing practices were required, particularly in regard to storage or reforwarding at the destination end." He added, "Distribution, in other words, would have to be carefully controlled, and the shippers, who were active competitors, doubted their ability to introduce and then enforce the necessary cooperation and discipline. . . . What these shippers really wanted, it soon developed, was a low rate but the unit train which they thought would make such a rate possible would only be operated whenever they were ready with 10,000 tons to move to the common destination. The shuttle concept the shippers flatly rejected as beyond their ability to handle."[75]

Undaunted by the failure to introduce unit-train shuttle service, the Rock Island, with Jervis's full backing, formulated another way to transport grain. In conjunction with the Frisco, the two companies independently proposed as of December 30, 1966, introduction of a combination of car reservations and incentives rates for export shipments of corn, milo, and wheat. As the railroads explained to the media: "For the first time, the shipper will know when he will get his cars, how many he will get, and when his shipment can be expected at destination." Among key features were provisions for reservations for eight cars or more that had to be made 15 days in advance and lower rates that grew when shippers reserved more cars. The equipment needed to be loaded within 24 hours after car delivery and unloaded within 48 hours after arrival at the port destination. (The old allowance was 48 hours loading time and seven "free days" at the port.) Again there was disappointment; the ICC, responding to conflicting interests in the grain trade, refused to endorse the Rock Island–Frisco plan. This negative action rightly reaffirmed Jervis's generally low opinion of the regulatory process.[76]

Jervis was not about to relent; the Rock Island needed every dollar. A profitable scheme was mandatory, for in 1967 an unusually sharp decline in wheat carloadings plagued the company. Much of this loss could be blamed on itinerant, unregulated truckers handling the lion's share of this traffic from Kansas, Oklahoma, and Texas. With ICC sanction, the railroad in 1968 finally operated the type of unit grain trains that it wanted. The agreement with shippers involved a limited time for loading and unloading and a reduction of rates that averaged 20–25 percent less than the former tariffs. Now Rock Island unit trains, one of which totaled a whopping 201 cars in a test run, made nearly five trips monthly between wheat centers such as Enid to Houston and Galveston compared to the previous average of 1.3 trips every 30 days.[77]

Part of the new grain car–pricing program involved targeting transport of corn and later soybeans from locations in Iowa. For some time corn from the eastern part of the state had moved on trucks to terminals on the Mississippi River for transfer to barges usually destined for Baton Rouge or New Orleans. Corn from western sections of Iowa had either been fed to livestock or sold to processors. In fact, the railroad handled only about 6 percent of the available corn from the Hawkeye state. "A farsighted Rock Island management was alert to the fact that economic opportunities awaited enterprising marketers skilled in innovation," boasted a company publicist. "Rock Island's marketing department had been staffed with bright, aggressive 'comers,' unfettered by obsolete traditions or practices. These men, together with a newly aligned group of progressive-minded pricing experts held over from the prior management, went after new business." The essence of this release was correct.[78]

The overall results were remarkable, although Jervis expected as much. In 1967 the movement of export grains to gulf ports stood at a disappointing 12.7 million bushels, but a year later it soared to 50.6 million bushels. Export corn alone accounted for nearly 2.5 million bushels, and this was almost entirely new business. Revenues jumped from $3.2 million to $10.3 million.[79]

This triumph did not go unnoticed. In 1969 the Railway Progress Institute awarded the coveted Silver Freight Car trophy to the Rock Island in recognition of "effective promotion of railroad freight traffic." The smiling president, along with several other Rock Island officials, including Al Hatcher, vice president for traffic, Norman Schultz, manager for pricing, and Ted Wells, marketing manager for grain and grain products, attended the gala award ceremony in Chicago. The subsequent positive publicity was wholly deserved.[80]

While movements of grain did not require high speeds, other shipments, particularly automobiles and parts, perishables, and TOFC, needed to move rapidly. With improvements to the track structure, longer passing sidings, and better motive power and equipment maintenance, the Rock Island enhanced freight train schedules, terminal operations, and interchange arrangements with connecting roads. By 1966 faster trains operated between every major destination. For example, the Chicago–Denver schedule dropped by 4 hours, and running times between Chicago, Twin Cities, St. Louis, and Texas were reduced by approximately 4 hours southbound and as much as 20 hours northbound. Early on, the company took additional pride in a classification system that "blocked" traffic to afford the longest possible haul, thereby minimizing switching and rehandling of cars at intermediate terminals. In August 1966, *Railway Age* gave the Rock Island and New York Central (NYC) prominent coverage under the headline "Freight Trains Adopt the Space Age." The story heralded the debut of two trains—*Gemini I* and *Gemini II*—that operated as "run throughs" between NYC's Elkhart, Indiana, yard and Rock Island's Silvis facilities, bypassing the congested Chicago terminal area. This "significant speedup" was also facilitated by the roads operating trains on a pool basis; locomotives and cabooses ran through between Elkhart and Silvis. There would be other coordinated freight arrangements, including a joint operation with Erie Lackawanna (EL) that began in early 1968. This service involved moving pre-blocked freight with pooled power between Marion, Ohio, and Silvis, cutting 24 hours off transit time. Resembling the Rock Island, the managements of NYC and EL, both experiencing financial difficulties, demonstrated a willingness to innovate with these run throughs.[81]

The Rock Island became especially pleased with the run throughs with the SP via Tucumcari and the overall improved service on what was the longest and most profitable haul. In fact, there was a test run conducted in 1968 in which a train with "a lot of power and ten or twelve freight cars and several office cars . . . and all green signals" bested the competing Santa Fe by several hours from Chicago to Los Angeles. This experiment, reflected a senior Rock Island operating officer, showed that "we felt that we could

Dear students:

The directing of a modern transportation enterprise by a young and imaginative management group is making railroading a challenging career.

A retired railroader of the last generation would hardly recognize his industry today. To say that the Rock Island and other American railroads are competing in the transportation arena with the latest equipment and techniques tells only part of the story.

The key to the success of any company, such as the Rock Island, is people. Recently the Rock Island has been singularly successful in recruiting and developing a management team of real ability.

We resort to the graduates of the nation's colleges and universities, with the hope of finding young men who can sustain our recently established momentum and put us into a position of leadership in the days ahead.

You are urged to give the Rock Island Railroad serious thought as a career possibility. It presents more challenging problems than many other railroads because the competitive situation is tougher. If you are intrigued, arrange to talk to our campus representative when he visits your school.

Cordially,

Jervis Langdon

Jervis Langdon, Jr.
Chairman and President

Just as he had done on the Baltimore & Ohio, Jervis sought to hire bright young college graduates at the Rock Island. *Transportation Careers* was a pamphlet the company distributed in the late 1960s. (Author's collection) compete with the Santa Fe with its highly attractive single-line operation." Such competition would be difficult albeit possible.[82]

Toward the end of Jervis's tenure, the company explored the feasibility of operating fewer but much longer trains, at least on the Southern Division. Designed to reduce crew costs and other expenses, these "monster freights," with their impressive lash-up of locomotive power, moved the available tonnage, but in the process they hardly established any speed records. The model may have been the CGW, which in the early 1950s had dispatched trains that might exceed 150 cars.[83]

Merger Mess

Whether at work or away from the office, Jervis had much on his mind. "It's a damned tough property to operate," he told Nancy Ford, a respected columnist for *Modern Railroads*. He could see improvements with the corporate structure, physical plant, and service operations and benefits derived from reducing the workforce by more than 1,000, a paring process that continued. Although the Rock Island did not appear headed toward imminent bankruptcy, the company was only limping along. In July 1967, David P. Morgan, editor of *Trains*, put it this way: "Rock Island lies gloomily on its sickbed." Net income was on a decided downswing: a positive $3.84 million in 1964, a negative $1.45 million in 1965, a positive $1.89 million in 1966, a negative $16.14 million in 1967, a negative $4.25 million in 1968, and a negative $9.29 million in 1969. Jervis was not wholly pessimistic, but he was realistic. Since his presidency began, the railroad had made real progress in bolstering freight traffic. Between 1964 and 1969, "Rock Island's share of 'the pie' in the central western district increased from 9.58 to 10.62 percent of cars loaded on line and from 10.12 to 12.39 percent of cars received," he observed. "But this achievement, representing a gain of about 156,000 carloads and reflected in steadily increasing freight revenues (at a rate generally in excess of the industry average), has not been able to overcome an even greater rise in operating expenses." The railroad still needed to spend much more to improve physical plant and equipment. Heavy grain trains, for example, at times pounded the delicate track structure, and the company's patching program often could not keep up. "Only massive infusions of cash which the Union Pacific stands committed to advance—once the merger is approved—will save the Rock Island and enable it to become a viable unit in a strong transportation system," Jervis again emphasized.[84]

When Jervis arrived in Chicago, the merger cards had already been dealt. After all, UP was determined to acquire the Rock Island and Rock Island shareholders anxiously awaited high-dividend-paying UP common stock, knowing that the robust UP was also rich in land and minerals. There was no interest in the C&NW financial package, even though it had a face value of about five dollars per share more than the UP offer. The combination of C&NW stock and collateral trust income bonds seemed too risky. On November 2, 1964, as one of his initial acts, Jervis sent a single-page statement to Rock Island stockholders reaffirming his determination to back the merger application and urging investor support. *"I therefore concur with the recommendation of all of the other Rock Island directors that you support the proposed combination with the Union Pacific and accept the Union Pacific Exchange Offer. Since the accomplishment of such a combination is a major objective, I, as your Chairman, will do everything in my power to bring it about"* (emphasis in original). Subsequently, shareholders gathered in Chicago on January 7, 1965, and overwhelmingly approved the merger.[85]

While Jervis supported the ICC application, he discovered to his alarm that the Rock Island lacked its own legal counsel to represent its merger position. When board members were asked why this was, Jervis learned that the company "could use the same counsel as the Union Pacific because, in their view, our interests were identical, and we both wanted this merger." This was dangerous. At Jervis's insistence, the Rock Island employed the Chicago firm of Kirkland, Hodson, Chaffetz and Masters as its own special counsel.

Jervis knew that the UP–Rock Island proposal, if approved, would have an enormous impact on the national railroad structure. A score or so of midwestern and western carriers saw their prosperity in the balance; for some the issue was survival. "We had nearly every western railroad against us." He could count on support or neutrality only from the "Northern Lines," namely, the Burlington, GN, and NP, which were in the process of seeking to become the Burlington Northern. The best way to achieve success for the Rock Island, Jervis believed, would be to have a broad settlement among the affected carriers *before* the ICC examiner held the customary prehearing conference. He especially sought talks with Ben Heineman, respecting him personally and appreciating his reasons for wanting to take control of the Rock Island.

The openness of Jervis to discussions among industry leaders did not set well with the UP. In the course of his early activities to push for merger, he told a reporter from the *Wall Street Journal* that he realized that there was growing resistance to the Rock Island–UP union, stating that "I hope that we can work to some adjustments and compromises here that may eliminate, or at least reduce some of this terrible opposition that we've got." Although Jervis recalled "I was pretty careful in what I said," he felt that overtures to opponents was a wise course of action. Finding "common ground" made sense. When Frank Barnett read the *Wall Street Journal* interview, he exploded. "We've got no intention of talking with these people. We don't want to try to work things out." Then Barnett demanded that Jervis make a retraction. He refused. Jervis warned Barnett, "It's going to be hard for you if you don't do some talking." Jervis, of course, realized that the Rock Island and UP had to bring in the U.S. Department of Justice in order to avoid violating the antitrust code, but he had already discussed the matter with the federal lawyer who had been assigned to the case. Jervis found him receptive to such conversations, but these never occurred, thanks to Barnett's rigid position. The attitude of the always patronizing UP hierarchy was that attorneys should manage the merger. Said Barnett: "Leave it up to the lawyers," and the UP would do so with disastrous results.[86]

Jervis and the UP disagreed on other matters of the merger proceedings. A likely sticking point in the application involved the substantial stake, about 24 percent, that the UP held in IC Industries, which controlled the Illinois Central Railroad. As Jervis put it, "This was kind of a thorn in their case." He went to Barnett and explained the situation. Even though Barnett did not believe that the financial relationship would be much of an obstacle, Jervis thought that they should discuss the matter with Roland Harriman, who chaired the UP board. "I think you fellows, if you're going to take the Rock Island over, you're going to have to get rid of the Illinois Central," he expounded. "I just think that you're not going to be able to get the Rock Island if you continue to hold the Illinois Central. And that's aside from all the opposition that's coming from the North Western and all the other railroads that are opposed." While Barnett and Harriman did not respond immediately, somewhat later Jervis received a telephone call from Harriman. "I'm sorry, I don't think we ought to let the Illinois Central holdings go. That has a lot of family connection and they go way back," a reference to E. H. Harriman's acquisition of IC securities early in the century. Jervis felt that sentimental attachments to anything connected with the senior Harriman made for bad business decisions.

The actions of Roland Harriman bothered Jervis. He also believed that Barnett should have acted more forcefully. "If Barnett had been on the ball, he would have seen what that problem was, and he would have advised Mr. Harriman that, sure, those holdings ought to be disposed of, as they were later on." This response to the IC issue only reaffirmed Jervis's low esteem for Barnett. "He was a tax lawyer and never understood railroading." Moreover, Barnett "had a bad habit with alcohol," a personal trait that irritated Jervis.[87]

Another annoyance, albeit minor yet indicative of the problems that existed between the two merger partners, involved the UP marginalizing the Rock Island. "I never will forget going into the board room of the Union Pacific [in Omaha]," recalled Jervis, "and there upon the wall was a great map of the Overland Route including the Chicago & North Western from Council Bluffs to Chicago, and you could hardly find the Rock Island on that map. It was there, but it wasn't!" Obviously, no one at the UP saw a need for an updated map, even though UP–C&NW Overland Route passenger service had been gone since 1955 and acquisition of the Rock Island now seemed likely.[88]

The red-letter date for the merger process became May 4, 1966, when hearings began on the Rock Island–Union Pacific proposal and the C&NW control application. Scores of lawyers who represented 19 railroads, news media personnel, C&NW, Rock Island, and UP employees, and other interested individuals crowded into a large room at the Conrad Hilton Hotel in downtown Chicago. Likely no one realized that formal hearings would stretch into 1969 and that it would not be until 1974 when the process would ultimately end. Jervis, though, was hardly sanguine about a speedy decision, expecting that the ICC would take at least several years to come to a final resolution.[89]

The hearings did not go well for the UP–Rock Island merger. Jervis and others who attended the first round of testimony were shocked by the performance of UP's Edd Bailey, one of the lead-off witnesses. "He just showed that he didn't know really what it [merger] was all about," remembered Jervis. "He stumbled around, he didn't have his facts straight, he spoke very hesitatingly, and he was just a disaster as a witness." And that performance unfortunately set the tone for the UP.

On the other hand, representatives of the C&NW performed well throughout the hearings. "The North Western was very well represented in the proceedings," reflected Jervis. "Ben Heineman himself was very close to it. . . . He had some very smart lawyers that he hired from Washington, antitrust lawyers, and he did an incredibly fine job in opposing the Union Pacific. He made the Union Pacific look awfully sick."[90]

The merger represented a life-or-death situation for the C&NW. Heineman and his associates and allies knew that this was David fighting Goliath, and they employed the tactics of delay, believing that the UP would become hopelessly mired in the official proceedings. Heineman cleverly brought in the Santa Fe as an ally. Santa Fe tentatively agreed to buy the Rock Island's southern lines and to lease trackage rights to St. Louis, a gateway that it wanted to serve. The C&NW also strengthened its position by launching a hard-sell

The Rock Island and Union Pacific worked hard to convince everyone that UP's acquisition of the faltering Rock Island was in the public interest. *The Merger Messenger,* an occasional newsletter, became such a public relations tool. (Author's collection)

public relations campaign that focused on the theme of "The Great Train Robbery" with the message that the Rock Island–UP merger would have the effect of making the strong stronger and the weak weaker. The UP, on the other hand, had its own advertising blitz that centered on these somewhat innocuous promises: "Improved Rail Service for the Nation; New Capital for Major Improvements in Rock Island Facilities; A Stronger Economy through Healthy Competition." There was virtually nothing said about Heineman's vision of a "strong regional transportation system for the Middle West." By the time that the hearings opened, the C&NW had spent $1 million and the UP three times as much in attempting to enhance their positions. Both sides, too, sought to drum up grassroots support, encouraging chambers of commerce, for example, to pass resolutions that backed their position.[91]

As the ICC hearings dragged on and Jervis gave repeated testimony, strains developed between the Rock Island and UP leadership. Not only did the iron-clad philosophy of the UP about negotiations with opponents irk Jervis, but he did not care for the unhappiness Omaha expressed, usually coming from Edd Bailey, about the improved physical condition and financial performance of the Rock Island. "Bailey called me up again and passed the word that we showed net income, much to everybody's surprise in 1966," reflected Jervis. "It wasn't very sound net income, but nevertheless it was black ink. He said, 'Oh, no. . . . You're not supposed to make any net income down there. We're supposed to come to your rescue, and that's only going to be if you continue to show deficits.'" Admittedly Jervis's successes were at odds with the failing corporation doctrine that was central to UP's legal justification for the merger. Furthermore the UP did not care for the Rock Island president's "passion for straight talk."[92]

Similarly, Jervis did not like how the UP managed a loan to cover acquisition of additional (and much-needed) covered hoppers. "We could have borrowed money elsewhere, but they [UP] wanted to, and they got an awfully good return on it," he related. "They insisted that in the movement of those covered hoppers, even though the title was then with us, be routed to favor the Union Pacific." The UP also refused to join the Rock Island in through rates where Rock Island had the greater mileage (via Denver, for instance), but insisted that the UP always have the long haul (via Council Bluffs, for example).[93]

Although the Rock Island received financing from the UP to expand the covered hopper fleet, the company in 1967 faced a temporary cash-flow tightness. So Jervis and Henry Crown asked the UP for a $2-million bridge loan. The answer was no, a callous act that infuriated them. "They wouldn't have lost any money, and yet they turned us down flat." The two men then walked over to the First National Bank of Chicago and immediately won approval for the loan. "We got it repaid in a couple of years."[94]

The struggle to achieve a Rock Island–UP merger distressed Jervis. "It has created a state of paralysis by this long period of indecision." While he had expected a prolonged battle, Jervis had thought that it was possible for the ICC to decide within a reasonable length of time. But by February 1, 1969, these ongoing hearings had generated a record of 43,201 pages of testimony, exhibits, and related documents. The bulk of the material dealt with threats of traffic diversion for every participating railroad concentrated on that issue.[95]

Jervis became more vocal about the need for railroads to set up a dialogue or machinery for arbitrating their inter-industry disputes. As he had believed earlier on matters of rates, there should be cooperation among carriers and not a nearly total reliance on the ICC. "Only a broad settlement among the warring railroads could have saved [the merger]," Jervis opined later. "But the kind of railroad leadership required to knock heads together was nowhere to be found, and the ICC was not inclined to exert pressure." Maybe the newly created Department of Transportation might "pound some sense regarding mergers into the chief executives of the nation's Western railroads," thoughts he shared with members of the National Transportation Institute. Jervis suggested that at the least the heads of the sparring roads should be invited to a meeting—"an informal dinner, if you please"—and be told to devise a concrete, feasible merger proposal. It would, in effect, be an ultimatum. "You could give them 30 days, have another dinner, and see if they can come up with a plan." He thought that these railroad executives, through the inspiration of governmental prodding, might learn that there had to be some "give" as well as "take" in merger talks.[96]

Then on March 5, 1968, a prehearing phase was held in the next stage of the merger proceedings. Attention turned to the C&NW application for control of the Rock Island with the expectation that the C&NW would also unite with the CGW and Milwaukee Road, creating a more unified midwestern transportation network. Four months later, testimony began regarding what impact a C&NW–CGW–Milwaukee Road system would have on a takeover of the Rock Island, and in August the process concluded. By now the merger proceedings had generated nearly 48,000 pages. (Ultimately, the total volume reached a staggering 150,000 pages of testimony, exhibits, briefs, petitions, and replies.) Subsequently, though, the C&NW–Milwaukee Road merger bid was abandoned, although the C&NW won regulatory permission to purchase the declining 1,500-mile CGW. The effect was that most of the testimony taken in the second phase was rendered superfluous.

More action (or arguably inaction) occurred on January 6, 1969, when all parties filed extensive briefs on the merits of the Rock Island–Union Pacific merger, the competing application of the C&NW for control, and the relief requested by various intervening railroads, ranging from the Missouri Pacific to the Western Pacific. All of this meant a decision delay and seemingly the only gainers were the lawyers, totaling 112 for the quarreling carriers and 57 who represented other parties. These actions reminded some observers of *Jarndyce v. Jarndyce,* a case described in the Charles Dickens novel *Bleakhouse* that went on forever.

Jervis came to believe that merger between the Rock Island and UP should not be the sole course of action. Perhaps the formal request for control that the C&NW had made should be seriously considered. It might be better, he thought, to fuse together several granger roads, namely, the C&NW, Milwaukee Road, Rock Island, and Soo Line, and after that restructuring with the accompanying consolidation of facilities and "line rationalization," the new and profitable company could seek out a transcontinental partner, probably either the SP or UP. Heineman himself had privately suggested a C&NW–CGW–Milwaukee Road–Rock Island combination that the UP should acquire at some future point. For some industry leaders, except those at UP, the building-block concept of merger seemed to be a practical alternative to UP and SP division of the Rock Island.[97]

If that scenario failed, perhaps the ICC, even though a "political creature," could at last demonstrate some much-needed leadership. Jervis thought that it would be appropriate for the ICC to demand that the strong western transcontinentals come forward with a mutually acceptable plan for dealing with the weaker roads, including the C&NW, Milwaukee Road, and Rock Island. Some scheme of absorbing such lines or other reconfigurations, he believed, would end the merger litigation before the troubled carriers slipped into bankruptcy and perhaps forced nationalization.[98]

By the late 1960s Jervis became increasingly convinced that the solution to the merger mess (not just between the Rock Island, UP, and C&NW) involved creation of two or possibly three mega-railroads or one privately owned railroad for the nation. As for the latter, Jervis, the realist, admitted that "one railroad for the entire United States is too much to expect." The former, though, was the better, more practical solution; after all, he saw value in the performance of Canadian railroads where two large, competing carriers, Canadian National and Canadian Pacific, dominated rail transport. Jervis liked the fact that single-line hauls would increase in length, for he had long contended that "a railroad's average haul is a key to profitability."[99]

Speaking in March 1968 at the Tenth Annual Transportation Conference, sponsored by the Texas Transportation Institute at College Station, Texas, Jervis publicly embraced the concept of fewer railroads, reiterating senti-ments expressed by John W. Barriger in his 1956 book *Super Railroads for a Dynamic American Economy,* and also soon after by Robert S. Macfarlane, president of the NP. He told an audience of transportation officials, policy makers, and academics that a major rethinking of railroads was essential for protecting the public interest. Jervis offered numerous reasons why this was true. He contended that interline service, for example, is costlier and slower than single-line service. "At an interchange point served by my railroad, I have personally discovered delays of 24 hours or more in receiving from a con-necting line carload traffic for which we already had the waybills and have been told that such service was standard." There was more. "At one of our principal gateways, the terminal company which Rock Island must use takes 20 to 30 hours to move business between railroads on different sides of the river. . . . In fact, for many carriers, through service at the gateways is so bad that on piggyback traffic, in order to save time, it is routine to move trailers over the highway between the terminals of 'connecting' railroads."

Other thorny problems plagued carriers. The 80 or so major railroads could never easily agree on car supply, per diem payments, and rate divisions, but substantially fewer railroads or just a single carrier would mitigate or solve these long-standing issues. Jervis recalled a disagreement between rail-roads in the South and East over how to split rates on citrus traffic originat-ing in Florida, which began in 1930 and still raged 38 years later! And with ICC decisions, disputes were often not really resolved. "No sooner does the ICC render one decision then the 'losing' railroads file a counter complaint to get even." The unresolved Rock Island–UP merger revealed once more that individual railroads were incapable of harmoniously working together, further hindering a functioning national transportation system.[100]

Exiting the Rock

Jervis still had to confront the realities of the day. By 1969 he reached the con-clusion that the "Rock Island isn't going to last much longer," even though from an operational standpoint, performance had improved. "Our share of the traffic, ton-miles in the West, was going up; our schedule performance was improving; our interchange with the Southern Pacific at Tucumcari was 100 percent better than it had been prior to the merger agreement." Jervis appreciated that the Heineman strategy of delay had worked well for the C&NW and understood why Heineman had made the plight of the granger roads a primary issue. In fact, Jervis held no animosity toward the C&NW. Yet the Rock Island needed a corporate partner, and the sooner the better.[101]

By 1970, the merger picture had changed noticeably. A Heineman C&NW was no longer a roadblock for the Rock Island. The C&NW faced increasing financial troubles and therefore terminated its bid for the Milwaukee Road and even offered its own assets for sale. The clever Heineman concluded that a better way to increase shareholder value would come not from unification but from investments *outside* the transportation sector. "To put it simply," he told the business press, "I've been discontented with the railroad industry and its long-range outlook under present circumstances, because its rate of returns is disgustingly inadequate." As the 1960s ended, Heineman oversaw a growing conglomerate, Northwest Industries, reflecting a strategy that several other carriers embraced. And in 1970, he endorsed the imaginative proposal submitted by his able protégé Larry Provo, who since 1967 had been C&NW president, that employees take over the railroad through a leveraged buyout. On October 5, 1970, the North Western Employees Transportation Company entered into an agreement with Northwest Industries to buy the Chicago & North Western Railway Company. However, the new Provo-led enterprise would seek to protect itself from the loss of interchange traffic with the UP.[102]

The departure of Heineman was considered to be a positive for the Rock Island–UP merger application. "Whatever reasons there may have been for prolonged litigation over the competing offers of Union Pacific and North Western have now disappeared," Jervis told company shareholders in early 1970, "and as a result, the ICC is free to move faster." He added, "Only massive infusions of cash which the Union Pacific stands committed to advance—once the merger is approved—will save the Rock Island and enable it to become a viable unit in a strong transportation system. Let us hope that the ICC, realizing the situation, will move and move fast."[103]

The ICC failed to provide a speedy, definitive response. The process would end anticlimactically in 1974, but on July 8, 1970, the initial decisional procedure by the hearing examiner Nathan Klitenic (his title later became administrative law judge) began to unfold. In a "syllabus," or digest, Klitenic approved the Rock Island–UP merger, but unification was subject to certain *undisclosed* conditions. Jervis was encouraged and told *Railway Age*, "Hopefully, the railroads involved in this litigation can now compose their differences and, before the case is submitted to the ICC for a final decision, reach a general agreement, using the examiner's recommendations as a base."[104]

But there was no immediate positive outcome for the backers of the Rock Island–UP merger. Complications followed. Klitenic became ill, and the ICC assigned the matter to another division, much to the unhappiness of numerous parties, including the Rock Island and UP. Then in April 1971, Klitenic, who had recovered his health, returned to the case. Five months later, the first volume of his report appeared. Again, Klitenic endorsed merger, but the vital subject of protective conditions and various applications of other railroads remained for development in subsequent volumes. Finally, on March 21, 1972, Klitenic issued volume 2. This report offered some detail as to what specific merger conditions would be imposed, but he deferred the rationale to a forthcoming volume 3. This final document, which was released on February 15, 1973, contained a "grand design" for restructuring the entire western railroad system. "The merger of the Rock Island into the Union Pacific, while approved," reflected Ted Desch, "was subjected to a host of sweeping conditions, most of which required unconditional acquiescence to the conditions as a prerequisite to consummation of the merger and subsequent sale of the southern half of the Rock Island to the Southern Pacific Railroad." He added, "Many were radically different from anything considered by the parties during the course of the lengthy proceedings." For example, the inclusion of the C&NW into the UP was made a condition for approval of the Rock Island merger into the UP, and the MOP was directed to merge with the Santa Fe.[105]

The industry response to Klitenic's volume 3 was overwhelmingly negative, and practically all of the affected railroads filed a petition for dismissal of the entire proceedings. The ICC refused, and additional hearings followed. When the UP refused to accept the onerous conditions that were part of what was a technically favorable decision, the process came to an ignominious end. In a 1990 letter to Frank Richter, editor of *Progressive Railroading*, Jervis summed up the merger mess succinctly: "It was a brawl from start to finish. . . . Here was a golden opportunity for the western lines with the informal concurrence of the ICC and the Department of Justice to work out (or at least try to work out) an overall merger pattern which could have avoided years of strife, saved millions of dollars, and provided a solid platform for 'seamless railroading.' "[106]

By December 3, 1974, when the ICC finally approved the merger, the Rock Island had declined. Derailments and slow orders plagued the road, and the company was a year away from its third corporate bankruptcy and seven years away from liquidation. The SP had become alarmed by the physical condition of the Rock Island, reducing its original $120-million offer to $40 million, an unacceptable price to the principal Rock Island investors. The UP was not interested at any price. "When the Union Pacific finally 'won' the war," observed historian Maury Klein, "there was nothing left to win."[107]

Jervis, though, was not part of the final merger happenings. In 1970, this "doctor of sick railroads" had reached that bewitching age of 65 and concluded that his tenure with the Rock Island should end. His decision to leave involved more than this milestone birthday on January 28, 1970. Jervis had become disgusted with the unwillingness of the UP to negotiate, especially with the C&NW. As he told Henry Crown shortly before he departed, "You've got to persuade the Union Pacific to sit down and talk about a compromise here, because otherwise I am sure that the conditions the commissioners are going to impose in their decision, even if they vote in favor of the merger, will be so onerous on the Union Pacific that they're going to reject it." Jervis, Crown, and a UP director did chat about the situation with Jervis urging the UP to buy the C&NW. The response by the UP was negative. "We [UP] couldn't do that. Don't have enough money and so forth and so on and all kinds of phony excuses." The UP was not about to change course. Much later in his life Jervis told a correspondent that "so far as I know, to the bitter end of the proceeding, no effort was ever made to reach an understanding with *any* of the opposing railroads."[108]

Soon thereafter Jervis informed Crown that he would leave. Earlier, Judge John P. Fullam Jr., the Philadelphia federal district court judge who had taken charge of the reorganization of the bankrupt Penn Central Transportation Company, contacted Jervis about becoming the lead full-time trustee. Jervis was not sure, thinking that if he were to join Penn Central, he would rather be president. Still, he wanted to remain an active railroader. Although Jervis loved Quarry Farm, he did not see himself becoming a gentleman farmer, and he was not about to stay at home twiddling his thumbs. So, in July 1970, a new phase of Jervis's career would commence.[109]

Just as most employees enthusiastically applauded the Langdon appointment, there was nearly universal sadness about his announced departure. "Langdon was thought of as a savior up to the last day," recalled a white-collar employee. "He was the last person to breathe fresh air into the Rock Island." Although Jervis's protégés Bill Dixon and Ted Desch took charge, they generally lacked the skills that their former boss possessed, and they confronted a worsening financial situation. Then, in late 1974, a coup of sorts took place when 45-year-old John Ingram, former head of the Federal Railroad Administration, assumed control. Quickly the common consensus among Rock Island employees was that "Ingram had the opposite impact of Langdon on the Rock Island. He was a real beast." Henry Crown soon realized that Ingram was "inept and inexperienced." The designing Ingram did much to wreck the Rock; the many accomplishments achieved under Jervis's imaginative and statesmanlike leadership turned to dross. Still, a successful financial liquidation would ultimately occur, and most shippers retained access to rail service.[110]

5 Rerailing Penn Central

Merger Disaster

In the weeks and months that followed the bankruptcy of the Penn Central Transportation Company (Penn Central) on June 22, 1970, the news media bombarded the public with startling revelations of the largest corporate debacle in American history. Initial shock rapidly turned into grave concern about the fate of Penn Central service and serious reflection on the future of the railroad enterprise. "We're an interchange industry, and everything that happens in our industry ripples right on through," observed Gregory DeVine, president of the C&O/B&O. "For days after the recent Penn Central difficulty, investors and the financial community were scared of all railroads regardless of the state of their finances. They just wouldn't talk to you." Some observers worried that the collapse might trigger a national recession. While an economic disaster did not follow, there was a lengthy struggle to untangle the corporate mess. Ultimately, failure of Penn Central led to landmark federal legislation, including a statute that on April 1, 1976, created the quasi-public Consolidated Railroad Corporation (Conrail).[1]

The unfolding of the stunning failure came only 871 days after the much-ballyhooed birth of Penn Central (briefly known officially—and appropriately—as the Pennsylvania New York Central Transportation Company). At 12:01 AM on Thursday, February 1, 1968, "Merger Day," two historic and giant rivals, New York Central (NYC) and Pennsylvania (PRR), joined to form the world's largest privately owned railroad, a company whose approximately 19,000 miles of lines stretched between New England and the Midwest and served the heart of industrial America and 12 of the country's 20 biggest metropolitan centers. Technically, Penn Central owned or controlled 186 rail and nonrail companies, including such semi-independent railroads as the Detroit, Toledo & Ironton (DT&I) and the Pittsburgh & Lake Erie (P&LE). At the end of 1968, based on a condition of the merger agreement, Penn Central became saddled with the bankrupt New York, New Haven and Hartford Railroad (New Haven). This 1,700-mile carrier dominated rail service in southern New England, but was in poor physical condition and in 1968 had lost more than $22 million. "The New Haven was ready for liquidation" was how Jervis described the property. The consolidated company, which after the New Haven takeover operated in 16 states, the District of Columbia, and two Canadian provinces, owned a staggering amount of rolling stock, including more than 4,200 locomotives (diesel and electric), 3,800 passenger cars, and nearly 175,000 freight cars. The roster even counted several hundred pieces of "floating equipment," including 21 tugboats that powered scores of carfloats.[2]

The process of corporate unification had been painfully slow and had come at a price, but there were great expectations. The Interstate Commerce Commission (ICC) had conducted 128 hearings and had dithered for a half-dozen years before approving the NYC–PRR merger proposal and in the process forced the PRR to dispose of its profitable stock holdings in the Norfolk & Western (N&W) and Wabash. Still, most commentators felt that the decision to permit formation of Penn Central was in the public interest. They expected this rail colossus to benefit customers, employees, and investors. The ICC emphasized the service advantages. "There will be single-line service between more points, with less route-circuity, less handling of freight, less switching of cars, and consequently less likelihood of damage, less time in transit and terminal, and easier tracing of equipment." Investors and management eagerly anticipated an estimated annual savings of more than $80 million, money to be derived from eliminating duplicate jobs, offices, shops, terminals, and trackage. The assumption existed, too, that Penn Central stock would be a good investment. Soon stock prices shot up to $86.50 a share, and the public regarded Penn Central as a blue-chip investment.[3]

For the first few months of Penn Central's existence, optimism prevailed, at least publicly. A company-inspired phrase called the carrier the "newest symbol for progressive railroading." President and chief operating officer Alfred E. Perlman echoed this sentiment, telling an industry trade journal in spring 1968, "Uncommitted to traditional approaches, the new company is gaining new strength and efficiency by adopting the best practices and procedures of each of the former companies and is dedicated to the improvement of service." And he further opined, "As savings from the merger are realized, Penn Central is prepared to make greater commitments to the modernization of the entire system." Even privately Perlman expressed optimism. On May 6, 1969, he wrote Perry Shoemaker, a retired railroad executive and industry consultant, "We have things turned around now, and we look for continued improvement." Initially the most repeated negative comment about the merger came from wags who thought that the distinctive Penn Central corporate logo suggested "two worms making love."[4]

What the able Al Perlman and other enthusiasts said publicly sounded good, indeed. But it did not take long before the upbeat rhetoric turned hollow. A plethora of problems erupted that could not be concealed, causing Penn Central to hemorrhage enormous amounts of money and in the process demoralizing everyone associated with the company.[5]

If backers of the coupling of the NYC with PRR believed that "all of the i's and t's had been dotted and crossed before Merger Day," observed an industry consultant, "they were either in denial or just too hopeful about the future success of Penn Central." For nearly 10 years, the NYC and PRR had a planning committee analyzing what needed to be done to unify, but this work was largely worthless. "While a great deal of effort was expended," noted a U.S. Senate Commerce Committee report in December 1972, "premerger planning turned out to be largely a paper effort." Moreover, during these discussions, major—even insurmountable—differences occurred. A protracted dispute erupted over what type of computer system would serve the combined companies. "The two roads had different computers that wouldn't mesh, and neither line's computer people would yield." Adding to the planning woes was an agreement that PRR president Stuart T. Saunders had arranged in 1964 with the 24 operating and shop-craft brotherhoods. In his desire to win critical union backing for the merger, he foolishly ignored his labor relations staff and other experts. In what became known as the [Charles] Luna-Saunders agreement, Saunders promised employees that once the NYC–PRR merger was consummated, Penn Central would rehire every worker with five years' seniority who had been furloughed between the time of the agreement and Merger Day. The new company also agreed to pay one year's severance for each five years of seniority to any employee laid off after the merger.[6]

When Penn Central began operations, two philosophies reigned about how best to consummate the union. NYC elements, the "green team" or "green hats" led by Perlman, wished to consolidate as quickly as possible, largely because of Saunders's expensive labor agreements and the pressing need to generate income. Earlier Perlman had told the *Wall Street Journal* that the gradual merger approach was "foolish." He explained, "It leaves you wide open to nuisance court suits by minority shareholders on some piddling saving or sell-off." PRR forces, the "red team" or "red hats" captained by Saunders, PC's chairman and chief executive officer, recognized the desire for cash, but they thought that unification should be more gradual, "bits and pieces." Both concepts had merit, although the latter would likely have been more successful; after all, the relatively slow process of the Baltimore & Ohio consolidation with the Chesapeake & Ohio generally had worked well.[7]

The actual merging process of NYC and PRR went badly. "It was just a goddamned operating mess," recalled an employee. There were tales of woe galore. Classification clerks did not know how best to route cars, and congestion in yards and sidings resulted. Connecting roads were unsure about where to deliver cars for interchange. Because of incompatible computers, waybills were prepared incorrectly or did not exist at all. At times, yard superintendents, overwhelmed when their facilities became jammed with cars, dispatched entire trains without vital paperwork. That rendered these cars without waybills effectively missing, the legendary "lost trains" of Penn Central. "Penn Central's illness has been diagnosed to me as a massive case of constipation," commented the president of a major carrier. "You can feed a lot of cars into their system, but nothing ever seems to come out." Further contributing to the chaos was that track connections between the former NYC and PRR lines and yards were often incomplete or entirely lacking. This meant that lengthy and costly delays occurred, often forcing crews to "die in service," since federal law prevented them from working more than 12 continuous hours. Moreover, track conditions deteriorated, resulting in frequent derailments and numerous "slow orders," even on principal arteries. The company also faced chronic car shortages and inadequately maintained equipment, especially motive power. Employee morale sagged, and shippers screamed. Soon some customers decided that they must find other ways to handle their freight needs, and scores of these good patrons constructed new plants or facilities on other railroads or turned to trucks. Their actions meant a permanent diversion of traffic. Almost immediately, operating costs skyrocketed and income plummeted.[8]

Further exacerbating this disappointing merger was the fact that former NYC and PRR personnel really did not care for one another. "They hated each other's guts" was probably a more accurate statement. NYC people thought that PRR employees showed arrogance and rigidity. Those who came from the PRR believed that their NYC counterparts lacked discipline and shared the wrong priorities. The PRR had long been a transporter of coal, ore, steel, and other heavy commodities while the NYC had concentrated on merchandise traffic. The PRR thus stressed volume, and the NYC embraced speed and service. NYC and PRR officials even bickered over trivial matters, including what to name the last car on a freight train. Should it be called a "caboose," which was the term used on the NYC, or a "cabin car," the nomenclature employed by the PRR? "They were opposites, and this proved fatal when their differing operating styles were brought together," concluded business writer Rush Loving Jr.[9]

The NYC and PRR were an odd couple in other ways. For more than a century, they had embraced dissimilar forms of governance. The former used a "departmental" structure, where managers reported directly to superiors in the central office; the latter practiced a "decentralized divisional" structure where the various regions operated almost as separate companies and divisional officers functioned largely independent of one another. On Merger Day, these diverse institutional administrative forms remained virtually intact.[10]

Differing worldviews and operating practices, however, could be altered and for the better. When the Erie and the Delaware, Lackawanna & Western (DL&W) joined to create Erie–Lackawanna in October 1960, the less progressive Erie corporate culture dominated, but within several years, due to mounting financial problems, the superior ways of the DL&W became commonplace under the leadership of William White. "Lackawannazation," observed an EL officer, "finally saved the company or at least until outside forces forced it into bankruptcy and then into Conrail."[11]

Unfortunately for the Penn Central, leaders from the old PRR team largely assumed control. "The man from the Pennsy always was above the New York Central man," wrote Charles Luna, president of the United Transportation Union (UTU). "The Pennsy management seemingly felt that their railroad had effectively 'acquired' the New York Central instead of merging with it as a coequal." This turn of events caused Perlman and former NYC associates to lose power, leave, or retire. The company lost key members of the former NYC marketing department, considered by many to have been one of the best in the industry. In August 1969, the Saunders group forced Perlman out. "Kicked upstairs" as vice chairman, he subsequently took the throttle of the Western Pacific Railroad, the "Wobbly Pacific," where he rehabilitated what had been a marginal carrier. Saunders and PRR associate David Bevan, chairman of the Penn Central finance committee, and their closest allies made other disastrous mistakes, including some that were highly questionable, perhaps even illegal. The objective was to have earnings statements as large as possible. "Saunders and Bevan knew how to use blue smoke and mirrors, and that seemed to be their business strategy with their Penn Central holding company that controlled the railroad," observed a bankruptcy attorney. "They thought that they could hide those astronomical operating losses at the railroad through some very creative accounting tricks and tactics." There would be real estate swaps, buy-ups of old bonds, equipment leases, and nonrailroad ventures, and these transactions created paper profits that masked monster railroad operating losses. Although the holding company reported a profit of $4 million for 1969 and the railroad revealed a deficit of $56 million, the actual numbers were much worse than the "happy figures," a real loss that exceeded $70 million for the former and more than $200 million for the latter. Even reports by the old-line auditing firm of Peat, Marwick and Mitchell failed to reveal the depths of Penn Central's money woes. Finally, on the eve of bankruptcy, the board, sensing the coming downfall and feeling pressure from bankers and the Richard Nixon administration, dumped both Saunders and Bevan.[12]

A personnel shake-up at the highest levels could not prevent calamity. Soon the federal government became the last best hope for economic survival. But these desperate efforts to secure loan guarantees failed, and this crushing setback at the hands of politicians understandably angered Penn Central officials. "They just don't seem to understand what's at stake," noted one source. "That $200 million may sound expensive, but it's going to wind up costing everybody a lot more if Penn Central doesn't get some help soon." Already Penn Central stock had plummeted, dropping from $35 per share in January to $6.50 in June. The inability to secure additional financing and to meet an impending loan maturity threw the company into the hands of the federal court. "The New York Central–Pennsylvania merger should never have happened," argued industry specialist Jim McClellan. "But once consummated, it was too large for private markets to deal with."[13]

Trustee

Once lawyers filed the legal papers in the U.S. District Court of the Eastern District of Pennsylvania in Philadelphia for reorganization of the Penn Central Transportation Company (since October 1, 1969, the wholly owned subsidiary of the Penn Central Company), a judge was needed to oversee the case. Fortunately, John P. Fullam Jr., a smart, conscientious, and honest jurist, took charge of the bankruptcy. This 49-year-old graduate of the Harvard Law School and onetime Democratic candidate for Congress quickly inquired about possible candidates for both the full-time position of lead or chief trustee and individuals who could assist on a part-time basis. Unlike some bankruptcy judges, Fullam was not about to appoint cronies or unqualified people. Soon the judge compiled a list of more than 50 nominees. Several industry leaders had recommended Jervis for principal trustee, and so Judge Fullam decided to contact him about such an appointment. Within a day, Jervis met with Fullam in his chambers and agreed to serve, although Jervis admitted privately that he preferred to be president. He would be joined by three prominent individuals, albeit part-time trustees: George P. Baker, former dean of the Graduate Business School of Business Administration at Harvard University who had served as vice chairman of the Civil Aeronautics Board during World War II; Richard C. Bond, retired president of the Philadelphia-based Wanamaker department store chain; and W. Willard Wirtz, secretary of labor in the John F. Kennedy and Lyndon B. Johnson administrations and a former law professor. Collectively, this quartet became the equivalent of a board of directors.[14]

Appointment as lead trustee in a bankruptcy case of the magnitude of Penn Central was universally considered a daunting task. "It was an absolutely terrible job," recalled James Hagen, a future Conrail president. Still, to some individuals the post was considered an administrative plum. John W. Barriger III, who had served with distinction with the Reconstruction Finance Corporation and later as president of the Chicago, Indianapolis & Louisville (Monon), P&LE, and Missouri-Kansas-Texas (Katy) railroads, desperately wanted the job. In fact, Barriger retired from the Katy to spend time in Washington, D.C., and elsewhere to lobby for the post. He was bitterly disappointed when Jervis won the appointment, causing tensions in their longtime acquaintanceship. But Judge Fullam was wise in not selecting Barriger. "Dad was becoming frail," noted a son, "and would fall asleep in meetings." Although Barriger on January 1, 1971, began a two-year stint as president of the bankrupt Boston & Maine Railroad, his health failed, and he died in 1975.[15]

With the new job assignment official, Jervis relocated his family to the Philadelphia area. In some ways this was a bittersweet move. Irene and the boys had enjoyed the Geneva, Illinois, community and Halsey and Charlie had thrived in the local schools. The new home for the family would be Solebury, Pennsylvania, in the heart of historic and bucolic Bucks County and within convenient driving distance to center-city Philadelphia. Unfortunately, the change in schools proved to be difficult for the 12-year-old Charlie, and his parents worried about a pervasive youth drug culture in their neighborhood. So within a year the Langdons returned to the Baltimore area, buying a home in a gated community on Gibson Island south of the city, a place where they had earlier vacationed. The boys attended private schools, and Irene threw herself into a variety of civic projects. Baltimore made sense for Jervis's work responsibilities. Since he spent an increasing amount of time in Washington, he faced an easier commute. He made frequent trips to Philadelphia, either taking the train or flying his plane.[16]

The Langdons could afford any location, yet they lived modestly. Jervis continued to be generous to deserving individuals, organizations, and causes. "His checkbook was always open," recalled Irene. When Jervis joined Penn Central, he did not take much of a pay cut. During his last year at the Rock Island he had earned $98,333 ($522,306 in 2006 funds), and the full-time trusteeship paid $95,000 annually. He expected to earn every penny. Noted the *New York Times*, "He anticipates that he will spend all of his time in the discharge of his duties as trustee." The salary for the lead trustee was considerably more than what the three part-time trustees received: Wirtz got $70,000, and Baker and Bond took $40,000 annually. The rationale was that Wirtz would devote up to 75 percent of his time on the railroad's business, and Baker and Bond would commit 40 percent of their efforts.[17]

When Jervis assumed his role as PC trustee in his posh office atop 6 Penn Central Plaza in downtown Philadelphia, he was no babe in the woods. He had closely followed the NYC–PRR merger case and had been deeply concerned about the fate of the new company. "Jerv anticipated the financial collapse of the Penn Central," recalled Irene. "He saw a lot of funny business going on there." He did not see unification as the sole cause of the trouble. "The merger may have hastened the bankruptcy by a few months or perhaps even a couple of years, but in no way was it responsible for Penn Central's collapse," he informed *Trains* editor David P. Morgan. "The causes were much more basic. For one thing, Penn Central's revenue level in relation to the size and scope of its plant, much of which had been built to handle an extensive passenger service, was far too large. For another, the escalation in costs had been disproportionate because of declining volume and heavy terminal operations." There were other reasons, including "divisions of rates on interterritorial traffic that were way out of line under the standards of the Interstate Commerce Act." Jervis knew that tensions existed between former NYC and PRR personnel and that the general physical condition of Penn Central was poor. He told *New York Times* reporter Robert Bedingfield that equipment needs were "almost desperate," and that meant inoperable motive power and excessively high per diem freight car costs. Commented an industry expert: "Langdon fully understood that he was about to run a company that was absolutely shot." Most of all, Jervis realized that the Penn Central bankruptcy was without precedent. The company's problems went far beyond those in the ordinary case of a railroad that was unable to meet its financial obligations. The real question involved viability. Could the PC produce enough revenues to cover operating expenses?[18]

Jervis offered much to the court and the railroad. He had respect both within and outside the railroad industry. "Judge Fullam was most astute in selecting Jervis, someone who had been active in railroading all of his life and who knew the problems, challenges, and opportunities of railroading in the East," observed Hays Watkins of the C&O/B&O. "He was an excellent choice, a real gem." John Clancy, a reporter for the *Philadelphia Inquirer,* wrote that "Langdon is described by fellow railroaders as a 'no-nonsense' executive. But his forthright manner and likeable personality have brought him few enemies." Jervis, of course, possessed a wide range of business skills. "He knew how to scrutinize operations, and he understood the art of diplomacy and compromise," remarked journalist Rush Loving. Jervis's family heritage, Ivy League education, previous accomplishments, especially on the Baltimore & Ohio (B&O), and commanding presence allowed him to be treated as an "equal" or at least listened to by powerful bankers and influential businessmen, railroaders, and politicians. Of great importance at Penn Central, according to James Hagen, was that "Langdon was above the fray, and that helped to make him extremely effective as the lead trustee and later as president." Not to be overlooked was his determination to succeed. "There's nothing more important to the future of the railroad industry than making Penn Central work." If a successful reorganization could not be achieved, the alternative, he believed, would be some form of nationalization, and that turn of events could have disastrous results for the American public. Jervis Langdon would be a committed trustee.[19]

There were, however, a few criticisms levied against Jervis's selection as lead or senior trustee. The recent celebration of his sixty-fifth birthday became a concern. "Some feel that his age is against him in what likely will be prolonged proceedings," noted the *Wall Street Journal.* "Langdon's no spring chicken." And was he too nice? After all, railroads typically embraced a militaristic style with stern leaders. Jervis's manner was different. "One of his basic objectives," a Rock Island executive told the press at the time of his Penn Central appointment, "is to make everyone right down the line feel like he's a part of the decision-making process." Critics thought that Jervis would not be the tough manager that the company required. "It's going to take some really drastic steps to save that line," remarked a railroad official. "We all like Jervis very much, and he'll have good industry support, but I'm afraid he's too much of a compromiser to effect the abrupt changes that are necessary."[20]

As with the B&O and Rock Island, Jervis, compromiser or not, wasted no time in assuming his role as lead trustee. He met with fellow trustees and sensed that they possessed varying degrees of talent. Jervis had had a long-time friendship with George Baker. In the 1950s both men had been active in the Transportation Association of America, a national organization that represented commercial transport, and later Baker had seen that his friend served as a member of the Visitor Committee at the Harvard Business School. Jervis soon found Baker to be a valuable colleague who was eager to share his considerable wisdom. Richard Bond was much less useful. "He was a nice fellow," remembered Jervis. "If you had any problems in Philadelphia, local problems, he was helpful to have there, but he didn't have any idea what the railroad business was all about. He never contributed anything." A Philadelphia newspaper in essence agreed with Jervis's assessment: Bond "should make an especially valuable contribution to the trusteeship by virtue of his intimate knowledge of the business climate in the city where Penn Central is headquartered." Willard Wirtz was a dud. "Wirtz wasn't a happy choice by any means." Jervis said, "He was brought on because of all the labor problems. Well, the labor people didn't want any part of him. In fact, he antagonized them. I thought he was more interested in promoting his own image than he was in trying to solve the problem of the bankruptcy." Moreover, Wirtz, a publicity hound, always wanted to speak for the trustees and the railroad.[21]

Another member of the team would be Robert W. Blanchette, who assumed the duties as counsel to the trustees at an annual salary of $60,000. And he was eminently qualified. Earlier Blanchette had been counsel to the trustees for the New Haven, and he also had some familiarity with Penn Central, having served briefly in 1969 as regional counsel in New England. "He was so outstanding in his qualifications all the way around, there wasn't ever a moment of question [about his appointment]," commented Jervis. Although Penn Central officials found Blanchette to be vain and at times a schemer, Blanchette respected Jervis, and the two men worked well together.[22]

A pressing priority for Jervis and the judge was to find someone to run the railroad. At the time of the bankruptcy Paul A. Gorman, retired chairman of Western Electric, manufacturing arm of American Telephone & Telegraph Company, who earlier had replaced Perlman and later the ousted Saunders, had stepped down. But what followed would not be good for Penn Central. William H. Moore ("Wild Bill" to some), the chief operating officer at the Southern Railway (SR) who had started at the bottom in 1941 as a pick-and-shovel track worker, became the new president. Although Moore "knew the Southern like the back of his hand," said Hagen, "he was a fish out of water on the Penn Central." Graham Claytor, president and chief executive officer of the SR, realized that Moore was not suited to lead the company forward because he was arrogant, authoritarian, and stubborn. The politically astute Claytor, who wanted Moore off the property so that the exceptionally able L. Stanley Crane could take charge of operations, persuaded Judge Fullam to pick Moore for the Penn Central job. Fullam agreed, in part because other men of talent had shown no interest, including Louis W. Menk of the Northern Pacific and soon-to-be Burlington Northern.[23]

The decision to hire Moore, this 55-year-old tough "old line" railroader, troubled Jervis. As he later told a reporter, "I could tell the day he arrived he wasn't going to suit us." Jervis also was not pleased with the $165,000 annual salary ($876,416 in 2006 funds) that was guaranteed to Moore for five years, although it was far less than the $279,000 a year paid to Saunders and the $250,000 given to Gorman.[24]

On July 22, 1970, the trustees began their labors. As part of their general work schedule, they met on Mondays with Judge Fullam to discuss the bankruptcy. Their first major activity, though, involved preparation of a "Preliminary Report Concerning Premises for a Reorganization," which the judge received on February 10, 1971. Another document, "Report of Trustees on Status of Reorganization Planning," followed on March 22, 1971.[25]

If reorganization were to take place on a traditional basis, Jervis and his co-trustees told Judge Fullam, four "tough conditions" had to be met in order to "lay a sound foundation." The company's monumental passenger losses had to be drastically reduced. The railroad had scores of money-draining long-distance trains, and commuter operations in the greater

New York City region were excessively expensive. Penn Central was also losing heavily on similar service in the Baltimore-Washington, Boston, Chicago, and Philadelphia commuter zones. Next, the railroad operated far too much trackage, especially a maze of twigs and branches. The company needed to rationalize its plant from approximately 20,000 to 15,000 or fewer miles, leaving a core of potentially profitable lines. The traffic density per route mile was low when compared with other regional carriers; in 1970 the N&W was 169 percent of Penn Central, and the C&O percentage stood at 177 percent. Another pressing need involved reversing the downward trend in business. Although erosion of heavy manufacturing in what was becoming the "rust belt" could not be altered, the trustees endorsed a modernization of pricing practices, including the right to make contract rates. And they did not overlook the need to modify labor work rules that "required the employment of 10,000 more people than necessary in an efficient operation."

The trustees informed the judge that they would fashion a workable solution. Jervis and his colleagues believed they were in "the best position to determine whether a plan can be submitted, and, if so, to prescribe its terms." It could be traditional restructuring or something quite different. What the judge learned was that Penn Central might be kept operating through a broad program of government subsidies; the railroad could be broken up for sale to connecting roads and new start-up shortlines, either privately or publicly owned; government could purchase the physical plant with a lease-back arrangement to Penn Central as the operator; or the road could be nationalized.[26]

These early reports revealed Jervis's handiwork. He expected that solving the problems of Penn Central would take creativity. After all, neither the NYC nor PRR, as individual properties, had had any real earning power after World War II. When compared with railroads in the South and West, they were marginal concerns, as were most other carriers in the East. Only those few eastern roads that hauled vast quantities of coal, much for export and under the most favorable operating conditions, produced decent earnings. The creation of a viable Penn Central was going to be a colossal challenge and far more than casual observers believed. Gross mismanagement alone had not caused the wreck of the Penn Central; the first trustees' report systematically outlined the range of long-standing problems that confronted the company.[27]

During the formative period as trustee, Jervis became particularly concerned about the size of Penn Central. The system map in several states resembled a plate of wet spaghetti, indicating that the company owned scores of branches and secondary lines that should shut down. With approval of his compatriots Jervis worked with Michigan congressman John Dingell to prepare legislation that would make it easier for railroads in reorganization to rid themselves of unwanted trackage. The proposal, although not enacted because politicians desired to maintain freight activities at current levels, was thoughtful and wholly practical.[28]

The trustees continued working in earnest. In September 1971, they told the judge that the next six months would be critical in reaching conclusions about the viability of Penn Central. Jervis insisted that the trustees needed additional data to determine the correct course of the reorganization. As in the past, he wanted facts before he endorsed a particular course of action. Specifically, he sought more information about anticipated levels of freight traffic and the railroad's ability to compete in the marketplace. Another question that required an answer, or at least a reasonably good estimation, was whether a rational labor pattern could be forged. Would creation of the federally supported National Railroad Passenger Corporation, better known as Amtrak, which had made its debut on May 1, 1971, have a pronounced positive impact on historic passenger train losses? Would arrangements made with state and local authorities for the financial support of commutation service, particularly in the New York–New Jersey and Philadelphia regions, significantly improve the bottom line? Would the recently launched effort to win regulatory approval to reduce excessive and costly capacity be successful, and what would be the real financial benefits of these line abandonments? On September 15, 1971, Jervis succinctly summarized the position of the trustees in an address before a meeting of the Railroad Systems and Management Association in Chicago. "If we do have the prospect of earning power, we can move ahead to reorganize the company in the traditional manner. If we don't have the prospect of earning power, we will acknowledge it and will try to develop a plan for reorganization short of nationalization."[29]

While the trustees met with each other and with the judge and began the process of collecting data, Bill Moore, the president, attempted to turn around the railroad. An early effort was the centralization of command. Moore stripped the six regional managers of most of their powers, leaving them with responsibility only for overseeing the daily operations of trains. Other formal duties, including control over maintenance of cars, tracks, and the like, would be centered in Philadelphia. Even though the company had received a combination of direct loans and guarantees that amounted to $100 million under terms of the Emergency Rail Services Act of 1970, money remained tight. Glaring equipment shortages plagued the road. "Even cabooses are short on the railroad," Jervis reported to the ICC during hearings on much-needed freight rate increases. "We have had many situations here in the last two weeks when freight trains couldn't be run because there were no cabooses." Moore and his associates concentrated on cutting operating expenses. Some yards were modernized, freight cars were used more efficiently, and a new computer system was installed. And the Moore team wisely tackled labor costs, focusing on the costly full-crew laws (or "excess crew laws," as the industry called them) that remained on the statute books in Indiana and Ohio. For most freight runs, the company was forced to assign five-man crews in Ohio and six-man crews in Indiana, when the railroad really only needed two or three trainmen. Through the cooperative lobbying actions of Penn Central and other carriers that served these states, legislators subsequently repealed measures that had made sense only in the days of steam and other obsolete technologies. Moore also pushed to improve the railroad's marketing efforts, especially for intermodal traffic. New and rebuilt equipment, including 137 road locomotives, helped as well.[30]

Although Bill Moore met with some success, he lacked good people skills. "He didn't know how to deal with people in a humane way to get anything done," recalled an associate. Jervis himself concluded that Moore failed to lead, and that weakness resulted in important staff people ignoring him. Furthermore, the company lost some capable employees who simply refused to work under Moore. Jervis's initial assessment of the Penn Central president remained valid.[31]

But Jervis developed real concerns about Moore's performance. He repeatedly asked Moore about the specific condition of the property, and Moore responded that it was improving and generally acceptable. "We [trustees] were trusting Moore," commented Jervis, "and he kept telling us there was no problem with the plant." But an inspection conducted by the Federal Railroad Administration reported that Penn Central failed to meet track standards and warned that the road might have to be shut down. This disturbing news "embarrassed the trustees and undercut Moore's credibility," recounted Rush Loving. In June 1972 the track situation had worsened dramatically in sections of New York and Pennsylvania when tropical storm Agnes devastated hundreds of miles of line, especially along the extensive watershed of the Susquehanna River. Irrespective of this act of God, Jervis knew that Moore must go, although the president had support among the trustees. And little did he realize that Moore had misinformed John Ehrlichman, the influential advisor to President Nixon, that "all was well with Penn Central and that we can solve the problems." Jervis would need to be patient.[32]

Coming of Conrail

Improvements under Moore and the trustees failed to revitalize Penn Central, even though between 1970 and 1973 losses fell from $325.7 million to $189 million and the company's operating ratio dropped from 92.08 percent to 82.73 percent. While there were positive trends, the basic problems were never solved. For one, Jervis's core concept, mileage reduction, was economically sound but politically unacceptable. This setback especially bothered him throughout his tenure at Penn Central. After all, the only available procedure was abandonment of individual lines, one by one. "Even the smallest segment required a separate application, questionnaire, hearings, briefs, and oral argument (if requested), with final ICC decision later," recalled Jervis. "In a strongly contested case, a review of the ICC decision by a federal district court might be required. And then, after years of multiple litigation, there was no assurance that the resulting smaller plan, with some applications granted and some denied, would constitute the viable smaller plant intended when the process was initiated." Arguably even more troubling for the railroad was the failure to achieve a breakthrough in attracting more traffic.[33]

Penn Central remained sickly, and most everyone affected worried about the future. William Johnson, who chaired IC, told railroad and government officials that "if Penn Central doesn't make it, we'll all be in trouble. If Penn Central leads to nationalization of the railroads, we're dead."[34]

Jervis understood the challenges that the bankrupt Penn Central confronted and gave matters much thought. He expressed his concerns and ideas for change in a lengthy "Point of View" article that the *New York Times* published on Sunday, April 1, 1973. Jervis explained succinctly the problems of excess capacity and unneeded workers that plagued the railroad. But he emphasized also the difficulties posed by a national network that consisted of approximately 70 large and often uncooperative carriers. Companies continued to battle regionally or one another over rate-making before the ICC, fearing major changes in the status quo. In one example Jervis noted that Penn Central had made a careful study, including market surveys, that prompted the railroad to propose for piggyback traffic volume rates that featured a strong incentive for round trips. "Although able to join in the proposal, the Penn Central's competitors, after failing to induce the ICC to suspend the proposed rates, shattered the experiment by publishing even lower rates on lesser volumes," wrote Jervis. "This was a counter move that drastically reduced the net earnings reflecting high equipment utilization promised by the original rates." In another case when Penn Central sug-

Jervis (*left*) stands in front of the Penn Central offices in Philadelphia, flanked by James Hagen, United States Railway Administration employee and later president of Conrail, A. M. "Al" Schofield, vice president for reorganizational planning, and Joseph Spring, a regional Penn Central manager. (Irene Langdon)

gested that Congress give the ICC power to make its findings retroactive and thus eliminate the incentive on the part of defending carriers in division controversies to stall, there were cries of anguish from roads in the South and West. "The interest of the owners of these lines is to hang on to their revenue proportions for as long as possible." The point that he made was that individual railroads fought each other on every possible front. And with the immediate crisis he revealed that "at no time since the Penn Central's bankruptcy has any other railroad (with a single exception) made a friendly suggestion as to how the Penn Central might help itself in its reorganization efforts or offered a helping hand." Jervis ended with this salient comment: "A national railroad system that does not act as a system is hardly a system at all."[35]

Although Jervis wanted railroads to work together, he explained in the *Times* essay that the hour had come to consider an organizational structure to preside over the operating units. "Possibly, this could be along the lines of the American Telephone and Telegraph Company, or a holding company pattern."

The advantages would be multifold. "Certainly a central control would bring order out of the present confusion; give a sense of direction to the individual railroad, and bring them together in providing better transportation service for the entire country." There was more. "It should also stop the interminable quarreling and eliminate the staggering expense that inevitably arises when railroads are forced to deal with each other." Jervis concluded his piece as such: "More importantly, central control (in whatever form attainable) would give the country the great advantages of a rail system that operated as a true system. The public would have the use of the most efficient routes without regard to interchange points, and car supply would be geared to national needs and not be limited by the financial ability of the individual carriers to make their contributions to the so-called national freight-car pool."[36]

While there was no meaningful response to the *Times* commentary, the continuing problems that vexed Penn Central and nearly a half-dozen other bankrupt carriers in the East caused industry leaders, investors, and others to fret about the possibility of nationalization, perhaps the type that had occurred in Great Britain in 1948. If a system like "Ma Bell" with its "Baby Bells" evolved, there would be no need for a federal takeover, and the private sector could effectively manage the American railroad network.[37]

Indicators may not have pointed to imminent nationalization, but they certainly anticipated greater government involvement. Jervis and his associates realized that Penn Central could not be continually going to Washington to seek money on a piecemeal basis. A permanent solution had to be found, and the sooner the better. On January 2, 1973, the trustees sent a report to Judge Fullam indicating that the railroad could not function without sustained aid from the federal government. Somewhat earlier Jervis had adroitly noted the realities of the situation. "I think the real problem facing Penn Central is that the railroad form of transportation in the northeastern part of the country may not be viable. In other words, no matter how efficiently operated or well managed they are, the Penn Central and in fact the other railroads in the Northeast may not be able to produce earning power." Later in January Bob Blanchette reinforced this troubling perspective by telling the court that Penn Central faced an immediate financial crisis.[38]

These dire predictions prompted railroad leaders, creditors, shippers, and politicians to consider the fate of the bankrupt carriers, most of all Penn Central. Jervis became heavily involved. In mid-January, for example, he talked with Frank Barnett, who chaired the Union Pacific board, and William McDonald, UP senior vice president, about practical ways to respond to a deteriorating northeastern rail situation. They agreed that nationalization of the railroad network must be avoided and that something positive had to happen. But Barnett and McDonald were not pleased when Jervis urged that rate divisions for western roads be made more equitable for Penn Central. And Jervis, often joined by Bob Blanchette, "Langdon's gun slinger with Congress," made frequent trips to Capitol Hill, meeting politicians and lobbyists to discuss the developing crisis. They spent time with the new secretary of transportation, Claude Brinegar, whom Jervis found to be bright, cordial, and understanding.[39]

Jervis and his colleagues received more attention when they revealed on February 1 that the railroad would require a staggering $600 to $800 million in federal assistance over the next three years to keep trains rolling. Jervis announced, "Only by catching up on maintenance and capital improvements neglected in the past 15 years can Penn Central be put in a position to provide the high quality of service demanded by an ever-increasing portion of the nation's shippers. Because of claims already accrued, neither the non-rail assets of the estate nor further borrowing can be looked to for the cash needs of the railroad. Indeed, with the railroad lacking funds to make it viable, with plant and equipment deteriorating, with tax claims and other post-bankruptcy claims eroding the estate available for pre-bankruptcy claimants, it would be a violation of the constitutional rights of Penn Central claimants to continue Penn Central rail service much longer under the status quo."[40]

But action from Washington was not immediately forthcoming. So what should be the strategy? Jervis concluded that the trustees needed to provoke a crisis. With approval from Judge Fullam, Penn Central announced that the size of train crews would be cut dramatically, an action that would produce substantial savings. If the brotherhoods struck for more than a few days, the court would allow the railroad to be shut down permanently. Service would be disrupted, perhaps forever on some lines, and the company's physical plant, rolling stock, and other assets would be sold.[41]

Union leaders, of course, were not happy with any cutbacks in the workforce, wanting to retain existing train crew sizes. Yet knowledgeable labor officials sensed that the trustees and the judge were not bluffing about ending service and liquidation. Al Chesser, general chairman of the UTU, the union that represented trainmen, understood that tens of thousands of jobs were at stake if Penn Central shut down. As a result of his creative thinking, labor decided to pressure lawmakers to respond to the needs of Penn Central with a walkout, but not one intended to last long or to destroy the railroad. "We've got to let Congress know what we're going to do," Chesser announced, "and we've got to have them stop the strike." And it was Chesser who made it clear to responsive politicians on Capitol Hill, including House Speaker John McCormick, Representative Harley Staggers, and Senators

Warren Magnuson and Mike Mansfield, that action needed to be taken immediately. These powerful lawmakers understood that a sustained stoppage in shipments of raw materials, components, and finished products that normally moved by rail would create massive disruptions within industry and commerce.

The strike occurred. But the walkout of 28,000 union members on February 8, 1973, was brief, as Chesser and his allies had intended. With freight and Amtrak and commuter passenger service disrupted, Congress responded with Senate Joint Resolution 59, which halted the stoppage with a 90-day cooling-off declaration and ordered Secretary Brinegar to provide a comprehensive report that would offer proposals for preserving essential rail service in the Northeast. The secretary faced a deadline of only 45 days. The one-day walkout caused only minimal problems for shippers and riders; in fact, workers returned to their posts even before President Nixon signed the emergency legislation. Yet the strike cost Penn Central precious dollars.[42]

All in all, this pleased Jervis. As he told the *New York Times,* "the seriousness of Penn Central's plight had finally been recognized by the general public." Jervis and most other informal individuals understood that the real issue in the strike was not the reduction of crew sizes but the desire of the trustees to force Congress and the Nixon administration to assist the bankrupt railroads, most of all Penn Central. Yet he wanted to reduce labor costs, and he reiterated his desire to trim the railroad roughly in half. The remaining 11,000 miles would still generate about 80 percent of the company's freight revenues.[43]

In order to keep pressure on Congress, Judge Fullam, working with Jervis and the other trustees, early in March 1973 issued a well-publicized report. "It was a real bombshell," said EL president Gregory Maxwell. The document indicated that in 1972 the bankruptcy estate had lost about a half-billion dollars, and to prevent further erosions it would be necessary for Penn Central to *shut down* on October 1, 1973. Assets would then be sold unless the federal government provided a permanent solution to the railroad's financial woes. "The property is becoming less valuable every day because we can't maintain it properly," Jervis told the ICC. Penn Central leadership was not about to play a passive role.[44]

The wheels of government began to turn. Secretary Brinegar came to understand that if Judge Fullam were to liquidate Penn Central, a transportation disaster of potentially monumental proportions would surely follow. And the secretary realized that the judge was obligated to protect the financial interests of the railroad's creditors and not the interests of the general public. In order to prevent what might be considered the natural flow of events,

Washington had no choice but to intervene; there had to be an alternative to liquidation.

Secretary Brinegar endorsed Jervis's assessment of what needed to be done with Penn Central and the other, smaller bankrupt carriers. By this time the Ann Arbor, Central Railroad of New Jersey (Jersey Central), Erie Lackawanna, Lehigh & Hudson River, Lehigh Valley, and Reading were under court protection. The secretary rejected nationalization and instead argued for a more efficient network of rail lines, selling off or abandoning non-core routes and eliminating unproductive jobs. Brinegar believed that rail transportation had a future in this troubled region. "In a word," he quipped, "quite clearly there is a healthy rail system trying to crawl out of the northeastern wreck."

Fortunately, Jervis and Brinegar were not alone with their compatible views about the fate of the bankrupts. Some influential industry leaders, including Frank Barnett, Graham Claytor, and Stephen Ailes, president of the Association of American Railroads, felt strongly about the need to avoid nationalization and the attractiveness of a privately operated, albeit streamlined company composed of the viable parts of the seven bankrupts, including Penn Central. And in June 1973 the appropriate bills entered the legislative process.[45]

Yet before the federal government responded in a meaningful way, the trustees filed with the court a dramatic report that contemplated retention and restructuring of Penn Central's non-railroad assets and sale of railroad properties to others. Although the possibility of a cessation of service hardly pleased Jervis, he considered the plan to be wholly warranted. Yet he and his colleagues held out hope that the legislative and executive branches might respond positively, providing an alternative to liquidation. "Should government assistance be forthcoming and provide the means of continued rail operations by the Trustees while a solution to the northeast railroad problem is evolved, the trustees will promptly amend their Plan to reflect this development."[46]

While hope grew for a "final solution to our problems," as Jervis put it, Penn Central got some intermediate federal assistance. In August 1973, the government loaned Penn Central $16.4 million, or an amount about equal to the losses sustained by storm damage the previous year, under the terms of the Emergency Rail Facilities Restoration Act of 1972. While the loan was good news, Jervis soon shared his concerns with the ICC, which after July 3, 1973, considered the Penn Central reorganization proposal on an expedited schedule. He restated the claim that the railroad required at least $200 million a year to function and that was much more than in any bill currently before Congress. These funds were needed to control erosion of the debtor's estate from the buildup of administrative claims and to confront the continued poor maintenance of the physical plant and rolling stock. "No one wants to close down the railroad," Jervis informed the Commission. "But we're fast approaching the time when we'll be completely out of money." He knew that he had to be blunt; the pressure for change had to be strong and ongoing. Commented Rush Loving, "Langdon pushed the envelope at Penn Central, and he knew that he had to get the public involved."[47]

It did not take long before the ICC made a decision. On September 28, 1973, the Commission rejected the trustees' plan, concluding, "Our review of the legislative history underlying Section 77 [of the federal bankruptcy code], its purpose, and the precedents interpreting Section 77 lead us to conclude that the . . . [Penn Central Transportation Company] plan cannot be considered a plan of reorganization either within the letter or the spirit of that statutory provisions." The ICC saw liquidation as wholly contrary to the public interest and agreed that a "Penn Central reorganization must be considered in the context of the entire eastern district problem which involves seven bankrupt railroads, and, that given certain external assistance, the restructuring of the entire railroad system of the northeastern quadrant of the country can be achieved."[48]

While the ICC conducted its hearings and deliberations, legislation to "save" railroad service in the Northeast moved through Congress. Industry personnel, including Jervis and Bob Blanchette, worked diligently with lawmakers to bring about some type of resolution to what was undeniably a rapidly growing crisis. Jervis teamed up with Frank Barnett, who played a key role in formulating the ultimate legislation, and this was a good strategy, for Barnett was "great on the hill." And Jervis did not ignore those lobbyists who represented the major auto and steel manufacturers, including General Motors and Bethlehem Steel. "Langdon greatly helped Penn Central's cause," remarked James Hagen, "by getting big shippers involved."[49]

Finally success came. In late 1973, Congress, in a bipartisan fashion, passed the Regional Rail Reorganization Act (popularly known as the 3-R Act), which President Nixon reluctantly signed on January 2, 1974. At last the nation had a policy toward railroads in trouble and did not have to rely on a nonprogressive ICC. This unique piece of legislation created the United States Railway Association (USRA), a government corporation designed to plan the restructuring of the rail system in the Northeast. The statutory instructions for the USRA included submission of a Preliminary System Plan (PSP) within less than a year to the Rail Services Planning Office of the ICC, which would hold hearings and evaluate the proposals. In this initial phase, Consolidated Rail Corporation, a railroad with government funding, would take over Penn Central together with portions of the smaller bankrupts, while the Chessie and Southern would extend their routes into Delaware, New Jersey, New York, and Pennsylvania over parts of the bankrupt Erie Lackawanna, Lehigh Valley, and Reading railroads. The new corporation would receive up to $1.5 billion of federally guaranteed loans for betterments, and in September 1975, the projected funding was set at $2.026 billion. What had happened was really revolutionary; only the temporary federal takeover of the railroads in December 1917 had been more drastic.[50]

Government personnel hammered out additional matters. Five months after the PSP was revealed, the Final System Plan (FSP) was announced, and in design it resembled the PSP. But largely because of concerns about labor costs, neither Chessie nor Southern acquired sections of the bankrupts, much to the disappointment of USRA operatives. The FSP, though, did endorse transfer of the busy Northeast Corridor to Amtrak and strategic trackage rights that would benefit the Delaware & Hudson, DT&I, Grand Trunk Western, N&W, and P&LE. Also the FSP called for approximately 6,000 miles of low-density lines to be abandoned, sold to other carriers, or publicly subsidized. In an impossibly short time, a dedicated USRA staff worked out the critical details. The process for a federally backed "bailout" had begun in earnest.[51]

Response to the 3-R Act was mostly positive. Although critics considered the measure as a glaring example of "Special Interest Socialism," most knowledgeable observers agreed with Joseph Albright, Washington correspondent for the *San Francisco Chronicle,* when he wrote that "if the Northeast rail bill had been defeated, there would have been little to stop the Penn Central creditors from carrying out their intention of shutting down the railroad and auctioning off the pieces to the highest bidder." He concluded, "Faced with that wrenching alternative, it is hard to fault Congress for acting when it did." The mandatory conveyance of the bankrupts to Conrail made sense.[52]

President

As lead trustee Jervis could not ignore the shortcomings of Bill Moore. When shortly before Christmas 1973 the Penn Central president had unfairly fired a division superintendent, the issue of Moore's employment was brought to a head. Yet that impulsive act alone would not permit dismissal. Jervis had been gathering evidence of Moore's failings, learning some disturbing facts.

Early in the bankruptcy Judge Fullam had ordered the sale of Penn Central's corporate aircraft. But the crafty Moore, who wanted this perk, negotiated with Scott Paper Company for the railroad to use an extra plane that Scott owned, "and the railroad would be billed each month for the equivalent value of toilet paper." A *Washington Star* story brought this scheme to light, and Jervis ordered the arrangement stopped. But there was more. Moore had had a valuable grandfather's clock that stood in his office sent out for repairs and then had the mended clock delivered to his home instead. More bothersome than theft of an antique timepiece was Moore's practice of sending railroad employees to perform work on his house and property in Potomac, Maryland, on company time. "This was unquestionably improper," concluded Rush Loving, "especially for a railroad that was receiving government subsidies." Jervis reported these matters to fellow trustees and the judge, and received their approval to dismiss Moore. On January 2, 1974, the same day that President Nixon signed the 3-R Act, Wild Bill left the railroad, with the press benignly describing the reasons as "policy differences." While some details of Moore's dismissal later appeared publicly, a brief ICC inquiry into his wrongdoings did not lead to criminal prosecution. Later Moore reimbursed Penn Central for the cost of his home improvements; he could afford to do so because his $165,000 annual salary continued until September 1, 1975.[53]

The firing of Bill Moore created a vacancy in the presidential suite. Yet the void lasted only momentarily. Judge Fullam asked his lead trustee to take command, and he gladly accepted. Although Jervis inquired if he could exercise the responsibilities of president while remaining a trustee, the answer was no. "[Judge Fullam] said, there's a conflict there and I want you over there as the direct operating head of the railroad." As for Penn Central trustees, the company continued to have three. (In late December 1972, Willard Wirtz had resigned to concentrate on labor law in Washington, D.C., and the judge decided not to replace him.) Judge Fullam, however, felt it necessary to name a successor to Jervis, and on January 11, 1974, he chose Bob Blanchette, legal counsel to the trustees. George Baker and Richard Bond remained, although in June the 70-year-old Baker resigned to enjoy his retirement years. Baker recommended his replacement, and the judge agreed. His successor also had a Harvard connection; the 40-year-old John H. McArthur was a professor of management and finance and an associate dean at the Harvard Business School.[54]

Being president of Penn Central would not be easy. "At age 68 Langdon has taken on his biggest challenge," observed a reporter for the Associated Press. After all, Penn Central remained the largest railroad in the East, experienced serious maintenance problems, desperately needed more freight revenues, owed more than $4 billion, and faced the complexities of implementing the 3-R Act. Then there was the need to work with various individuals and groups. "Politicians especially always wanted to talk to the big guy, and that meant Langdon," observed James Hagen. "I don't know where he found time to do all of the things that the presidency demanded."[55]

Jervis was up to the challenge. He employed the same hands-on approach to management that he had used so effectively at the B&O and Rock Island. "I tried to operate this railroad as joint responsibility with the general managers," he recalled. "We really tried to get a kind of a family concept about this." Jervis would fly out to various on-line locations to meet with these officials. "One meeting would be Monday morning in Pittsburgh. The general managers were all there, and we'd talk our problems all over, and the next week it would be Chicago, and the next week it would be in Detroit, and in New Haven the next week after that." These gatherings produced results. "Everybody was free with suggestions, and the quality of the service really did improve."[56]

Just as Jervis had done at the Rock Island, he hired Bill Dixon. On November 15, 1974, the capable Dixon, who had struggled as Jervis's successor as Rock Island president, became vice president for staff. Jervis wanted to tap Dixon's special talents, which he had demonstrated on the Rock Island and most notably as director of industrial engineering for the B&O. It was a choice that pleased both men and benefited Penn Central.[57]

It would be out of these meetings with supervisors and additional gatherings with shippers that an array of solid suggestions were converted into policies and programs that improved the health of Penn Central. Ship-A-Train exemplified this creative thinking. In 1972, the railroad offered a rate reduction of 25 percent when a shipper moved 60 or more highway trailers or containers in a single train. Under the Langdon presidency, the service was refined and marketed extensively, proving particularly popular among customers in Chicago. In what amounted to an express service, Penn Central trains delivered cars to the New York City terminal facilities in about 24 hours, and the competitive rates, coupled with general dependability, enabled the company to recapture a considerable volume of business that formerly had moved on the highways. The railroad also focused on overnight piggyback service on shorter runs, for example, between Chicago and Detroit and between Buffalo and New York. "We did what we could in promoting service," related Jervis. "Every morning we watched it like hawks. I can't say that the earnings improvements were startling [because] . . . this kind of service takes time to develop."[58]

Jervis did not mistakenly judge performance. Published reports indicated that a higher degree of shipper satisfaction existed than had been true earlier in the bankruptcy or prior to 1970. The bedeviled Penn Central was somewhat less so. Commented Harry Deck, director of transportation for Armstrong Cork Company, "Penn Central has become a very dedicated, service conscious railroad. . . . Everyone we deal with is most helpful and in practically all instances [they] have been successful in eliminating or correcting whatever problems we have had." George Sperry, traffic manager for National Distillers and Chemical Corporation, happily remarked, "Transit time between Indianapolis and Bridgeport [Connecticut] has been cut in half." And J. F. Stoerrie, traffic manager for the Budd Company, rated the railroad "high on cooperation and willingness to do everything possible to solve problems." But he saw room for improvement, largely in the area of track maintenance. "However, as we all know, this is due to their poor financial condition." *Railway Age* agreed with these testimonials. "Of 95 shippers surveyed by Railway Age, 53% now give PC a 'good' rating on service reliability. Only 9% rate PC service as poor. PC gets an even higher plus vote—58%—for attention to costumer needs."[59]

This trend in better consumer relations continued. In 1975 Penn Central instituted a program to measure on-time service. As the year progressed, the number of cars that experienced lengthy delays dropped. The railroad's improving service was reflected in an increasing market share, rising from 33.1 percent in 1970 for railroads in the Eastern District to 35.9 percent five years later. Other statistics bore out these improvements. Gross-ton-miles per freight train hour, a good indicator of operating efficiency, looked promising. Following a serious decline at the beginning of the bankruptcy and then negatively impacted by the recession of 1974 that reduced traffic and inflated fuel and material costs, Penn Central's record was as follows:

Year	GTM per FTH
1972	61,816
1973	65,644
1974	65,258
1975	67,650

While in absolute terms this performance was below the average of prosperous carriers, the trend had taken a positive direction. Yet during the first two years of Conrail operations, performance when compared with Penn Central's dropped off substantially, 62,686 for 1976 and 62,518 for 1977.[60]

Jervis realized that because of a lack of capital, Penn Central would not have raceways between principal terminals, but the goal was to improve service as much as resources allowed. "We had some large stretches of railroad that were down to 30 miles an hour for high speed freight service that was supposed to be 60 miles an hour," he recalled. "But even so, we were able to improve service because we were working at it. Sometimes if you're just determined to improve, even though the conditions haven't improved much, you can get a better showing just because of your determination." He was right. It was a remarkable showing because in early 1974, for example, over 8,200 miles of line had to be slowed down, some to less than 10 miles an hour, and the number of derailments had increased by more than 100 percent over the previous year.[61]

As with his presidencies on the B&O and Rock Island, Jervis pushed toward modernization. One example took place in early 1975 when Penn Central completed a new computer-centered system that provided close control of nearly $380 million in materials and supplies it purchased annually from thousands of manufacturers and vendors. The railroad received critical acclaim for this Material Accounting and Purchasing System, or MAPS, and the expenditure shortly paid for itself. Jervis was particularly pleased that MAPS could forecast cash requirements for future purchases. But funds were not being wasted. As he told Secretary Brinegar in February 1974, "We are making every effort to husband our cash and to stay close to projections."[62]

Jervis never ignored ways to protect vital revenues. In 1975, he became worried about the possibility of federal legislation that would permit construction of coal-slurry pipelines, and especially proposed amendments to the Mineral Leasing Act that were designed to clear the way for this coal transport alternative. Penn Central depended heavily on coal shipments, which in 1974 represented more than a quarter of its freight volume, and other carriers relied on this traffic. "The nation must face up to the fact that it cannot permit the most profitable segment of railroad traffic to be siphoned off and still have a viable railroad system," Jervis told the U.S. House Interior Committee. "If the railroads are essential, they must be afforded the widest opportunity to attract and handle traffic at a profit; if they are not, they should go the way of the horse and buggy. Otherwise, they will forever be dependent on public support." Fortunately for the railroad industry, a combination of forces, including the growing environmental movement, nipped in the bud this drive for coal-slurry pipelines.[63]

By the advent of Conrail, April 1, 1976, Jervis was only moderately satisfied with how events had played out. Other than liquidation, there really was no other practical option at hand. Although he was proud of some successes that were part of his tenure at Penn Central, he admitted that glaring failures had prevented efforts to achieve a nonpublicly assisted reorganization. The quest to build up traffic density on Penn Central really had not worked. Attempts to create a core railroad, a company with about half the size of the original plant, also had not materialized. "I can still hear the screams of anguish from the state capitals in Penn Central's territory," he wrote *Trains* editor David P. Morgan in 1977, "the smaller communities and shippers (with perhaps one car a month), and individual congressmen offended at any proposal to curtail rail service regardless of deficit." Efforts to increase freight volume, concentrating on highway business that could be diverted to piggyback, likewise proved a disappointment. A combination of motor carrier competition and ICC rate decisions hindered profitable intermodal growth.

If monumental changes, which Jervis heartily embraced, were to be forthcoming, there would not have been any need for the quasi-public Conrail. Deregulation or measures that gave railroads greater control over line rationalization and rates likely would have made possible reorganization of Penn Central on an income-producing basis. But he understood the facts of political life. "What makes economic sense in the transportation business often is unacceptable politically," he wrote to University of California at Berkeley business professor Michael Conant, "and in this country it is the political sense that usually prevails." As early as January 1977, Jervis had noted privately that "Conrail is not a solution." It merely bought time, pending a more realistic approach to the problem. Jervis desired megamergers. "The number of operating units in the national system must be drastically reduced, and railroad service, still highly competitive, must be truly transcontinental (East–West, North–South), with traditional regional boundaries completely eliminated and forgotten." As in the past, he wanted government to accept the principle that every efficient railroad operation must earn a fair profit. In those instances where this would not be possible and the service was needed in the public interest, a subsidy would become mandatory. In time the drastic changes Jervis had in mind would mostly come to pass.[64]

But Jervis would not be at the Conrail throttle. He concluded that it was time to become a *former* railroad president. As with his departure from the B&O and Rock Island, employees expressed sadness about his decision not to lead the new carrier. "In just 10 days, Conrail will be a reality. I'm looking forward to that event—as are all my fellows—with a great anticipation and expectation," wrote a junior Penn Central officer from Chicago. "We've been

On March 24, 1976, this employee-sensitive executive presented the coveted "President's Safety Trophy" to the Central Region of the Penn Central Transportation Company in Pittsburgh. Penn Central executives surround Jervis. (Irene Langdon)

pleased with the announcements of appointments but missing is the name of a man we've grown to respect and revere. . . . Yours. You have done so very much for us and our company. You could continue doing so with Conrail, even though eminently qualified for a richly deserved retirement." And a chairman of a local UTU local in Buffalo told the outgoing president, "A few years ago I had the honor to hear you address the Pennsylvania State Union Meeting of the United Transportation Union at Hershey. Your message on that day was an *honest appraisal* of the most difficult tasks that lied [*sic*] ahead for all members of the Penn Central Family, and asked the cooperation of all, in order to attain success in making Penn Central a profitable railroad." He added: "In my judgement, Sir, you did not fail, for you inherited an industry with no funds, and then an economic recession, which made your task an impossible one, you did by your leadership raise the moral of the employees from a low point to its present day high." Both assessments were correct, and they were deeply appreciated by this railroad executive who liked people.[65]

Although not playing an active role in Conrail, the former Penn Central lead trustee and president had left a legacy. The Langdon years had made positive, long-lasting changes; the groundwork had been laid for a later revolution at the railroad, resulting in Conrail becoming a profitable and respected company.

6 Still Railroading

Penn Central Estate

On April 1, 1976, Conveyance Day (C-Day), the quasi-public Consolidated Rail Corporation (Conrail) absorbed much of the Penn Central Transportation Company. Yet the corporate shells of Penn Central and the other bankrupts that joined Conrail remained to manage property and assets not taken by the government. The presence of these "estates" allowed Jervis to continue a relationship with his former employer. In a sense he was unique. "When Conrail took over, all the management went over, except for me." Yet at age 71 Jervis was not about to leave what he considered to be the fascinating business of railroading. Even though he viewed the years after the Penn Central presidency as his "retirement" time, he remained involved, undertaking a variety of professional activities and commenting on an industry that at times changed rapidly.[1]

Although Jervis would work as a consultant for the Penn Central estate, he simultaneously served as counsel to the Atlanta-based law firm of Alston, Miller & Gaines, later Alston & Bird, and would so do from 1976 to 1983. His close connection with Robert Blanchette at Penn Central may have provided his entry to the prestigious law firm with important railroad clients, for after C-Day Blanchette had become the managing partner. Alston, Miller & Gaines, which operated a busy office at 1800 M Street, N.W., in Washington, D.C., focused on corporate law with important railroad clients and took advantage of its close ties with President Jimmy Carter. Jervis worked mostly out of the Washington branch, but he flew his twin-engine Aztec to Atlanta whenever necessary.[2]

In the complicated restructuring of the eastern bankrupts, not all railroad trackage or all controlled companies entered the Conrail orbit. The several railroad estates, including Penn Central, were left with a range of assets that included rail lines, real estate, mineral holdings, investments in other firms, and even historical artifacts and documents. "There was much more meat on these carcasses than anyone really imagined," observed an Erie Lackawanna operative about these former carriers. The retained assets needed to be sold to satisfy debts, particularly back property taxes, and to add value to investors. During this sorting-out process, representatives from Central Railroad of New Jersey (Jersey Central), Erie Lackawanna, Lehigh Valley, and Reading met regularly to discuss their mutual interests, focusing on how to deal with Conrail and the federal government. Penn Central personnel also became interested. "The Penn Central because of its size felt above us," recalled Erie Lackawanna executive Harry Zilli Jr., "but it got involved later when it was apparent that the little bankrupts generated some excellent ideas." Everyone realized that these estates possessed value; they enjoyed substantial tax loss carry-forwards, and that, together with the eventual federal payments for properties that Conrail acquired and sale of assets, allowed the former bankrupts either to move into nonrailroad businesses or to liquidate successfully.[3]

For Penn Central, Judge John Fullam and the trustees presided over the estate and attempted to maximize value before the bankruptcy was finally terminated in 1994. For the first few years after Conrail, Penn Central sought Jervis's expertise in rail evaluation conveyance proceedings that the Regional Rail Reorganization Act (3-R Act) of 1973 mandated. This measure created a three-judge special court to set valuation of the conveyed properties. This was tricky work because the law required that compensation be based on "constitutional minimum value." But according to attorney Harry Silleck, "nobody knew exactly what this meant!" And the 3-R Act contained more murky provisions. It insisted that the court consider "other benefits" that accrued to the estates under the statute and told the court to weigh any "compensable unconstitutional erosion" of the estates' assets. Yet the law did not offer any rules of procedure determining these valuation figures. By the end of 1976, matters had become clearer, although not fully resolved. It was in this environment that Penn Central needed assistance from Jervis to prepare for the evidentiary hearings. And this he did before the final and satisfactory settlement was reached in late 1980. "I testified on the main valuation cases," Jervis recalled. "Had to go to Washington and stay there for a long time. I had to work awfully hard preparing the testimony and the cross-examinations, and the government attorneys went after me for three or four days." Federal officials sought to make payouts for the assets of the bankrupts as low as possible, but he helped to validate the claims of the Penn Central estate.

The trustees also relied heavily on Jervis's knowledge and skills in the sale of several major rail subsidiaries that were not conveyed to Conrail. These included the Pittsburgh & Lake Erie (P&LE); Toledo, Peoria & Western (TP&W) (50 percent interest owned by Penn Central); and the Detroit, Toledo & Ironton (DT&I). These railroads were of similar size and importance and possessed considerable value.[4]

When it came to the disposal work, Jervis initially concentrated on the P&LE. This well-built, multitracked 211-mile railroad stretched from Pittsburgh northwestward to Youngstown, Ohio, and had long been controlled by the New York Central (NYC). Historically, the P&LE had been principally a hauler of raw materials used in steel making, and that role continued. Then, in 1966, the P&LE joined with the C&O/B&O and Pennsylvania (PRR) to build the 35-mile Waynesburg Southern Railroad, which provided service to new coal mines in northern West Virginia. Jervis knew the P&LE well. In the mid-1930s, he had worked for the parent NYC. And the Baltimore & Ohio (B&O) had had trackage rights over the P&LE for its through passenger and freight trains between McKeesport and New Castle Junction, Pennsylvania. Jervis had also kept abreast of the Waynesburg Southern project.[5]

With the P&LE disposal, Jervis supervised the gathering of factual information. Soon this data, which included statistical materials on traffic, rolling stock, real estate, and the like, appeared in a printed prospectus that the estate sent out to likely purchasers for bids. Although there would be various offers, the estate ultimately agreed to sell the P&LE to the "Pittsburgh Group," investors associated with the local Melon banking interests. Jervis and the estate were pleased; the approximately $60-million selling price was considered a fair value for a railroad that had experienced better days. Unfortunately, the steel industry in the greater Pittsburgh and Youngstown areas was in sharp decline, with the Ohio city becoming the national poster child for the developing "rust bowl." The final sale agreement took place on May 15, 1979.[6]

Next Jervis concentrated on disposal of the DT&I. This largely Ohio carrier extended from Detroit in a generally southerly direction to Ironton on the Ohio River, a distance of nearly 360 miles. As a mostly north–south route, the DT&I crossed a number of east–west carriers, allowing for frequent interchange connections. Unlike the formative years of the P&LE, the DT&I consisted of relatively weak predecessors. A renaissance came after 1920 when industrialist Henry Ford took control of the unified property and rebuilt and reequipped it. But the iconoclastic Ford became disenchanted with railroading and so in 1929 sold the DT&I to the Pennroad Corporation, an affiliate of the PRR. The relationship with PRR continued. In 1963 the DT&I purchased the 300-mile Ann Arbor Railroad from the Wabash Railroad, the latter mostly owned by the PRR. The Ann Arbor unit fared poorly, falling into bankruptcy on October 15, 1973. In time the railroad underwent liquidation, with the State of Michigan acquiring and then leasing much of the trackage to independent operators. Although the Ann Arbor for the DT&I was a loser, provisions by government policy makers for C-Day relieved the DT&I of the burden of the Ann Arbor and granted trackage rights over Conrail between South Charleston, Ohio, and Cincinnati. This arrangement provided the DT&I access to the busy Cincinnati gateway and direct connections with the Louisville & Nashville and the Southern railroads. Adding to the DT&I's increased strategic value was a new, creative management.[7]

Sale by the estate of the DT&I paralleled the P&LE process. Jervis participated in fact finding and preparing a perspective for bids. The disposal, however, became somewhat more complicated than with the P&LE. He believed that the public interest would best be served with the DT&I being sold to a "group of railroads rather than one individual railroad." And it appeared that this would happen. On May 31, 1977, Norfolk & Western (N&W) and Chessie System announced that they planned to purchase jointly the DT&I for $15 million. Then the Southern entered the picture, offering more than $22 million. N&W and Chessie remained interested and surpassed the Southern offer with a bid of $23.6 million. The estate then signed an agreement with N&W/Chessie, although technically the N&W and B&O, a unit of Chessie, would be the buyers.

The sale story, though, was not finished. Grand Trunk Corporation, the American unit of Canadian National Railways (CN), wanted the DT&I trackage to strengthen the position of its Grand Trunk Western (GTW) in the ever-changing picture of railroading. Therefore, GTW appealed to the Interstate Commerce Commission (ICC) for control and challenged the N&W/Chessie application, arguing that the sale would have a "serious impact . . . on the competitive position and solvency of smaller railroads—especially GTW." This challenge to what the estate had considered a fait accompli bothered Jervis. The GTW had not made a specific dollar offer, and he questioned the ability of GTW to pay a fair price. So the battle for control of the DT&I raged. Ultimately, a variety of forces came into play, including the proposed plans of a Chessie and Seaboard Coast Line merger, the anticipated union between N&W and Southern, and the willingness of GTW to pay more for the DT&I than N&W/Chessie. On April 1, 1980, the estate agreed to a $25.2 million price, and soon the ICC approved the deal, which sizably expanded the DT&I.[8]

A more straightforward sale came with the liquidation of the estate's position in the TP&W. The core 242-mile road operated between Effner, Illinois, on the Indiana border, and a connection with the PRR, through Peoria to Keokuk, Iowa, on the Mississippi River, with a short branch that connected with the main line of the Atchison, Topeka & Santa Fe (Santa Fe) at Lomax, Illinois. The TP&W benefited from its access to the sprawling manufacturing districts of Peoria and East Peoria. The company had a checkered financial past and gained momentary fame during a bitter strike in 1947 when someone assassinated the owner-president, George P. McNear Jr. After World War II, the TP&W emerged as a bridge route between the PRR and Santa Fe and offered the potential to serve as an efficient outer belt around the congestion of Chicago. In the 1950s, Ben W. Heineman, who headed the Minneapolis & St. Louis (M&StL), recognized the strategic value of the TP&W and sought to take the property. With his M&StL and with potential ownership of the Chicago, Indianapolis & Louisville (Monon), he planned to forge a competitive alternative to the Chicago gateway. In a defensive move, the Santa Fe acquired the TP&W and sold a half-interest to the PRR.[9]

In 1976 the TP&W, which served several large customers and an active bridge route, became a stronger property. With the coming of Conrail, TP&W took control of the 62-mile former PRR line between Effner and Logansport, Indiana, allowing for direct interchange with both Conrail and N&W and providing a more complete route around Chicago. It did not take Jervis and the estate long to consummate a $3 million deal with the Santa Fe to buy out the estate's interest. The arrangement took place in 1979, and four years later the TP&W was merged into the parent road.[10]

Board Member

During the immediate years following his Penn Central presidency, much more occupied Jervis than property valuations and sales of estate assets. He remained a member of the board of directors of Amtrak and served a term as chair. In his customary way, Jervis contributed to the passenger railroad. "Jervis was always well prepared for the monthly meetings that usually lasted

As a member of the Amtrak board, Jervis, who is representing Penn Central, attends a planning meeting about the Northeast Corridor Improvement Project. He stands on the far left. Alan Boyd, head of Amtrak, is seated on the far right, and behind Boyd is Lou Thompson, the Department of Transportation representative on the Amtrak board and director of the NCIP. (Irene Langdon)

one or two days," recalled fellow board member Robert Downing, who represented Burlington Northern. Downing noted that Jervis pushed for Amtrak's acquisition of the Northeast Corridor from Penn Central. That transaction, which involved an expenditure of $87 million, enabled Amtrak to become more economically and politically stable, although Jervis correctly had reservations about Amtrak ever making money outside the corridor between Boston and Washington, D.C. Moreover, he "helped Amtrak greatly by sorting out the problems with rolling stock and dealing with [Charles] Luna of the UTU and assisting in creating new relationships with public commuter agencies." Jervis enjoyed working with one of his "boys" from the B&O, Paul Reistrap, who had served since 1975 as Amtrak president and chief operating officer. Reistrap remembered that Jervis "made quick and clean decisions" and "cared enormously about making long-distance passenger travel a success, being practical and not nostalgic."[11]

Less important than Jervis's involvement with Amtrak was his ongoing service to the board of the 116-mile Richmond, Fredericksburg & Potomac Railroad (RF&P). This well-positioned and profitable company served as a link between Washington, D.C., and Richmond, Virginia, and was used extensively by Chessie, Conrail, Seaboard Coast Line, and the Southern. Jervis contributed to RF&P, especially "in diplomatically handing the various railroad personalities that were on the board of directors."

But in the fall of 1978, Jervis severed his ties to both the Amtrak and RF&P boards to accept a director's seat at the Delaware & Hudson (D&H) Railway. The formal election took place on February 28, 1979. The reason for joining this 1,671-mile Albany-based railroad was simple. The president, Kent Shoemaker, who had taken charge in March 1978, had asked him to serve. Jervis gladly gave up two well-paying board assignments for a position that paid negligibly. As one of "Jerv's boys" from the B&O, Bill Collins, D&H vice president for administration and strategic planning, put it: "Jervis did not come for glory or for coin." Collins once overhead a conversation in which Jervis explained succinctly why he accepted the D&H post: "A couple of my boys are there." This included Shoemaker, who in the early 1960s had been a rising star on the B&O. Jervis, in fact, gladly resigned from the other boards, wishing to avoid any appearance of a conflict of interest. Amtrak operated over the D&H, and the D&H held trackage rights into RF&P's Potomac Yard. Yet the ICC would not have considered these board relationships a violation of the law.[12]

Jervis found the D&H to be an exciting railroad. The coming of Conrail had made the D&H, which Norfolk & Western (N&W) had controlled since 1968 through its Dereco holding company, a more important property. The historic core, which amounted to approximately 750 miles, included principal lines that ran between Albany and Montreal, Quebec, and between Albany and Wilkes-Barre, Pennsylvania. But United States Railway Administration (USRA) personnel, most of all Jim McClellan and James Hagen, had worked hard to make the D&H competitive with the gestating Conrail, obtaining for the D&H in the USRA's final system plan trackage rights between Binghamton and Buffalo, Wilkes-Barre and Philadelphia, Allentown/Bethlehem and Newark, and Wilkes-Barre and southern connections (Potomac Yard) at Alexandria, Virginia. A critical restriction of this arrangement was that with the exception of the Bethlehem Steel plant in Bethlehem, Pennsylvania, D&H was not permitted to serve customers located along these new routes. A larger D&H was not the sole attraction for Jervis, although he believed that it could be "a strong competitor of Conrail in a territory which it monopolizes at present." As in the past, Jervis wanted a competitive, privately owned railroad system.[13]

Jervis liked how Shoemaker managed the property. In an early action, Shoemaker wisely decided to expand the board from seven to nine members. Although the two N&W representatives, Robert Claytor and John Turbyfill, were "bright and knowledgeable but only listened," the other directors, local people, were far less talented. They had little railroad-related knowledge or experience. As one executive put it, "Except for Claytor and Turbyfill, there was little timber on the board." Initially Shoemaker sought to appoint William Scranton, the former governor of Pennsylvania and a vocal advocate for freight rail competition in the Northeast, but he was too busy to accept. Yet Scranton wanted D&H to have capable direction, and so he recommended an energetic Athens, Pennsylvania, neurosurgeon and businessman, Dr. Arthur King, who served as chief-of-staff at the Robert Packer-Guthrie Medical Center in Sayre, Pennsylvania. Dr. King, who shared Jervis's passion for trains, had recently been president of the Railroad Task Force for Northeast Region, Inc., and "his election recognizes the extensive D&H operations in Pennsylvania and the need for representation from that area." Dr. King and Jervis became good friends, often traveling together to D&H meetings, and this kindly physician advised Jervis on personal medical matters and later, after a surgery, helped to monitor his health.

Not only did Shoemaker create a stronger board of directors, but he also attracted young, smart railroaders because "they liked the dynamic organization" and understood that N&W "generally maintained a 'hands-off' policy in [D&H's] affairs." These individuals often willingly took pay cuts to join the Shoemaker team. In some ways the D&H resembled Jervis's B&O of the early 1960s. No wonder Jervis enjoyed being associated with the company. Shoemaker himself admitted that he was imitating the Langdon managerial style.[14]

The D&H did not appear to be headed for bankruptcy; in fact, the opposite seemed to be happening. The company was improving its physical plant, rolling stock, and freight volume. By the early 1980s D&H trains handled approximately 180,000 cars annually, and possibilities for more business seemed likely, especially additional shipments generated by Agway, Bethlehem Steel, and International Paper.

Jervis worked hard as a D&H director. "He could be called at any time of the day or night to assist us," recalled Bill Collins. "Jervis was a selfless individual. If he didn't fly from Elmira to Albany, he might leave by car at 4 AM for the drive to the board meeting." Although he never had a close call with his airplane, Jervis once wrecked a rental car, having fallen asleep at the wheel. When he arrived late for the meeting, he remarked, "Mr. Hertz will not be happy with me."

Jervis's contributions were significant and appreciated. Since he knew so many individuals in government and within the industry, especially executives at Conrail, he provided his D&H associates with "lots of people insights." Jervis also commented on existing marketing practices and proposed marketing initiatives, particularly as they pertained to paper and intermodal traffic. There would be fresh options, since with passage in 1980 of the Staggers Act partial rate regulation had at last occurred. And as he had done previously at the B&O, Rock Island, and Penn Central, he heartily endorsed cooperation between departments. Particularly gratifying were new marketing efforts that had transportation and mechanical department personnel working together in a more closely coordinated environment to produce improved service results, recalled Shoemaker and Collins. "Jervis was especially helpful in such projects where results came from the cooperation of two or more departments. He also vigorously encouraged ingenious ways of bolstering D&H's cash flow, such as through the recovery and sale of coal that had been mixed into fills and roadbeds during the railroad's construction many years before."

Jervis, Shoemaker, Collins, and other insiders realized that the D&H faced a host of challenges. Even having new access to major gateways and ports hardly guaranteed long-term profitability. The company was in a somewhat unusual position vis-à-vis the railroad industry, being owned by a carrier that really did not want any involvement. In the early 1980s, however, the N&W did desire something: corporate union with Southern Railway. Although eventually the ICC approved creation of giant Norfolk Southern, regulators demanded resolution of the fate of the D&H. "Until that happened," recalled Bill Collins, "the merger could not go through and the N&W and Southern were losing money each day that they stayed apart." So what would be D&H's ultimate future?

Several scenarios seemed probable. There could be inclusion of the D&H in the future Norfolk Southern, providing long-haul entry between the South and Canada and New England. Another possibility might be corporate independence, but with initial financial backing from Norfolk Southern. N&W had used accelerated depreciation and other bookkeeping tactics to extract money from its ownership of the D&H; N&W officials bragged that they had never put a penny into the D&H. Still another solution might be a third party acquiring the road.[15]

Jervis reflected hard on the future of the D&H. He understood why New York officials wanted the company to maintain its headquarters in Albany and to serve local industries well. Jervis appreciated the willingness of state transportation personnel to support the railroad, for example, by buying ties and "loaning" them to the D&H for track rehabilitation within the state.

Jervis concluded that it would be better for an independent D&H to seek union with another railroad, actually railroads. He then played a role in getting businessman Timothy Mellon, the 39-year-old descendant of the Mellon banking family of Pittsburgh, involved with the D&H. And the State of New York liked this approach. The concept was to unite the D&H with two other struggling northeastern properties, Maine Central Railroad and Boston & Maine Corporation, but to allow D&H to remain a separate entity with offices in Albany. If completed, the three roads would operate nearly 4,000 miles of line and possess the potential of becoming a strong regional combine.

By the latter part of 1981 the three-way union had taken shape, although regulatory and legal matters would continue into early 1984. The controlling company would be Mellon's Guilford Transportation Industries, Inc., headquartered in Durham, Connecticut. And in the case of the D&H, the holding company took ownership with a nominal capital investment, $500,000 (500 shares at $1,000 per share and no debt obligations), because N&W wished to rid itself of the property as quickly as possible.

But arrival of Guilford turned out badly for Jervis, his friends, and the D&H itself. Mellon and his associates did not honor various commitments that had been made to Shoemaker and the D&H board. And almost as soon as Guilford took charge, Shoemaker was fired and replaced by Charles McKenna, a former PRR and Penn Central operating official. Other "Shoemaker's boys" either resigned or were dismissed. "When Guilford started, it had some fine people," Jervis told the director of the rail division for the New York Department of Transportation, "but they have all left or been fired. Tim [Mellon], who knows nothing about the business, has delegated authority to those who think they know but actually don't."[16]

Still, Jervis remained on the board, having good reasons for not resigning. Most of all, he felt a strong sense of responsibility to the D&H and hoped that he might provide counsel that would help to stabilize the company and bring back to life the fragile rail network in New England. As in the past, Jervis wanted to protect employees from acts of corporate mischief.

Then in 1983 Jervis resigned. He could not take the destructive actions committed by the Guilford organization. Once Mellon and his associates became involved, Jervis could not prevent or control their decisions. As he told Bill Collins, who had left the D&H in fall 1982, "Bill, we were simply snookered." Dr. King also quit, for he "absolutely hated the Guilford people." Business matters had occasionally upset Jervis, but he became truly angry with the Guilford affair. Yet as a friend observed, Jervis refrained from attacking Mellon personally or any other individual in his organization, saying that "he was frustrated with Guilford." Frustrated he was.[17]

Under Guilford control, the D&H languished and then perished. Management seemingly cared little about customer service, which was so important to Shoemaker and Jervis. There had appeared the possibility of increasing business by at least 45,000 cars annually through the MC–B&M/D&H alliance. That did not happen; rather, traffic over D&H dropped dramatically, amounting to less than 40,000 cars annually. Guilford representatives annoyed International Paper and its traffic manager so much that the paper giant went almost totally to truck transport, even at a substantial cost to itself. "One of D&H's biggest shippers," explained Jervis in 1985, "has practically abandoned the railroad because they can't find anyone to speak with about service and rates." Finally, on June 20, 1988, the D&H slipped into bankruptcy. Due to insufficient cash reserves, the road ceased operations, and soon the ICC appointed the New York, Susquehanna & Western Railway as interim operator. A year later, court-appointed trustees sought bidders for the D&H, and several parties, including Guilford itself, showed interest. In January 1990, Canadian Pacific Ltd. won with a $25 million offer, and on June 10, 1990, this rail behemoth, through its subsidiary CP Rail, took possession of the D&H.[18]

About the time Jervis left the D&H board, Mortimer B. Fuller III, who headed the Genesee & Wyoming Railroad, asked him to join the G&W board. In the mid-1980s, Fuller and his associates were in the process of operating much more than the company's first line, a 14-mile tap road that hauled rock salt from a mine in western New York to interchange connections with several Class 1 carriers. With rate reforms that came with the Staggers Act, excess trackage created by mega-mergers, and the desire to end dependence on a single commodity, the G&W considered other rail investments. Jervis was interested, but he told Fuller, "I'm too old to be a board member." Even though Jervis was in his late seventies, he still became involved with the G&W. "He liked what we were doing," said Mark Hastings, a G&W executive. And Fuller explained the role that Jervis assumed: "Jervis was a shadow director," meaning that he attended the regular quarterly board meetings and the annual strategic planning session, but he lacked a vote. Yet G&W paid him the same as a duly elected director. Even though Jervis accepted this compensation, he never filed an expense report.

Fuller, who was careful about hiring consultants and recruiting board members, initially had come in contact with Jervis in late 1982 or early 1983. At that time Jervis served as special counsel for Grand Trunk Corporation (GTC), which controlled GTW, Central of Vermont (CV), and the Duluth, Winnipeg & Pacific, and he analyzed bids for the disposal of the CV, properties all in the CN domain. Fuller was interested in the CV, but ultimately the CN board in Montreal decided not to sell. During this time Fuller learned that he and Jervis had much in common. A native of Scranton, Pennsylvania, Fuller knew friends of Jervis, including a classmate from Cornell University. And as a student at Princeton, Fuller had studied the career of Mark Twain. Most of all, Jervis impressed Fuller and others at G&W with his understanding of the complexities of the industry. "Jervis simply possessed a vast array of very useful knowledge."

This railroader with knowledge and connections offered Fuller and G&W considerable advice. This included details about two former B&O pieces of trackage that became profitable G&W units, the Buffalo & Pittsburgh and the Rochester & Southern railroads. Jervis also provided comments about how to deal effectively with Class 1s, pointing out perceptively that "they were really customers as well." He remained involved with the G&W until the end of his professional career in the mid-1990s, when he had passed the age of 90. Jervis found the G&W to be a creative and money-making concern that operated various shortlines and switching roads, and before his death the company grew even more impressively. He knew that shortline groups like G&W could shrewdly pick up castoff properties from the Class 1s and, through innovative and aggressive attention to customer needs, produce handsome profits.[19]

In addition to serving as either an active or "shadow" board member in his post–Penn Central career, Jervis also took on individual consulting jobs. One involved work for the GTC, and the contact was made through Basil Cole, former vice president for legal administration at Penn Central who earlier had worked for GTC. William McKnight, a Grand Trunk executive, was highly impressed with Jervis's skills in the matter of the Central of Vermont review, although he was surprised that "Langdon did his own clerical work" and used "a really old typewriter."[20]

In a memorandum dated May 20, 1983, to GTC president John H. Burdakin, Jervis offered a sophisticated analysis of what needed to be done with the CV, succinctly listing and explaining several options. He warned Burdakin, "Unless GT or CN is willing to make good on these growing cash deficits, bankruptcy is inevitable, and in the case of CV, bankruptcy spells liquidation under direction of the bankruptcy court. Deregulation in the

U.S. and the emergence of Guilford would speed the process." Jervis recognized the need to slash operating expenses and to provide greater service satisfaction to customers, believing that an independent operator could meet these requirements.[21]

What troubled Jervis about his work on the CV was that he had made contacts with possible purchasers and appeared to have an interested party that would "pay more than I thought the property was worth." But then CN backed out. The CN chairman "changed his mind. He decided that the Canadian National ought to keep the Central of Vermont because he loved to come down to Vermont and realized that he had a railroad. He had no reason at all. He was a politician. Except for the operating people, the directors were politicians." Jervis found that annoying.[22]

What Jervis recommended in the case of the CV ultimately transpired. In the process that led to the privatization of CN in late 1995, several routes were placed on the auction block, including CV. RailTex, a leader in making unprofitable lines shed by Class 1 carriers into viable properties, took control of CV on February 3, 1995, and renamed the operation the New England Central Railroad. Five years later, RailTex became part of RailAmerica, Inc., an even larger operator of regional, shortline, and terminal railroads.[23]

This indefatigable railroader took on other assignments, and his employers included the Illinois Central, Monongahela, and Soo Line. His connections within the industry, including Paul Reistrup, made these jobs possible. Jervis noted that as a consultant he focused on matters of "possible sales or acquisitions, or unification." But he also reviewed traffic matters; in the case of the Monongahela, this included how best to move coal. As with other activities, he worked hard, charged modest rates, and did solid work. Although specific employers might not follow his advice, they seriously considered his reports.[24]

Industry Observer

For decades, Jervis had been expressing his thoughts on the railroad industry in professional journals, trade publications, newspapers, and speeches. In his twilight years, though, he shared his opinions in letters to friends, politicians, government officials, and industry leaders, in "op-ed" pieces for newspapers and magazines, and interviews with journalists. "Reporters from the *New York Times* called Jerv frequently for information and help," remembered his wife, Irene. "Sometimes Jerv was published under his name, and other times he simply helped the reporter with the correct information."[25]

The fallout of Penn Central captured Jervis's attention. Indeed, he expended considerable energy writing about Conrail, both in the immediate post–Penn Central period and later in the mid-1980s when the government moved to privatize the railroad. Jervis had been involved in the birth of Conrail, and he kept abreast of happenings.

Jervis became alarmed about the failure of Conrail management to turn around the property. Not only was the balance sheet frightening, but so too was poor customer performance. In July 1978 he told *Washington Star* reporter Stephen Aug that the percentage of freight cars that arrived at their destination within a day of their scheduled time had plunged from 76.5 percent at the time of the Conrail takeover to only 56 percent in the preceding March. Although Jervis was reluctant to scold management publicly, he suggested that "it may be that the local division superintendents aren't given enough authority, or the general managers." Something had to be done. Jervis wanted a thorough examination of Conrail's five-year economic outlook, intimating that such a study would show that Conrail's "earning power for the operation as it's presently being conducted is not likely to be obtained." Conrail, he believed, still operated too much trackage and had to respond to the steady erosion of business in its service territory. Both matters would be difficult to manage. A drastic retrenchment, reducing the railroad's size to 7,000 or 8,000 miles, would be "politically unacceptable," and federally subsidized truck competition and restrictive railroad rate regulation would be hard to change.[26]

Jervis continued to express doubts about Conrail. In a lengthy piece that appeared a year later in the *Wall Street Journal,* he noted that the company's operating figures remained alarming. "In almost every instance they are worse than those of the bankrupts it's inherited, and the trends are in the wrong direction." Service, too, remained unacceptable. "Conrail has provided poor service, and its customers have turned to competing rail carriers as well as other modes." Jervis suggested strong medicine. He did not believe that government planners or consulting firms could remedy the situation; instead, he felt that "more astute management could probably correct many of the service deficiencies but that in itself would not result in the kind of earning power so badly needed." Jervis argued for "total and complete deregulation." The only requirements after deregulation would be "first, a continuing obligation to keep the public informed as to services offered together with prices; second, a commitment to provide unprofitable rail service if an acceptable subsidy is offered; and third, adequate labor protection." Unless something happened soon, nationalization seemed inescapable. As he had noted somewhat earlier, perhaps a Canadian National Railways model might work for the hard-pressed Conrail and other struggling railroads in the region. Fortunately, the promise of a better regulatory atmosphere could permit private enterprise to make Conrail a success.[27]

In personal correspondence Jervis reiterated his opinions, albeit at times somewhat more sharply stated than in his public pronouncements. He remained guardedly optimistic about the future of Conrail. Jervis thought that better management could energize the property. He was pleased when on January 1, 1981, Edward Jordan, a onetime insurance executive from California, left the presidency for a teaching post at Cornell. His successor, L. Stanley Crane Jr., a former chief executive at the Southern, loved railroads and was a capable leader. "Stan Crane following the miserable management of Jordan (with employee morale at the very bottom) will produce results that give a glimmer of hope for the future," he wrote to Chessie CEO Hays Watkins. Jervis believed, and rightly, that Jordan, while a "sharp cookie" and a "very fine gentleman," paid too much attention to outside consultants rather than operating, marketing, and other company personnel, and lacked the ability to make tough decisions.[28]

And it would be Jervis who played a role in getting Crane for Conrail. As he later related, "The Conrail performance got worse and worse and worse. I got hold of the creditors at one point and told them that they had to change the top management. They had to get a railroad man in there as president. And they agreed without question and who should we get? Well, I said, Stan Crane is one of them that you've got to think about and the other one is Graham Claytor." Added Jervis, "I don't think Graham Claytor is available, but you can probably get Stan Crane. He's about ready to retire from the Southern, and they got him." In his traditional modesty, he noted, "I can't say that I was the only one to recommend him. I think he'd been thought of by others, too."

The new Crane administration made a difference. Within a few years it would be a combination of deregulation and Crane's keen insights, careful negotiations, and painful contractions of jobs and enhanced service that pushed Conrail into the black, an event that surprised many, but not Jervis. Everyone involved with Conrail was pleased when in June 1983 the U.S. Railway Association issued a report to Congress that indicated it was a "profitable carrier." The standing joke that Conrail really should be named "Conjob" no longer made much sense.[29]

Conrail remained on Jervis's mind. Although the railroad had turned the corner financially, he was concerned with the lack of competition in sections of the East and Northeast. "The hundreds of shippers and receivers who today have no choice if railroad service is to be used should have an escape from Conrail." Furthermore, "competition might help Conrail by forcing it to improve its service." In several outlets, including *Traffic World,* Jervis suggested that portions of some of the bankrupts be severed from Conrail to create parallel routes. Some melding together of parts of the former Erie Lackawanna, Jersey Central, Lehigh Valley, and Reading might offer a viable alternative for some rail users. The earlier "Alphabet Route," which comprised several regional carriers (Nickel Plate, Pittsburgh & West Virginia, Western Maryland, Reading, and Jersey Central), had competed effectively with single-line service over the B&O and PRR.[30]

Jervis became even more interested in the Conrail saga when in 1983 the business-minded Ronald Reagan administration announced its intention to dispose of the government's 85 percent stock interest and to allow the private sector to take ownership. Soon the issues became who would buy Conrail and whether the property would remain in one piece or be sold piecemeal. Would labor take over? Would another railroad, most probably Chessie, Norfolk Southern, or Santa Fe, make an acceptable offer? Would some outside financial group seek control? Or would there be a public stock offering? Transportation Secretary Elizabeth Dole chose Norfolk Southern over the other 15 entities that submitted bids, feeling that its financial package was the best and that with its "deep pockets" it could afford to operate the property effectively.[31]

While the Dole decision delighted Norfolk Southern and its supporters, the announcement angered Stanley Crane. Since Conrail had been radically transformed into an efficient, money-making carrier, he believed that Conrail should remain independent. Moreover, Crane did not think that Norfolk Southern would operated Conrail properly, and therefore he wanted Conrail to continue as a stand-alone property. Crane felt that a single Conrail would avoid anticompetitive problems, protect railroad jobs, and maximize the financial return to the federal government.[32]

During this high-profile controversy Jervis openly sided with Crane. In a op-ed piece that appeared in the June 10, 1985, issue of the *Baltimore Sun,* he summed up his feelings. "Clearly, an operation so well established and so eminently satisfactory should be allowed—indeed, encouraged—to continue, as would result from a public sale of its stock." Jervis drove home the point that the federal treasury had a better chance of benefiting if Norfolk Southern did not become the owner. "The government is likely to receive more than the $1.2 billion offered by NS. According to the investment house of Morgan Stanley, the public sale transaction has a value to the government of approximately $1.8 billion, including $1.2 billion in cash and an incremental $600 million in tax revenues. In addition, the proposal would permit the government to share in any appreciation of the price of Conrail's stock through the issuance of purchase warrants for 1 million shares of Conrail common stock." And in a letter to the *New York Times* published on June 17, he reminded readers that "with the express concurrence of the Southern Railway, Norfolk & Western excluded the Delaware & Hudson from the Norfolk Southern merger because it was an 'intolerable burden' with 'no hope.' In its relations with its one-time family members, the Erie [Lackawanna] and Delaware & Hudson, the Norfolk & Western's principal role was limited to taking large tax credits amounting to millions of dollars." And he asked, "What reason is there to believe that if Conrail falters in the years ahead, its treatment by Norfolk Southern would be any different from the brush-off the Erie and the Delaware & Hudson got?" To Jervis, then, the answer was a "no-brainer."

Even though Jervis was not as influential politically as he had been when he headed the B&O, Rock Island, and Penn Central, he did what he could to work behind the scenes to prevent Norfolk Southern from acquiring Conrail. In one instance, Jervis lobbied to prevent Mario Cuomo, the new Democratic governor of New York, from publicly favoring Norfolk Southern, a position that the state transportation department had urged. He told the governor numerous reasons why the offer should be rejected, including antitrust violations and a grossly inadequate price. Instead, the governor should back an independent Conrail because such a position would benefit New York: "Why destroy, certainly demoralize, a service that is serving the state with great efficiency and understanding and promising to do better?" Admittedly this was a small deed, but it was something that Jervis, as always, felt obligated to do in order to foster a better railroad industry.[33]

Jervis's collective actions for the stand-alone Conrail cause gratified many, including Crane. "You have been such an enormous help to us throughout our battle to go public," Crane wrote Jervis in April 1987, "that I cannot begin to thank you." This letter and others like it surely pleased Jervis.[34]

Although Jervis never claimed clairvoyant powers, his analysis of the Conrail sale turned out to be correct. The privatization went well, and the railroad became eminently successful under Crane and his successors. On March 26, 1987, a public stock offering of 58,750,00 shares sold for $28 per share, and a decade later it would cash out at $115 per share when CSX and Norfolk Southern jointly bought the property. CSX took most of the principal lines of the original New York Central, and Norfolk Southern acquired key segments of the former PRR. Arguably the more than $10-billion cost meant that both railroads vastly overpaid for Conrail.[35]

Jervis also took satisfaction in other contemporary happenings. For one thing, the fate of the Rock Island delighted him. "The Rock Island's liquidation was successful—completely so. Every creditor was made whole, including every bond holder. Every stockholder was wholly reimbursed. And what is critically important, in the public interest, every segment of Rock Island's plant, its many rights of way, terminals both large and small, were sold for appropriate consideration. Freight service throughout Rock Island's territory was comparable to what it had been in the past, or better."[36]

Perhaps nothing gratified Jervis more than the new direction of the railroad industry. In a draft of a 1987 essay for "*Trains* Turntable" that he called "An Old Railroader Tries to Look Back," he applauded the Staggers Act. Relating the measure to Penn Central, Jervis argued that "if Staggers had come 10 years earlier, the PC bankruptcy could have been averted—not by the management then in place but by a fresh new management such as rescued Conrail in 1981." But, understandably, he made clear that the quest for a stronger railroad sector had not been easy. "Industry support for Staggers had come slowly and at the last minute. In fact, for many earlier years, many railroads had embraced full regulation—as affording protection against their rail competitors." As he related, "Back in the [late] 1950s, Bill Brosnan, Ben Heineman, and the writer, representing the three major rate jurisdictions in the country, testified before Congressional Committees in support of a competitive rate rule that would give railroads greater latitude in meeting truck and barge competition." He remembered well that there was major industry unhappiness with this way of thinking. "Dissenting railroads including the PRR recoiled and told their friends in Congress that greater freedom to compete with trucks and barges would make it easier for railroads to compete among themselves. The PRR, in short, resisted any impairment of its right to complain to the ICC about lower coal rates proposed by the B&O." Jervis wanted competition, whether intra- or intermodal, and Staggers, creative consumer-oriented management, and cooperative labor would surely bring about a meaningful railroad rebirth.[37]

By the mid-1990s, events in what unmistakably had become a revitalized industry further pleased Jervis and convinced him that he had been "mostly on the right track for decades." In an unpublished letter to the *New York Times,* he reviewed the recent past. "In the early 1980s, the federal government saw the light, and partial *deregulation* of the railroads came into being. Conrail came to life under a new *railroad* management that—with the indispensable help of deregulation—was free to develop its best competitive capabilities and do so at a profit under private control." Jervis added: "The American freight train system today is becoming competitive again, and it is leaner, tougher, and better managed."[38]

The Quiet Years

Jervis gradually left railroading. In an autobiographical sketch composed late in his life, he noted that he served as special counsel to Mortimer Fuller and his Genesee & Wyoming holding company: "This assignment continued in 1996 on a reduced basis." His work for Fuller's profitable assortment of railroads had remained his only professional activity; Jervis was 91. Throughout his later years he continued to read about the industry, talk to former associates, including his beloved "boys" from the B&O, maintain an active correspondence, and produce an occasional piece for publication. In a May 1995 letter to the editor of the *Journal of Commerce*, he repeated his longtime argument that, even in the era of deregulation, freight rates, in this case those made by Conrail, had to be carefully considered. "I would . . . hope that in addition to studying where rates could be increased to help cover its cost of capital, Conrail will give equal attention to increases where rates should be reduced to serve the same purpose."[39]

But railroad-related matters did not consume all of Jervis's attention. He continued to take great interest in the governance and operation of Park Church in Elmira. As with other commitments, he faithfully attended church meetings, a dedication that occasionally surprised the minister and staff. And he kept on being a avid reader, especially of biographies and English history. As in the past, Jervis also remained a doting husband and father.

Physically, Jervis was changing; he could not stop the aging process. In 1976 Jervis received a serious health scare. Twice he had cancerous growths removed from his bladder at Johns Hopkins. In 1998 the physician in charge told him that he would not die from bladder cancer, and there was jubilation in the Langdon household.

Concerned about his health, Jervis and Irene made a major decision about Quarry Farm "that was really tough for him." The farm had been their primary residence since 1976 when he left Penn Central, but in 1982 they returned to Gibson Island, partly to be near Johns Hopkins while Jervis underwent cancer treatments. They decided that the best way to manage the site was to seek its permanent protection. With outside legal and preservation guidance, they signed an instrument of gift that gave Elmira College the main house, the maid's cottage, the barn, and seven acres of adjoining land that included the site of Mark Twain's writing study. This was a logical choice; after all, shortly before his death in 1952, the senior Langdon had given the college the small wooden study used frequently by Mark Twain.

Although Jervis never considered himself a gentleman farmer, he attended to supervisory tasks at Quarry Farm. Usually a coat and always a tie were part of his attire. (Irene Langdon)

The family wanted to curb the occasional acts of vandalism and liked the idea of a protected public display for this important structure. So 30 years after the initial gift to Elmira College, the core of Quarry Farm was officially transferred. President Leonard Grant agreed that the Langdon homestead would be used solely as a peaceful retreat where Twain scholars could read, write, and reflect. Such a policy also fit nicely with Elmira faculty members who shared a professional interest in Twain. Unfortunately, the college veered from its contractual promises, causing Jervis to fret about the place's fate. Said Irene, "Quarry Farm became the worm in the apple."[40]

Nevertheless, Jervis's specific vision for the Center for Mark Twain Studies turned out to be successful. Scores of Twain scholars from throughout the world, including foremost authorities, have spent time at Quarry Farm and often presented their scholarship in local public lectures and in a rich variety of publications. And the Center has hosted five quadrennial international conferences on The State of Mark Twain Studies. Without doubt, this Center has added substantially to the reputation of Elmira College as a liberal arts school.[41]

Irene Langdon photographed her husband, who was then in his late eighties, a few months before he flew his beloved Aztec for the last time. (Irene Langdon)

Less troubling to Jervis than the fate of Quarry Farm, but nevertheless a hard decision to make, involved his choice in the late 1980s to stop flying and to sell his beloved Aztec. He adored the wild blue yonder, but admitted to friends that "my reflexes are not as good as they once were." He indicated to an acquaintance that he might buy a smaller, single-engine airplane that "would be easier for me to fly." But he never did.[42]

Still Jervis continued to drive, and cataract surgery helped to make that possible. As in the past he never cared about owning new, luxury automobiles. A car for him was a means of transportation and not a status symbol. Toward the end of his life driving usually meant a daily trip to the post office in his 1986 Pontiac from the couple's comfortable home on West Hill Road A outside Elmira. (In 1989 Jervis and Irene had returned to Elmira, first to a

It's Christmas 1999, and Jervis enjoys a book, *Flying the Hump,* which recounts aspects of his own experiences in Southeast Asia during World War II.
(Irene Langdon)

house on Hillcrest Road and later to their last residence, "where there are no steps—except one!") Then, in 2001, at 96, Jervis surrendered his driver's license, largely at the insistence of his son Halsey, who rightly worried about matters of safety.[43]

As Jervis approached the end to his long, productive life, fellow railroaders continued publicly to recognize his numerous accomplishments. As early as 1971, *Railway Age,* the industry's premier trade journal, had named him "Railroader of the Year," an award that had dated from only 1964. More recognition followed. In 1990 the Cooperstown Conference, sponsored by the Eastern General Managers' Association, inducted Jervis into its Hall of Fame, with a plaque being displayed at the Baltimore & Ohio Railroad Museum in Baltimore. The formal citation read in part: "Jervis Langdon Jr. was a voice for America's railroad industry in the halls of Congress and elsewhere. For nearly half a century, he spoke in support of legislation designed to improve the competitive position of the nation's railroads." Somewhat later a group of B&O retirees, Retired Administrators of the B&O Railroad, Its Affiliates and Successors (RABO), led by Ray Lichty, one of "Jerv's boys," made him the honorary president of the organization. This thrilled Jervis, for "I always have considered myself to be a B&O man."[44]

It was common for business associates to visit him and Irene, especially after the couple had moved permanently to Elmira from Gibson Island in 1989. Jervis remained interested in their activities, and he took pleasure in discussing matters that involved the industry. "I try to keep current." Not long before Jervis died, Bill Collins brought to the Langdon house a large set of railroad maps, and Jervis got down on his hands and knees to ask about specific line sales and abandonments. "He was genuinely excited to review these maps."[45]

But age took its toll. As Irene put it, "A general decline occurred." During the last three years of his life, Jervis used a cane and then a walker, and his once razor-sharp memory faded. About six months before his death, he contracted pneumonia, although he recovered. Not long after his last birthday, Jervis began to sink due to congestive heart failure. For the final three days of his life, Jervis and his family benefited from the services of hospice. On Monday, February 16, 2004, Jervis Langdon Jr. died quietly in his sleep surrounded by Irene, three sons, and other family members. "He just wore out." Now this visionary railroader belonged to history.[46]

NOTES

1. The Making of a Railroader

1. *Baltimore Sun,* February 17, 2004; interview with E. Ray Lichty, Baltimore, October 22, 2005.

2. "A Service of Celebration for the Life of Jervis Langdon Jr., April 3, 2004," The Park Church—Elmira, N.Y., video in possession of E. Ray Lichty, Hunt Valley, Md., hereafter cited as Langdon video; Carl Hayden, "Jervis Langdon Jr.: A Life (1905–2004)," Langdon papers, in possession of Irene Langdon, Elmira, N.Y.; interview with Irene Langdon, Elmira, N.Y., September 16, 2006; *Elmira Weekly Advertiser,* April 17, 1869; Eva Taylor, *A History of the Park Church, 1846–1981* (Elmira, N.Y.: Park Church, 1981), 3–24.

Thomas Kennicut Beecher was pastor of Park Church from 1854 to 1900. He was the son of Lyman Beecher, eminent preacher and reformer, and the nephew of Henry Ward Beecher, Catharine Beecher, and Harriet Beecher Stowe.

3. Robert D. Jerome and Herbert A. Wisbey Jr., eds., *Mark Twain in Elmira* (Elmira, N.Y.: Mark Twain Society, 1977), 236–37; Resa Willis, *Mark and Livy: The Love Story of Mark Twain and the Woman Who Almost Tamed Him* (New York: Atheneum, 1992), 14; Jervis Langdon Jr., "Jervis Langdon, Mark Twain's Father-in-Law," Langdon papers; Joseph B. McCullough and Janice McIntire-Strasburg, eds., *Mark Twain at the Buffalo Express* (DeKalb: Northern Illinois University Press, 1999), xix; *Elmira Weekly Advertiser,* August 9, 1870, clipping in Langdon papers.

4. Langdon, "Jervis Langdon, Mark Twain's Father-in-Law"; Peter Eisenstadt, ed., *The Encyclopedia of New York State* (Syracuse: Syracuse University Press, 2005), 499; Ida Langdon, "Elmira's Langdon Family," *Chemung County Historical Journal* 4 (December 1958): 51; H. Roger Grant, *Erie Lackawanna: Death of an American Railroad, 1938–1992* (Stanford, Calif.: Stanford University Press, 1994), 1–2; Robert F. Archer, *Lehigh Valley Railroad: "The Route of the Black Diamond"* (Burbank: Howell-North Books, 1977), 135.

5. Eisenstadt, *The Encyclopedia of New York State,* 499; *New York Times,* December 23, 1871; Willis, *Mark and Livy,* 18.

6. Langdon, "Jervis Langdon, Mark Twain's Father-in-Law"; Susan L. Crane to W. H. Siebert, September 14, 1896, Langdon papers.

7. Langdon, "Jervis Langdon, Mark Twain's Father-in-Law"; McCullough and McIntire-Strasburg, *Mark Twain at the Buffalo Express,* 286; *New York Times,* December 23, 1871.

8. Jerome and Wisbey, *Mark Twain in Elmira,* 236–37; Langdon, "Elmira's Langdon Family," 52; Ron Powers, *Mark Twain: A Life* (New York: Free Press, 2005), 242.

9. Langdon, "Elmira's Langdon Family," 52; Jervis Langdon Jr., "Charles Jervis Langdon (1849–1916)," Langdon papers, *Telegram* (Elmira, N.Y.), November 19, 1916.

10. Jerome and Wisbey, *Mark Twain in Elmira,* 36–43; Irene Langdon to author, October 8, 2006; Irene Langdon interview, September 16, 2006; *New York Times,* December 17, 1952; Jonathan Kendell, "Steeped in History," *Smithsonian* 37 (September 2006): 98; "The Elmira Years: A Mark Twain Anthology," *Chemung Historical Journal* (October 1987).

11. Langdon, "Charles Jervis Langdon (1849–1916)"; *Telegram,* November 19, 1916.

12. Langdon, "Charles Jervis Langdon (1849–1916)"; Edward Hungerford, *Men of Iron: The History of New York Central* (New York: Thomas Y. Crowell, 1938), 352–56.

13. Langdon, "Charles Jervis Langdon (1849–1916)"; "Charles Jervis Langdon," *National Cyclopedia of American Biography* (New York: James T. White, 1937), 31; *Telegram,* November 19, 1916.

14. *Elmira Star-Gazette,* November 20, 1916; *New York Times,* December 3, 1916.

15. Jerome and Wisbey, *Mark Twain in Elmira,* 236–37; interviews with Irene Langdon, Elmira, N.Y., August 5, 2005, and September 16, 2006; *New York Times,* October 10, 1964.

16. Jervis Langdon Jr., "Jervis Langdon (1875–1952)"; *Elmira Star-Gazette,* December 17, 1952; Morris Bishop, *A History of Cornell* (Ithaca, N.Y.: Cornell University Press, 1962), 378; *New York Times,* December 17, 1952.

Shortly after the death of the senior Langdon, Elmira journalist Frank Tripp reviewed his character. "Demagogs, self-seekers, bigots and isms have waved their arms, frothed their mouths and spent their words in futile effort to rock Jervis

Langdon off the pedestal of reason upon which he always stood. . . . Many a time his calm logic, mild words and determination for right and decency have swayed the very men who sought to wear him down."

17. Jervis Langdon diary, Langdon papers.

18. Langdon, "Jervis Langdon (1875–1952)"; *Elmira Daily Advertiser,* February 21, 1883; Irene Langdon interview, August 5, 2005; Irene Langdon to author, February 6, 2006.

19. Jervis Langdon diary; Irene Langdon to author, February 6, 2006.

20. Irene Langdon interviews, August 5, 2005, and September 16, 2006; Langdon, "Jervis Langdon (1875–1952)."

21. Langdon, "Elmira's Langdon Family," 56.

22. Irene Langdon interview, August 5, 2005; *Elmira Star-Gazette,* February 17, 2004.

23. Irene Langdon interviews, August 5, 2005, and September 16, 2006; Irene Langdon to author, February 15, 2006; Jervis Langdon Jr., "Jervis Langdon Jr. (1905–)."

24. Irene Langdon interview, August 5, 2005; *Elmira Star-Gazette,* March 10, 1970; *Who Was Who in America* (Chicago: A. N. Marquis, 1943), 744; Jervis Langdon Jr., "Surprise Visitor from Home," *Chemung Historical Journal* 38 (December 1992): 4197.

25. *Elmira Star-Gazette,* January 17, 1958; Irene Langdon to author, February 15 and March 15, 2006.

26. *Who's Who in Railroading* (New York: Simmons-Boardman, 1930), 313; *Elmira Star-Gazette,* July 12, 1937.

Since Edward Loomis objected to being called "Ed," Jervis referred to him as "Uncle Edward." Irene Langdon to author, February 19, 2007.

27. Irene Langdon interviews, August 5, 2005, and September 16, 2006; Irene Langdon to author, February 15, 2006.

28. William James Cunningham, *The Present Railroad Crisis* (Philadelphia: University of Pennsylvania Press, 1939).

Jervis kept the Cunningham publication in his personal library, even after he had disposed of most of his railroad-related holdings.

29. Irene Langdon interview, August 5, 2005; Jervis Langdon diary, Langdon papers.

30. Irene Langdon interview, August 5, 2005.

31. Irene Langdon to author, February 15 and March 1, 2006, Jervis Langdon diary, Langdon papers.

32. Irene Langdon interview, August 5, 2005; Jervis Langdon Jr., "The Class of 1927," *1927 Cornellian* (Ithaca, N.Y.: Cornell University, 1927), 147.

33. Cornell University official transcript, Jervis Langdon Jr.; Irene Langdon to author, February 15, 2006; Jervis Langdon Jr., "Jervis Langdon Jr. (1905–)"; Wallace Notestein to Allan Nevins, April 22, 1927, Langdon papers.

In his essay for the *1927 Cornellian,* Jervis wrote, "We had selected our college because, not being mathematically, nor agriculturally, nor architecturally inclined, there seemed to be no other place to go. We accepted our fate in good spirits, and announced that we were going to be cultured gentlemen instead of trained specialists."

34. Irene Langdon to author, February 15 and March 1, 2006; Anthony Kenny, ed., *The History of the Rhodes Trust, 1902–1999* (Oxford: Oxford University Press, 2001), 100–101, 103–104, 107, 132–33; Jervis Langdon diary.

35. Kenny, *The History of the Rhodes Trust*, 24.

36. Irene Langdon interviews, August 5, 2005, and September 16, 2006; Irene Langdon to author, September 22, 2006; *1927 Cornellian*, 200–201, 327, 414; *New York Times*, January 9, 1931; Jervis Langdon Jr., "Jervis Langdon Jr. (1905–)."

37. Jervis Langdon, "Reunion Address, 1992," Langdon papers; *Elmira Star-Gazette*, February 20, 2004; Irene Langdon interview, August 5, 2005; Bishop, *A History of Cornell*, 490.

38. Langdon, "Reunion Address, 1992"; *Cornell Daily Sun*, February 7, 1927.

39. Langdon, "Reunion Address, 1992"; *Cornell Daily Sun*, September 23 and December 17, 1926.

40. *Cornell Daily Sun*, October 2, 1926; Bishop, *A History of Cornell*, 485.

41. Langdon, "Reunion Address, 1992"; *Cornell Daily Sun*, April 3, 1926.

42. Langdon, "Reunion Address, 1992."

Although Jervis was probably correct about the *Sun's* commentary about world affairs, editorials that he wrote about the Statute of Westminster that designated the Crown as the "symbol of the free association of the members of the British Commonwealth of Nations" eventually may have had an impact on the post–World War II Constitution of Japan, specifically "The Emperor shall be the symbol of the State and of the unity of the people with whom resides sovereign power." In a letter to Jervis, dated July 26, 1989, from University of Maryland political scientist Theodore McNelly, there is a discussion about the influence that Jervis's commentaries in the *Sun* had on his colleague at the newspaper, Charles Kades, who after World War II chaired the steering committee that revised the Japanese Constitution of 1889. "While Kades at first seemed doubtful that he had been influenced by the example of the Statute of Westminster, it was clear that he had been greatly impressed by your writing on the topic," wrote McNelly. "I suggest that perhaps he had been 'subliminally influenced' by the Statute of Westminster and that even if the Statute had not inspired the origination of the 'symbol' in the Japanese Constitution, the example of the Statute of Westminster may have predisposed him to accept the idea." Added McNelly, "Several weeks ago when I was in Japan, a Japanese professor showed me a letter from Kades in which Kades refers to the notion that he may have been subliminally influenced by Westminster. It seems quite possible that the language of your articles as well as the text of the Statute of Westminster itself may have had at least some influence on the wording of the Japanese Constitution."

43. Quote from the *1927 Cornellian*, 151

44. *Cornell Daily Sun*, December 6, 1926.

45. Langdon, "Reunion Address, 1992."

46. *Cornell Daily Sun,* December 12, 1926.

47. Ronald Steel, *Walter Lippmann and the American Century* (Boston: Little, Brown, 1980), 174–77; Jervis Langdon diary.

48. Jervis Langdon diary; Robert E. Cushman to "Mr. Langdon," June 6, 1927, Langdon papers.

49. Notestein to Nevins; Irene Langdon interview, August 5, 2005; Langdon video.

50. Jervis Langdon diary; *Railway Age* 110 (March 29, 1941): 596; Archer, *Lehigh Valley Railroad,* 141, 154, 157, 194, 197, 204–205, 207.

51. David Vrooman, "An Interview with Jervis Langdon," September 13–14, 1996, Railroad Executive Oral History Program #1, John W. Barriger III National Railroad Library, St. Louis, hereafter cited as Vrooman-Langdon interview; Stuart Leuthner, *The Railroaders* (New York: Random House, 1983), 126.

52. Vrooman-Langdon interview; "Six Reasons Why I Believe the Railroads' Future Is Bright," *B&O Magazine,* November 1957, 2; *Baltimore Sun,* February 17, 2004; *Kansas City Star,* February 28, 1966; Jervis Langdon Jr., "Jervis Langdon Jr. (1905–)."

53. Kermit L. Hall, *The Magic Mirror: Law in American History* (New York: Oxford University Press, 1989), 218.

54. Vrooman-Langdon interview; Cornell transcript.

55. Irene Langdon interview, August 5, 2005; *Elmira Star-Gazette,* September 21, 1931; *New York Times,* January 9, 1931, February 8, 1953.

56. Irene Langdon interview, August 5, 2005; interview with Theodore Desch, Chicago, October 10, 2006.

2. Railroad Lawyer

1. Interview with Milton G. McInnes, Southbury, Conn., June 5, 1989.

2. Vrooman-Langdon interview.

3. Ransom E. Noble Jr., *New Jersey Progressivism before Wilson* (Princeton, N.J.: Princeton University Press, 1946), 100–120; Harley L. Lutz, *The Taxation of Railroads in New Jersey* (Princeton, N.J.: Princeton University Press, 1940), 43–68; Richard J. Connors, *A Cycle of Power: The Career of Jersey City Mayor Frank Hague* (Metuchen, N.J.: Scarecrow Press, 1971), 87–88, 103, 135; Dayton David McKean, *The Boss: The Hague Machine in Action* (New York: Russell & Russell, 1940), 43–45.

4. Vrooman-Langdon interview; *Railway Age* 93 (October 7, 1933): 510; *Before the New Jersey State Board of Tax Appeals: Brief of Petitioners,* July 15, 1933; *The Central Railroad Company of New Jersey, et al. vs. J. H. Thayer Martin, State Tax Commissioner of the State of New Jersey, et al.,* United States District Court, District of New Jersey, November 1, 1939; George W. Hilton, "What Went Wrong and What to Do about It," *Trains* 27 (January 1967): 38.

5. John Sherman Porter, ed., *Moody's Manual of Investments: Railroad Securities* (New York: Moody's Investors Service, 1935), 1858–1956; Kurt C. Schlichting, *Grand Central Terminal: Railroads, Engineering, and Architecture in New York City* (Baltimore: Johns Hopkins University Press, 2001), 8–29.

6. Vrooman-Langdon interview. See Albro Martin, *Enterprise Denied: Origins of the Decline of America Railroads, 1897–1917* (New York: Columbia University Press, 1971).

7. Jervis Langdon Jr., "Jervis Langdon Jr. (1905–)"; Vrooman-Langdon interview; Stuart Leuthner, *The Railroaders* (New York: Random House, 1983), 126.

8. Vrooman-Langdon interview; *Historical Statistics of the United States, Colonial Times to 1957* (Washington, D.C.: Bureau of the Census, 1960), 429; Leuthner, *The Railroaders,* 126; interview with Charles Smith, Cedar Rapids, Iowa, October 13, 2006; Michael Kudish, *Railroads of the Adirondacks: A History* (Fleischmanns, N.Y.: Purple Mountain Press, 1996), 274.

9. Vrooman-Langdon interview; "I.C.C. Files Suit to Dismiss Spotting Order Injunction," *Railway Age* 101 (September 19, 1936): 425–26.

10. Vrooman-Langdon interview; *New York Times,* June 25, 1961.

11. Ian S. Haberman, *The Van Sweringens of Cleveland: The Biography of an Empire* (Cleveland: Western Reserve Historical Society, 1979), 50–64, 89–104.

12. Porter, ed., *Moody's Manual of Investments,* 1116–46.

13. Herbert H. Harwood Jr., *Invisible Giants: The Empires of Cleveland's Van Sweringen Brothers* (Bloomington: Indiana University Press, 2003), 100–280, 292–96.

14. McInnes interview; *Erie Railroad Magazine* 33 (February 1938): 8.

15. *Railway Age* 104 (January 8, 1938): 133, (January 22, 1938): 197.

16. Minutes of the board of directors, Erie Railroad Company, January 3, 1938, Pennsylvania State Archives, Harrisburg; Jesse H. Jones, *Fifty Billion Dollars: My Thirteen Years with the RFC, 1932–1945* (New York: Macmillan, 1951), 143.

17. *Historical Statistics of the United States,* 435; Joseph Borkin, *Robert R. Young, the Populist of Wall Street* (New York: Harper & Row, 1969), 116–17; H. Craig Miner, *The Rebirth of the Missouri Pacific, 1956–1983* (College Station: Texas A&M University Press, 1983), 6–7.

18. Henry S. Sturgis, *A New Chapter of Erie: The Story of Erie's Reorganization, 1938–1941* (privately printed, 1948), 3–4, 7–9.

19. Author's interview with Jervis Langdon Jr., Akron, April 26, 1990, hereafter cited as JL interview; Leuthner, *The Railroaders,* 127; Haberman, *Van Sweringens,* 31–49.

20. Sturgis, *A New Chapter of Erie,* 15–20.

21. JL interview; Leuthner, *The Railroaders,* 127.

22. *Summary of Erie Railroad Company Reorganization before the Interstate Commerce Commission, Finance Docket No. 11,915* (Cleveland: Erie Railroad Company, 1942); *In the Matter of Erie Railroad Company Reorganization, Finance Docket No.*

11,915, Exception on Behalf of the Chesapeake and Ohio Railway Company to the Proposed Report of the Examiner (Cleveland: Gates Legal, October 2, 1939).

23. JL interview; interview with Charles Shannon, Arlington Heights, Ill., October 1, 1988; "Wm. Wyer & Co. Organized in 1940" (ca. 1954), 1.

24. "Shareholders Share in Proposed Erie Plan," *Railway Age* 107 (November 18, 1939): 317–18; "I.C.C. Hears Erie Oral Argument," *Railway Age* 107 (November 18, 1939): 802–803; "Commission Approves Erie Reorganization Plan," *Railway Age* 108 (April 20, 1940): 712–14; *Wall Street Journal,* November 16, 1939.

25. *Summary of Erie Railroad Company Reorganization;* Sturgis, *A New Chapter of Erie,* 29.

26. Interview with Irene Langdon, Elmira, N.Y., August 5, 2005; Irene Langdon to author, April 30, 2006; Lew Townsend, "Penn Central's Flying Trustee," *AOPA Pilot* (November 1970): 43; Langdon, "Jervis Langdon Jr. (1905–)."

27. Irene Langdon interview.

28. *Railway Age* 110 (March 29, 1941): 596; "B&O Railroad Company News," press release, November 21, 1956, Langdon papers.

29. JL interview; Leuthner, *The Railroaders,* 127.

30. Jervis Langdon Jr., "Over the Hump to China, 1942–1945," *Chemung Historical Journal* 38 (December 1992): 4193; Charles F. Romanus and Riley Sunderland, *Stilwell's Mission to China: The China-Burma-India Theater* (Washington, D.C.: Department of the Army, 1953), 289, 307–308, 348.

31. JL interview; Langdon, "Over the Hump," 4193–94.

32. Langdon, "Over the Hump," 4194–95.

33. Leuthner, *The Railroaders,* 127.

34. Langdon, "Over the Hump," 4194–95.

35. Ibid., 4195–96; Charles F. Romanus and Riley Sunderland, *Time Runs Out in CBT: China-Burma-India Theater* (Washington, D.C.: Department of the Army, 1959), 5–34; *Pittsburgh Press,* May 2, 1963.

36. Langdon, "Jervis Langdon Jr. (1905–)"; Langdon, "Over the Hump," 4196.

37. JL interview; Landon letter to "Dear Mother," October 29, 1945, Langdon papers.

38. Irene Langdon interview; interview with Paul Reistrap, Baltimore, June 24, 2006; Irene Langdon to author, May 17, 2006.

The Langdon divorce received public attention. The *Washington Post* on May 20, 1949, revealed that Jean had filed suit for "maintenance of herself and her three children against Jervis Langdon Jr., whom she described as a lawyer and a man of 'great wealth.'" Her suit also asked the District Court to restrain Jervis from going to Nevada to divorce her and demanded that he be ordered to pay her $1,800 that she claimed to have spent for medical bills while Jervis served in the military. Based on entries in Jervis's father's diary, there is reason to suspect that Jean's obsession with golf and her striving for personal wealth contributed to the marital split.

39. JL interview; Harwood, *Invisible Giants,* 295.

40. Irene Langdon to author, February 19, 2007; *Washington Post,* September 12, 1946; R. E. G. Davis, *Airlines of the United States since 1914* (London: Putnam, 1972), 339.

About the time Jervis joined Capital-PCA, the company officially renamed itself Capital Airlines, dropping the reference to what had been Pennsylvania Central Airlines. In 1961 United Airlines took control of the then faltering air carrier.

41. JL interview; *Railway Age* 122 (February 1, 1947): 294.

42. Irene Langdon to author, May 17, 2006; JL interview; Leuthner, *The Railroaders,* 127.

As late as 1990, Jervis continued to find fault with ongoing railroad practices. "During my 54 years in the industry it was consumed by one deep controversy after another usually bearing directly or indirectly upon joint line operations, such as mergers, divisions of through rates, per diem charges, and other aspects of interline movements," he told Frank Richter, editor of *Progressive Railroading.* "Instead of working together in the interest of efficient joint line operations, connecting lines were at each others' throats for long periods of time. Division cases, for instance, would often last for 10 years or more. Lawyers' fees ran into the millions." Jervis Langdon to Frank Richter, January 8, 1990, Langdon papers.

43. JL interview; *Guideposts Taken from the Statutes and the Decisions of the Courts and Interstate Commerce Commission for Procedure in Division Cases* (n.p., n.d.), 9.

44. See, e.g., James C. Cobb, *The Selling of the South: The Southern Crusade for Industrial Development, 1936–1980* (Baton Rouge: Louisiana State University Press, 1982), and *Industrialization and Southern Society, 1877–1984* (Lexington: University Press of Kentucky, 1984); Bernard L. Weinstein and Robert E. Firestone, *Regional Growth and Decline in the United States: The Rise of the Sunbelt and the Decline of the Northeast* (New York: Praeger, 1978).

45. JL interview; "Fighting Briefs Filed in Division Cases," *Railway Age* 130 (May 7, 1951): 56–57 and (May 14, 1951): 94, 96.

46. JL interview; Jervis Langdon Jr., "Criteria in the Establishment of Freight Rate Divisions," *Cornell Law Quarterly* 39 (Winter 1954): 213–36.

47. News release, Southeastern Presidents' Conference, April 28, 1953, Langdon papers; "Jervis Langdon to Head Southeastern RR Group," *Railway Age* 134 (May 4, 1953): 15; JL interview; interview with Albert W. Clements Jr., Willow Valley, Pa., October 22, 2005.

48. L. M. Abott to Jervis Langdon Jr., April 24, 1956, Jervis Langdon Jr. Collection, Hagley Museum and Library, Wilmington, Del.; Mark Rose, Bruce E. Seely, and Paul F. Barrett, *The Best Transportation System in the World: Railroads, Trucks, Airlines, and American Public Policy in the Twentieth Century* (Columbus: Ohio State University Press, 2006), 97–104.

49. Irene Langdon interview; Irene Langdon to author, February 19, 2007; Sam to Lee, September 27, 1902, Langdon papers.

50. Irene Langdon interview; *New York Times,* November 22, 1956; minutes of directors, B&O RR Co., book 3, January 18, 1956, 137, in possession of CSX Corporation, Jacksonville, Fla.

51. JL interview; *B&O Magazine,* October 1958, 14; *Baltimore Evening Sun,* September 18, 1958.

52. G. H. Pouder, "The Langdon Story," *Baltimore: The Business Magazine of Metropolitan Baltimore,* November 1962, 14; John F. Stover, *History of the Baltimore and Ohio Railroad* (West Lafayette, Ind.: Purdue University Press, 1987), 266–69; JL interview.

53. James D. Dilts, *The Great Road: The Building of the Baltimore & Ohio, the Nation's First Railroad, 1828–1855* (Stanford, Calif.: Stanford University Press, 1993), 49–80, 159–69; Herbert H. Harwood Jr., "History Where You Don't Expect It: Some Surprising Survivors," *Railroad History* 166 (Spring 1992): 114–15, 119.

54. Stover, *History of the Baltimore & Ohio Railroad,* 65–117, 141–62, 180–200, 215–31. See also David M. Vrooman, *Daniel Willard and Progressive Management on the Baltimore & Ohio Railroad* (Columbus: Ohio State University Press, 1991).

55. Interview with Herbert H. Harwood Jr., Harrisburg, Pa., September 29, 2005; interview with William J. Dixon, Sarasota, February 25, 2006.

56. JL interview; *Baltimore Sun,* January 4, 1961, December 3, 1965; *New York Times,* May 31, 1960; B&O 1961 annual report, 6.

57. JL interview; *Baltimore Sun,* December 2 and 3, 1965.

58. JL interview; E. Ray Lichty, "If Only He'd Had Some Money: Jervis Langdon Jr.," *Sentinel* 26 (Second Quarter 2004).

59. JL interview; *Baltimore,* clipping in Langdon papers.

60. Jervis Langdon Jr. to H. E. Simpson, February 12, 1959, Langdon papers.

61. Jervis Langdon Jr., "6 Reasons Why I Believe the Railroads' Future Is Bright," *B&O Magazine,* November 1957, 2; Jervis Langdon Jr., "Now—An Open Door on Rates," *Railway Age* 145 (August 18, 1958): 22–24.

62. Memorandum, Langdon Collection.

3. B&O President

1. Jean Strouse, *Morgan: American Financier* (New York: HarperCollins, 1999), 321–22; William Norris Leonard, *Railroad Consolidation under the Transportation Act of 1920* (New York: Columbia University Press, 1946), 301, 316–18; Richard L. Saunders Jr., *Merging Lines: American Railroads, 1900–1970* (DeKalb: Northern Illinois University Press, 2001), 47–99; Herbert H. Harwood Jr., *Invisible Giants: The Empires of Cleveland's Van Sweringen Brothers* (Bloomington: Indiana University Press, 2003), 27–85; *The Railroad Merger Problem,* pamphlet (Washington, D.C.: Government Printing Office, 1963), 13.

2. Interview with Gregory W. Maxwell, Moreland Hills, Ohio, February 19, 1988; Richard Saunders Jr., *The Railroad Mergers and the Coming of Conrail* (Westport, Conn.: Greenwood Press, 1978), 87.

3. Maury Klein, *History of the Louisville & Nashville Railroad* (New York: Macmillan, 1972), 485–86; Saunders, *Merging Lines,* 138–41.

4. "Railroads Clearing Tracks for a Comeback—an Industry Appraisal," *Francis I. du Pont & Co. Investornews,* February 1960, 9; Saunders, *Merging Lines,* 143; David Vrooman, "An Interview with Jervis Langdon," September 13–14, 1996, Railroad Executive Oral History Program #1, John W. Barriger III National Railroad Library, St. Louis.

5. Saunders, *Merging Lines,* 143–44; "ICC Hearings on B&O–C&O Unification Underway," *B&O Magazine* 48 (July 1961): 1.

6. Saunders, *Merging Lines,* 145; Rush Loving Jr., *The Men Who Loved Trains: The Story of Men Who Battled Greed to Save an Ailing Industry* (Bloomington: Indiana University Press, 2006), 28; Herb H. Harwood Jr. to author, November 28, 2006.

7. H. Roger Grant, *Erie Lackawanna: Death of an American Railroad, 1938–1992* (Stanford, Calif.: Stanford University Press, 1994), 76–100; *Moody's Transportation Manual, 1963* (New York: Moody's Investors Service, 1963), 1134; interview with Frederick N. Rasmussen, Baltimore, June 24, 2006; Saunders, *Merging Lines,* 187; *Baltimore Sun,* December 14, 1960, June 18, 1961; minutes of directors, B&O, book 4, May 18, 1960, 29, in possession of CSX Corporation, Jacksonville, Fla.

8. Saunders, *Merging Lines,* 187; minutes of the executive committee, B&O, book 11, July 19, 1960, 212–13, in possession of CSX Corporation, Jacksonville, Fla.; *B&O Magazine* 47 (August 1960): 3 and (September 1960): 2–3; Howard E. Simpson, *Recollections of a Railroad Career* (privately printed, 1976), 21–22.

9. Vrooman-Langdon interview; David Vrooman, "An Interview with Hays Watkins," August 15, 1996, Railroad Executive Oral History Program #2, John W. Barriger III National Railroad Library, St. Louis; Simpson, *Recollections of a Railroad Career,* 22; Walter Tuohy to Howard E. Simpson, July 25, 1960, in possession of E. Ray Lichty, Hunt Valley, Md.

10. Saunders, *Merging Lines,* 187–88; B&O 1960 annual report, 14; "B&O Oral History Program, Jervis Langdon Jr., Baltimore, October 25, 1995."

11. David P. Morgan, "That Which Is Unthinkable," *Trains* 20 (October 1960): 5; minutes of the executive committee, B&O, book 11, July 19, 1960, 214.

12. Saunders, *Merging Lines,* 188–89; minutes of directors, B&O, book 4, September 21, 1960, 67–68; *Baltimore Sun,* December 14, 1960.

13. Vrooman-Langdon interview; interview with Rush Loving, Harrisburg, Pa., October 1, 2005; David P. Morgan, "What Price B&O?" *Trains* 21 (November 1960): 12; Stuart Leuthner, *The Railroaders* (New York: Random House, 1983), 128; Jervis Langdon, "Maryland and the Port of Baltimore Miss the Old B&O," May 10, 1988, Langdon papers.

14. Saunders, *Merging Lines,* 189–90; *Baltimore Sun,* January 12, 1961.

15. *Baltimore Sun,* June 18, 1961; Loving, *The Men Who Loved Trains,* 30–32.

16. Interview with Herbert H. Harwood Jr., Harrisburg, Pa., September 29, 2005.

After joining the B&O in 1957, an employee heard a rumor that Langdon would be president. Interview with Robert P. Fetter, Abington, Va., November 15, 2006.

17. *New York Times,* June 25, 1961.

18. Fetter interview; Herbert H. Harwood Jr., "Some Random Notes on B&O's Organization and People before and after Langdon," in possession of author; minutes of directors, B&O, book 2, 227; interview with William J. Dixon, Sarasota, February 25, 2006; interview with Albert W. Clements Jr., Willow Valley, Pa., October 22, 2005.

19. "Major Changes in Top Management," *B&O Magazine* 48 (June 1961): 4; interview with George M. Beischer, Baltimore, October 21, 2005; interview with Paul Reistrap, Baltimore, June 24, 2006.

20. See, e.g., William H. Whyte, *The Organization Man* (New York: Doubleday, 1956).

21. Simpson, *Recollections of a Railroad Career,* 2; *Railway Age* 122 (February 1, 1947): 295; Rasmussen interview; minutes of directors, B&O, book 4, May 17, 1961, 150.

22. Rasmussen interview.

23. Dixon interview; interview with Herbert H. Harwood Jr., Baltimore, October 21, 2005.

"In fairness [to Simpson]," observed Harwood, "costing rail service—especially merchandise freight—was extremely difficult and required sophisticated techniques that were in their experimental infancy. The C&O pioneered the 'basic' formula in the late 1950s, but, of course, nobody at C&O paid attention." Harwood letter.

24. Vrooman-Langdon interview; minutes of directors, book 4, December 20, 1961, 197; Harwood interview, October 21, 2005; B&O oral history.

Lloyd Baker left the B&O at the end of 1963. Jervis successfully blocked awarding Baker 60 percent of his annual salary for a period of five years beginning January 1, 1964. Minutes of directors, B&O Railroad, book 5, November 18, 1963, 63.

25. Clements interview.

26. Interviews with Irene Langdon, Elmira, N.Y., August 5 and 11, 2005; Reistrap interview; *Kansas City Star,* February 28, 1966.

27. Fetter interview; minutes of directors, B&O Railroad, book 4, June 1, 1961, 151.

28. Irene Langdon interview, August 5, 2005; Jervis Langdon Jr., "Jervis Langdon Jr. (1905–)," Langdon papers; Clements interview; Reistrap interview.

29. Vrooman-Langdon interview; *Moody's Transportation Manual, 1963,* 1135; Herbert H. Harwood Jr., *Royal Blue Line: The Classic B&O Train between Washington and New York* (Baltimore: Johns Hopkins University Press, 1990), 167–70; B&O 1957 annual report, 5.

30. *Moody's Transportation Manual, 1963,* 1135; Howard Simpson, "Call for Teamwork," *B&O Magazine* 47 (January 1960): 21; "The Snow!" *B&O Magazine* 48 (March 1961): 2–5.

31. Dixon interview; interview with Kent Shoemaker, Minneapolis, November 4, 2005; Vrooman-Langdon interview.

32. Howard Simpson, "To All B&O Men and Women," *B&O Magazine* 46 (March 1959): 1; Howard Simpson, "Meanwhile . . . ," *B&O Magazine* 48 (February 1961): 3.

33. Dixon interview; Reistrup interview; Shoemaker interview.

34. B&O 1961 annual report, 5; Vrooman-Langdon interview; minutes of directors, B&O Railroad, book 4, January 17, 1962, 211.

35. Dixon interview; *Baltimore Sun,* November 18, 1963; David P. Morgan, "B&O Comes Back," *Trains* 24 (February 1965): 26.

36. David Vrooman, "An Interview with Paul Reistrup," February 27–28, 1997, Railroad Executive Oral History Program, John W. Barriger III National Railroad Library, St. Louis; minutes of directors, B&O Railroad, book 4, January 17, 1962; Shoemaker interview; interview with Raymond Holter, Hunt Valley, Md., October 21, 2005; Harwood interview, October 21, 2005; Reistrup interview.

37. Shoemaker interview; B&O Oral History; Dixon interview; Russell F. Moore, ed., *Who's Who in Railroading in North America* (New York: Simmons-Boardman, 1964), 136; "W. J. Dixon Appointed Industrial Engineer," *B&O Magazine* 48 (October 1961): 3.

When the B&O officer recruited Dixon, he asked him, "Why don't you come down here from that trolley line [New Haven] and join a real railroad?" Dixon was happy to comply. Interview with William Dixon by Robert Fetter, Sarasota, February 12, 2005.

38. Interview with E. Ray Lichty, Baltimore, October 21, 2005; Shoemaker interview.

39. Fetter interview; H. Roger Grant, *The Railroad: The Life Story of a Technology* (Westport, Conn.: Greenwood Press, 2005), 133–34; newspaper clipping, August 1, 1970, in Langdon papers.

Ironically, at the time the B&O embraced the DATAmatic 1000, the Pennsylvania Railroad decided to terminate its computer operations because of budget restraints. "It would take five to seven years for the Pennsy to catch up," likely a factor in the company's deteriorating financial health during the 1960s. Fetter interview.

40. Dixon interview; *Wall Street Journal,* September 15, 1970.

41. Shoemaker interview; Lichty interview; *For Those Who Think Ahead!* (Baltimore: Baltimore & Ohio Railroad, n.d.), 1–6.

42. Kent Shoemaker, "A Difficult Recruit," manuscript in possession of author.

43. Vrooman-Langdon interview; Harwood interview, October 21, 2005; Beischer interview.

44. Harwood interview, October 21, 2005; Herbert H. Harwood Jr., "Langdon and TOFC," manuscript in possession of author; "For B&O Piggyback: Revolution Begins," *Railway Age* 154 (June 24, 1963): 70; *New York Times,* September 11, 1966; Vrooman-Langdon interview.

45. Vrooman-Langdon interview; *Railway Age* 152 (January 8, 1962): 33.

46. "More Streamlining," *B&O Magazine* 48 (September 1961): 7; minutes of directors, B&O Railroad, book 4, September 20, 1961, 180.

47. Holter interview; *Railway Age* 152 (March 26, 1962); Harwood interview, October 21, 2005.

48. Holter interview; Harwood letter; Maury Klein, *The Life and Legend of E. H. Harriman* (Chapel Hill: University of North Carolina Press, 2000), 445.

49. Dixon interview; Vrooman-Langdon interview; *Columbus Citizen Journal,* April 18, 1963.

Jervis attended various meetings about car supply, and in one case he made a lasting impression. "Many remarks were made regarding the different types of cars that were in short supply—DF cars, covered hoppers, box cars, etc.," recalled Harry Hinds, who in the early 1960s was division sales manager at Decatur. "Someone mentioned air slide cars. Mr. Langdon moved forward in his seat at the head table. After a lengthy discussion, Mr. Langdon interrupted, asking, 'What is an air slide car?' He was probably the only man in the room that didn't know. What endeared him to the sales force at that moment was the fact he was a big enough man to admit it. A lesser man would have gone back to Baltimore and read up on air slides."

50. Harwood interview, October 21, 2005; "Diesel and Car Repair Programs Stepped Up," *B&O Magazine* 48 (August 1961): 5; "Progress Report on New B&O Car Repair Program," *B&O Magazine* 48 (November 1961): 6–7; "Diesel Repairs Keeping Pace with Other B&O Improvements," *B&O Magazine* 48 (December 1961): 6–7; "Computer Helps B&O Schedule Car Repairs," *Railway Age* 161 (October 16, 1961): 9–10.

51. "B&O Testing the Auto-Porter," *B&O Magazine* 48 (September 1961): 1–3; "B&O Completed Auto-Porter Tests," *B&O Magazine* 48 (December 1961): 5, 23; *Railway Age* 151 (October 2, 1961): 23; Paul Reistrup to E. Ray Lichty, September 4, 2006.

52. "Tunnel and Bridge Obstructions between Chicago and Jersey City to Be Cleared by December 16," *B&O Magazine* 48 (November 1961): 4–5; "All Clear for 12' 6" Trailers from Chicago to Jersey City," *B&O Magazine* 49 (January 1962): 1; Vrooman-Langdon interview.

53. "Completion of Major Tunnel Improvement Program Links the East and the West, for Handling of Massive Freight Shipments over All B&O Lines," *B&O News-Chessie News* 1 (November 30, 1963): 8–10.

54. *B&O Magazine* 46 (May 1959): 1, and 48 (October 1, 1961): 8–9; B&O 1959 annual report, 7; minutes of directors, B&O Railroad, book 4, October 17, 1962, 254; *Baltimore Sun,* November 18, 1963.

55. "High-Speed Freight Schedules Set by B&O," *Railway Age* 154 (January 28, 1963): 43; *Trains* 23 (February 1963): 9; William F. Howes Jr., "A C&O/B&O Memoir," *Chesapeake and Ohio Historical Magazine* (September 2003): 1.

56. *Moody's Transportation Manual, 1963,* 1134–35.

57. "B&O Reveals Plan to Cut Coal Rates," *Railway Age* 153 (July 9, 1962): 7; Shoemaker interview; Dixon interview.

58. *Baltimore Sun,* November 19, 1962; *Wall Street Journal,* July 3, 1962; Peter Lyon, *To Hell in a Day Coach: An Exasperated Look at American Railroads* (New York: J. B. Lippincott, 1968), 208–209.

59. Vrooman-Langdon interview.

60. "What's Ahead for Unit Trains?" *Railway Age* 156 (April 20, 1964): 20.

61. E. Ray Lichty to author, September 5, 2006.

62. Vrooman-Langdon interview.

63. Beischer interview; "Braking Those Gold Stripers," *Railway Age* 157 (September 14, 1964): 28–29.

64. Vrooman-Langdon interview; Shoemaker interview; "B&O Reveals Plan to Cut Coal Rates," 7.

65. Vrooman-Langdon interview.

66. *Railway Age* 157 (November 1964).

67. B&O 1963 annual report, 5.

68. *New York Times,* October 12, 1962.

69. David J. DeBoer, *Piggyback and Containers: A History of Rail Intermodal on America's Steel Highway* (San Marino, Calif.: Golden West Books, 1992), 43–44; *New York Times,* March 8, 1964.

70. Herbert H. Harwood Jr., "Langdon and TOFC," manuscript in possession of author; Vrooman-Langdon interview.

71. *Railway Age* 154 (March 25, 1963): 58; B&O Oral History; Harwood, "Langdon and TOFC"; *New York Times,* September 11, 1966; "The B&O Piggyback Revolution," 70.

72. Vrooman-Langdon interview; B&O 1961 annual report, 3.

73. Vrooman-Langdon interview; undated clipping from *Washington Post,* Langdon papers; interview with William Howes Jr., Jacksonville, June 18, 2006.

74. Holter interview; "School Tours to Washington," *B&O Magazine* 48 (April 1961): 1; Vrooman-Langdon interview; Reistrap interview.

75. Vrooman-Langdon interview; Fetter interview; Harwood letter.

76. Vrooman-Langdon interview; Reistrap interview; Vrooman-Reistrup interview.

77. Interview with Harry Stegmaier, Harrisburg, Pa., September 30, 2005; *Railway Age* 154 (February 25, 1963): 78; Harry Stegmaier, *Baltimore & Ohio Passenger Service: Route of the Capitol Limited,* vol. 2 (Lynchburg, Va.: TLC, 1997), ix, 25.

78. *Railway Age* 153 (October 15, 1962): 52; B&O Oral History; Vrooman-Langdon interview; *Trains* 22 (March 1962): 15.

79. Reistrap interview.

80. Irene Langdon interview, August 5, 2005.

81. Irene Langdon to author, April 12, 2006; interview with Irene Langdon, September 16, 2006.

82. *News-American* (Baltimore), February 16, 1964.

83. Clipping in Langdon papers.

84. *Baltimore Sun,* February 4 and February 10, 1963; *Moody's Transportation Manual* (New York: Moody's Investors Services, 1964), 1099; Fetter interview.

Early in 1964, the C&O increased its ownership of the B&O by acquiring about 727,000 shares from the NYC and Alleghany Corporation.

85. *Baltimore Sun,* May 1, 1962; C&O 1962 annual report, 8; "C&O Plus B&O—and How Many Others?" *Newsweek* (January 14, 1963): 53–54.

86. B&O 1962 annual report, 4; "B&O Rehabilitation Plan Is Announced," *Railway Age* 154 (February 11, 1963): 9, and 156 (February 17, 1964): 36; Fred Rees Toothman, *Working for the Chessie System: Olde King Coal's Prime Carrier* (Huntington, W.Va.: Vandalia, 1993); B&O 1963 annual report, 1–2; minutes of directors, B&O Railroad, book 5, January 20, 1964, 74; Tom Shedd, "Two Roads 'Put Science into the Track,'" *Modern Railroads* 19 (February 1964): 53–54.

87. Quoted in Saunders, *Merging Lines,* 199.

88. Walter J. Tuohy to Jervis Langdon, n.d., Langdon papers; B&O Oral History; Toothman, *Working for the Chessie System,* 129; Reistrap interview.

89. Jervis Langdon, "The Old B&O Railroad Is an Integral Part of CSX," July 24, 1996, Langdon papers; *Moody's Transportation Manual* (New York: Moody's Investors Service, 1988), 246; *Baltimore Sun,* February 10, 1963; Richard Saunders Jr., *Main Lines: Rebirth of the North American Railroads, 1970–2002* (DeKalb: Northern Illinois University Press, 2003), 148–50.

90. "The New Men," *Forbes* (January 15, 1963): 17; "Jervis Langdon Jr.," *The Traffic Club Record* (October 1964): 17; "B&O Comes Back," *Trains* 24 (February 1964): 23–24.

91. Interview with Norman Murphy, Baltimore, October 21, 2005; minutes of directors, B&O Railroad, book 5, July 15, 1963, 29.

92. Irene Langdon interview, September 16, 2006; "B&O Museum Big Hit," *Railway Age* 157 (July 13, 1964): 38.

93. Harwood, *Royal Blue Line,* 93, 96.

94. *Baltimore Sun,* October 19, 1961, September 22, 1996.

95. Norman Murphy to Jervis Langdon Jr., August 29, 1996, in possession of author.

96. Murphy interview; minutes of directors, B&O Railroad, book 5, September 21, 1964, 126.

97. Fred Lazarus IV to Jervis Langdon Jr., October 14, 1996, in possession of author.

98. Ron Dunn, "Testimony to Jervis Langdon," in possession of author.

99. Langdon, "The Old B&O Railroad Is an Integral Part of CSX."

100. Frederick C. Osthoff, ed., *Who's Who in Railroading in North America* (New York: Simmons-Boardman, 1968), 415; *Railway Age* 156 (February 17, 1964): 36; David P. Morgan, "Can B&O Save Its Varnish?" *Trains* 24 (August 1964): 3; Reistrup interview; "For B&O Passenger Men—an 'Or-Else' Task," *Railway Age* 157 (September 28, 1964): 50, 54.

101. Reistrup interview.

102. Morgan, "Can B&O Save Its Varnish?" 3; Reistrup interview; "On the B&O, 'First Class' Meant Just That," *Classic Trains* 6 (Fall 2005): 88–89.

103. Morgan, "Can B&O Save Its Varnish?" 3, 6–7; Vrooman-Reistrup interview; "B&O's Big Bid for Business," *Railway Age* 156 (March 23, 1964): 19; *New York Times,* April 13, 1964.

104. Reistrup interview; Vrooman-Reistrup interview; interview with William Howes Jr., November 2, 2006; *Railway Age* 157 (September 7, 1964): 34; B&O public timetable, April 25, 1965.

The company showed movies on the *Capitol Limited* in one of the coaches and in a section of the twin-unit diner. On the *National Limited,* movies were available only in one of the coaches.

105. Morgan, "Can B&O Save Its Varnish?" 6; Reistrup interview.

106. Russell F. Moore, ed., *Who's Who in Railroading in North America* (New York: Simmons-Boardman, 1959), 27–28; *Railway Age* 156 (March 2, 1964): 35; "B&O's Product Planning Bureau," *Railway Age* 156 (April 17, 1964): 45; Harwood interview; Harwood letter; Shoemaker interview; Fetter interview.

107. Lichty interview; Harwood interview; Herbert Harwood Jr. to author, November 24, 2006.

108. B&O Oral History; Dixon interview.

109. Harwood letter; Vrooman-Langdon interview.

110. *Railway Age* 154 (May 13, 1963): 7.

111. Vrooman-Langdon interview; *Wall Street Journal,* September 25, 1963; B&O Oral History; Harwood letter; minutes of directors, B&O Railroad, book 5, September 21, 1964, 124; Harwood interview.

In early 1963 Jervis had engaged Wyer, Dick & Company to examine the economic aspects of the Reading and Jersey Central as they related to the B&O. This type of careful study, which recommended greater B&O involvement, helped to convince Jervis that the Reading held considerable value. Minutes of directors, B&O Railroad, book 5, September 17, 1963, 47.

112. Shoemaker interview; Kent Shoemaker, "Jervis Langdon's Railroad Career," January 2006, manuscript in possession of author; B&O Oral History; Vrooman-Langdon interview; minutes of directors, B&O Railroad, book 5, April 20, 1964, 92; Maury Klein, "Interview with Jervis Langdon Jr.," March 15, 1988, Maury Klein papers, John W. Barriger III National Railroad Library, St. Louis.

113. Toothman, *Working for the Chessie System,* 155; Dixon interview; Reistrup interview.

114. Dixon interview; "Tuohy of C&O Gets New Hat at B&O," *Railway Age* 157 (October 19, 1964): 7.

115. Minutes of directors, B&O Railroad, book 5, October 8, 1964, 129–30; Klein-Langdon interview; Toothman, *Working on the Chessie System;* interview with Helen Delich Bentley, Hunt Valley, Md., October 22, 2005.

Unlike the golden parachutes that corporate boards would later commonly give, Jervis really got little at the time of his early retirement. He and his wife were granted a joint and survivor annuity at the rate of $635.56 per month, effective February 1, 1965. He also received $18,875 of deferred compensation that would be paid after January 1, 1966. Earlier in 1964, though, at the insistence of Walter Tuohy, the B&O board had raised Jervis's annual salary to $100,000. The C&O would reimburse the B&O "for a portion thereof in consideration of joint services performed for both companies by the President." See minutes of directors, B&O Railroad, book 5, April 20, 1964, 92.

116. B&O Oral History; Langdon, "The Old B&O Railroad Is an Integral Part of CSX."

117. Lichty interview; Fetter interview; Bentley interview.

4. Running the Rock

1. Interview with Irene Langdon, Elmira, N.Y., August 5, 2005; interview with Ted Desch, Chicago, October 9, 2006.

2. William Edward Hayes, *Iron Road to Empire: The History of the Rock Island Lines* (New York: Simmons-Boardman, 1953), 9–39, 54–57; H. Roger Grant, ed., *Iowa Railroads: The Essays of Frank P. Donovan Jr.* (Iowa City: University of Iowa Press, 2000), 168–75.

3. Hayes, *Iron Road to Empire,* 98–105, 109–53; Don L. Hofsommer, *The Tootin' Louie: A History of the Minneapolis & St. Louis Railway* (Minneapolis: University of Minnesota Press, 2005), 29–30, 33, 35–43.

4. Hayes, *Iron Road to Empire,* 157–89.

5. Don L. Hofsommer, *The Southern Pacific, 1901–1985* (College Station: Texas A&M University Press, 1986), 100; interview with William Hoenig, Cedar Rapids, Iowa, October 13, 2006.

6. Hayes, *Iron Road to Empire,* 190–221.

7. John Sherman Porter, ed., *Moody's Manual of Investments: Railroad Securities* (New York: Moody's Investors Service, 1935), 365–66.

8. Grant, *Iowa Railroads,* 195–96; Dan Butler, "John D. Farrington," in Keith L. Bryant Jr., *Railroads in the Age of Regulation, 1900–1980* (New York: Facts On File, 1988), 140–42.

A wonderful statement of how John Farrington instilled pride among Rock Island employees and their families is found in Hugh Hawkins, *Railwayman's Son: A Plains Family Memoir* (Lubbock: Texas Tech University Press, 2006), 70.

9. *Career Opportunities in Railroading* (Chicago: Chicago, Rock Island & Pacific Railroad, n.d.); *Moody's Manual of Investments: Transportation* (New York: Moody's Investors Service, 1953), 187, 201; Louis A. Marre, *Rock Island Color Pictorial Volume 1* (La Mirada, Calif.: Four Ways West, 1994), 5.

10. *Des Moines Sunday Register,* February 3, 1952; David P. Morgan, "Trouble on the Prairie," *Trains* 26 (December 1965): 3; interview with William J. Dixon, Sarasota, February 25, 2006.

11. "An Address to the New York Society of Security Analysts by John W. Barriger, March 16, 1956," Jervis Langdon papers, in possession of Irene Langdon, Elmira, N.Y.; H. Craig Miner, *The Rebirth of the Missouri Pacific, 1956–1983* (College Station: Texas A&M University Press, 1983), 45–46; "Jenks of the Rock Island," unidentified clipping in Langdon papers; "J. D. Farrington Resumes Rock Island Presidency: Other Executive Changes Result from Resignation of D. B. Jenks to Become Missouri Pacific President," box 93, Chicago, Rock Island & Pacific Railroad Collections, University of Oklahoma Libraries Western History Collections.

12. Miner, *The Rebirth of the Missouri Pacific,* 47–49; "Mr. Jenks in Shirtsleeves," *Railway Age* 171 (October 25, 1971): 5.

Henry Crown (1896–1990) lived a Horatio Alger life. Born Henry Krinsky to poor Jewish immigrants in Chicago, Crown left school in the eighth grade, worked at odd jobs, and at the age of 23 borrowed $10,000 to found the Material Service Corporation with his brothers. In time this sand, gravel, and concrete business boomed, and in 1959 Crown merged the firm into the General Dynamics Corporation. During World War II, Crown served as a colonel in the Army Corps of Engineers and produced inflatable decoy landing barges that saved hundreds of lives in the invasions of France and the Philippines. After the war, Crown's business interests also included communications, hotels, meat packing, sports teams, and a syndicate that acquired the Empire State Building in New York City. Crown, though, was a generous individual, liberally supporting hospitals, museums, and universities.

When Downing Jenks left the Rock Island for the MOP, Farrington assumed the Rock Island presidency until May 8, 1961.

13. Interview with George H. Durbala, Harrisburg, Pa., September 29, 2005; interview with George Niles, Cedar Rapids, October 12, 2006; Frank N. Wilner, *Railroad Mergers: History, Analysis, Insight* (Omaha: Simmons-Boardman Books, 1997), 203; Desch interview; Maury Klein, "Interview with Jervis Langdon Jr.," March 15, 1988, Maury Klein papers, John W. Barringer III National Railroad Library, St. Louis.

14. See Julius Grodinsky, *The Iowa Pool: A Study in Railroad Competition, 1870–1884* (Chicago: University of Chicago Press, 1950).

15. H. Roger Grant, *The North Western: A History of the Chicago & North Western Railway System* (DeKalb: Northern Illinois University Press, 1996), 102–104, 182–84.

16. Maury Klein, *Union Pacific: The Rebirth, 1894–1969* (New York: Doubleday, 1989), 516–18; Dixon interview.

17. Klein, *Union Pacific,* 517–18; Richard Saunders Jr., *Merging Lines: American Railroads, 1900–1970* (DeKalb: Northern Illinois University Press, 2001), 216–28, 329–32.

18. Klein, *Union Pacific,* 518–19.

19. Hofsommer, *The Southern Pacific,* 265–67.

20. Klein, *Union Pacific,* 521; Klein-Langdon interview; "Rock Island–Union Pacific Merger Chronology," Langdon papers.

21. Grant, *The North Western,* 213; Klein-Langdon interview; "Rock Island– Union Pacific Merger Chronology."

22. Klein-Langdon interview; *Wall Street Journal,* October 7, 1964; "Many Suitors," *Forbes,* January 15, 1966, 43; *Railway Age* 158 (May 31, 1965): 112.

At the time of Jervis's appointment at the Rock Island, there had been rumors about his employment after the B&O. "There has been much speculation in financial circles as to what the restless Mr. Langdon's future plans might involve," noted a reporter for the *Wall Street Journal* on October 7, 1964. "As recently as two weeks ago, reports were widespread that he was slated to head a Western railroad, far larger than the Rock Island and not in the middle of a battle for control."

At the board meeting on October 8, 1964, Henry Crown reported that "as the members knew, for over two years they had been seeking someone to head the Company, and about two weeks ago he learned that Jervis Langdon Jr. . . . might be available for that position." Board minutes, Chicago, Rock Island & Pacific Railroad Company, October 8, 1964, 4, box 66, Rock Island Collections.

23. David Vrooman, "An Interview with Jervis Langdon," September 13–14, 1996, Railroad Executive Oral History Program #1, John W. Barriger III National Railroad Library, St. Louis; board minutes, January 20, 1969, 15, box 68, Rock Island Collections.

Later Jervis blasted individuals, particularly CSX executive John Snow, who received compensation in the millions of dollars. "I think it's ridiculous! I think it's bad for the railroad industry. . . . You've got to consider all the people who are doing the work on the railroad."

24. *Wall Street Journal,* October 9, 1964; Durbala interview, September 29, 2005.

25. Klein-Langdon interview; "Western Railroads Collide on Mergers," *Business Week,* March 19, 1966, 140.

26. Rock Island 1964 annual report, 4; board minutes, May 17, 1965, 16, box 67, Rock Island Collections.

27. Rock Island 1964 annual report, 4–5; Rock Island 1965 annual report, 5; minutes of the executive committee, Chicago, Rock Island & Pacific Railroad Company, April 12, 1965, 16, box 66, Rock Island Collections; Hoenig interview, October 13, 2006; "Many Suitors," 43; Bill Marvel, *Rock Island: Volume II, 1965–1980* (Edison, N.J.: Morning Sun Books, 1995), 6.

28. Rock Island 1964 annual report, 5; Dixon interview.

29. Rock Island 1964 annual report, 5; Durbala interview, September 29, 2005; James G. Pate to Merle M. Miller, January 10, 1966, Rock Island Collections; Hoenig interview, October 13, 2006.

30. Desch interview; Klein-Langdon interview; *Transportation Careers* (Chicago: Rock Island Lines, n.d.); Jervis Langdon, "A Few Suggestions for Self-Improvement," luncheon address to the Railway Supply Association, Chicago, September 15, 1965; interview with Bill Collins, Loudonville, N.Y., February 26, 2007.

Two top officials whom Jervis pushed out before they had reached retirement age were Elden Tharp, vice president of traffic, and O. W. Limestall, vice president of operations. See board minutes, March 8, 1965, 4, box 66, Rock Island Collections.

31. Dixon interview; *Wall Street Journal,* January 22, 1969.

32. Klein-Langdon interview; interview with William Hoenig, Walnut Creek, Calif., February 17, 2006; "G. W. Kelly," box 67, Rock Island Collections.

There is no question that Kelly had performed well. One director wrote, "[Kelly] reorganized practically every phase of the Company's operations and property maintenance programs, introduced modern practices and procedures, including training of personnel, and raised the competitive standing of the Company to a high level." See box 67, Rock Island Collections.

On January 27, 1969, Gerald T. Kelly, G. W. Kelly's son, wrote Jervis the following heartfelt comment: "You, he [his father] respected more than anyone in his life, and justifiably so." See box 68, Rock Island Collections.

33. Desch interview; executive committee minutes, February 21, 1966, box 67, Rock Island Collections; Klein-Langdon interview; Dan Cordtz, "The Fight for the Rock Island," *Fortune,* June 1966, 142.

34. Hoenig interview, February 17, 2006; Durbala interview, September 29, 2005.

35. Interview with Daniel Sabin, Cedar Rapids, October 13, 2006; interview with Bill Davis, Overland Park, Kans., June 25, 2007; interview with George Durbala, Cedar Rapids, October 13, 2006.

36. Durbala interview, September 29, 2005; Rock Island 1964 annual report, 7; "Rock Island and Workers Profit from Suggestions," *Railway Age* 159 (September 13, 1965): 12.

37. Hoenig interview, October 13, 2006; Vrooman-Langdon interview.

38. Interview with Irene Langdon, Elmira, N.Y., August 5, 2005; Lew Townsend, "Penn Central's Flying Trustee," *AOPA Pilot* (November 1970): 44.

39. Interview with Irene Langdon, Elmira, N.Y., September 16, 2006.

40. Vrooman-Langdon interview.

41. Rock Island 1966 annual report, 10–11; "Rock Island Moving Operations," *Railway Age* 160 (April 18, 1966): 64; Durbala interview, September 29, 2005.

42. Rock Island 1965 annual report, 11; Dixon interview; Durbala interview, September 29, 2005.

43. Hoenig interview, October 13, 2006.

44. Rock Island 1965 annual report, 11; Durbala interview, September 29, 2005; *Des Moines Register,* January 7, 1968; "Data-Phone Cuts Paperwork for Suppliers and P&S Departments," *Railway Age* 160 (June 20, 1966): 20–21.

45. Rock Island 1966 annual report, 13; "Booming Industrial Complex on Ol' Man River," *Forbes* 95 (June 15, 1965): 32–33.

46. Rock Island 1965 annual report, 13; Rock Island 1967 annual report, 10.

47. Rock Island 1965 annual report, 14–15; *Railway Age* 160 (June 13, 1966): 7; Rock Island 1969 annual report, 7.

48. Rock Island 1965 annual report, 14; Rock Island 1966 annual report, 15; Rock Island 1969 annual report, 8.

49. "TOFC: Rock Island Aims at a 100% Increase," *Railway Age* 159 (October 25, 1965): 36–37; executive committee minutes, August 21, 1967, 4, box 67, Rock Island Collections.

50. Interview with Rush Loving, Baltimore, June 23, 2006; Rock Island 1969 annual report, 7; Rock Island 1966 annual report, 14; "TOFC/COFC: 'There Is Still Tremendous Potential,' Says the Rock Island," *Railway Age* 168 (October 26, 1970): 38–39.

51. "Address by Donald S. Chishom, Marketing Manager–Chemicals and Petroleum to the Des Moines Chapter of Delta Nu Alpha, April 25, 1968," Rock Island Collections.

52. Executive committee minutes, October 16, 1962, 2, box 67, Rock Island Collections.

53. Desch interview; author's interview with Jervis Langdon Jr., Akron, April 26, 1990; *Centerville* (Iowa) *Iowegian,* November 1, 1968.

54. Desch interview.
Not long after Jervis arrived, he backed scrapping the lightweight *Talgo Train,* which the company had acquired in 1956. As he told members of the board, "This train proved to be so unsatisfactory that it was transferred for a time to suburban service, but in that service also the cost of maintenance and repairs became prohibitive." Although the railroad attempted to sell the train, efforts failed, and so this experimental equipment became junk. See board minutes, March 8, 1965, 5–6, box 66, Rock Island Collections.

55. Desch interview; Rock Island 1964 annual report, 4.

56. "MTT, Alias Red Circle," *Trains* 25 (March 1965): 8.

57. "RI Plans Revision of Passenger Operations," *Railway Age* 160 (April 4, 1966): 7; *Wall Street Journal*, March 31, 1966; Rock Island 1965 annual report, 5; *Des Moines Register*, September 20, 1968; *Trains* 28 (April 1968): 6.

58. *Railway Age* 162 (June 5, 1967): 34; *Des Moines Register*, March 23 and May 1, 1967.

59. Desch interview; *Des Moines Register*, July 24 and 25, 1967; public timetable, Chicago, Rock Island & Pacific Railroad, March 2, 1969; "RI Adds Parlor Cars to Two 'Rockets,'" *Railway Age* 162 (March 27, 1967), 7.

60. "Train Runs End," *Rocket* 30 (November/December 1970): 15.

61. Grant, *The North Western*, 203; "Good News for North Western Commuters," *Carbuilder*, January/February 1960; "Rock Island Commuters Get New Cars," *Railway Age* 158 (January 4–11, 1965): 42; Rock Island 1969 annual report, 11–12.

62. Grant, *The North Western*, 225.

63. Dixon interview; "People—New Opportunity on RI," *Railway Age* 165 (November 18, 1968): 8.

64. Rock Island 1965 annual report, 13.

65. Desch interview; J. G. Pate, "Rock Island—'Where the Action Is,'" box 93, Rock Island Collections.

66. Dixon interview; Rock Island 1965 annual report, 4; Klein-Langdon interview.

67. Rock Island 1966 annual report, 4; G. W. Kelly to Jervis Langdon Jr., March 16, 1966, box 67, Rock Island Collections; *Des Moines Tribune*, January 24, 1968; "New Type Deck Cuts Bridge Costs," *Railway Age* 161 (November 14, 1966): 21–22; Hoenig interview, October 13, 2006.

68. Hoenig interview, October 13, 2006; *Slow Order Status Report*, June 6, 1969, box 1, Windsor Collection, University of Iowa Special Collections.

69. Dixon interview; Klein-Langdon interview.

70. Rock Island 1964 annual report, 7; Rock Island 1965 annual report, 4, 13–14; Rock Island 1968 annual report, 10; "RI: Budget Goes Up as Deficit Comes Down," *Railway Age* 160 (January 3–10, 1966): 7.

71. Dixon interview; G. W. Kelly to Jervis Langdon Jr., March 18, 1966, box 67, Rock Island Collections.

72. Durbala interview, September 29, 2005; Rock Island 1965 annual report, 13, 15.

73. Hoenig interview, February 17, 2006.

74. Dixon interview.

75. "RSMA Seminar, Knickerbocker Hotel, Chicago, Ill.," Jervis Langdon Papers, Hagley Museum and Library, Wilmington, Del.

76. Rock Island 1965 annual report, 13–14; *Wall Street Journal*, November 19, 1966; *Railway Age* 162 (January 16, 1967): 7; "Incentive Rates from RI," *Railway Age* 162 (April 10, 1967): 34.

77. Dixon interview; Rock Island 1968 annual report, 4–5, 8–9; "Confirming Old Suspicions," *Trains* 29 (November 1968): 7.

78. *You Are Witnessing the Birth of a Market* (Chicago: Chicago, Rock Island & Pacific Railroad Company, n.d.); Rock Island 1967 annual report, 9.

79. Jervis Langdon Jr., "Grain Transportation on the Rock Island Lines," *Grain Transportation Symposium Proceedings* (Ames: Iowa State University Extension, 1970), 9–12.

80. "IC, Rock Island, Southern, PC Win RPI Awards," *Railway Age* 167 (December 1, 1969): 11; Rock Island 1969 annual report, 9; "Rock Island Receives Silver Car Trophy," *Traffic Manager,* November 1969, 3, 18.

81. Rock Island 1965 annual report, 11–12; Rock Island 1966 annual report, 10–11; Rock Island 1968 annual report, 10–11; "Freight Trains Adopt the Space Age," *Railway Age* 161 (August 8–August 15, 1966): 11; "Joint Operation Set Up by RI, EL," *Railway Age* 164 (April 22, 1968): 12.

82. Hoenig interview, February 17, 2006.

83. Steven Allen Goen, *"Down South" on the Rock Island: A Color Pictorial, 1940–1969* (La Mirada, Calif.: Four Ways West, 2002), 108; Dixon interview. ·

84. Nancy Ford, "Inside Track," *Modern Railroads* (May 1967): 47; *Moody's Transportation Manual* (New York: Moody's Investors Service, 1970), 827; *Wall Street Journal,* September 15, 1970; David P. Morgan, "Needed: A Better Idea," *Trains* 27 (July 1967): 3; Rock Island 1969 annual report, 4.

85. Cordtz, "The Fight for the Rock Island," 204; Klein-Langdon interview; "To Rock Island Stockholders," November 2, 1964, Langdon Papers, Hagley Library.

86. Klein-Langdon interview; "Jervis Langdon Remarks about the CRIP–UP Merger Attempt in Conversation with TED [Ted Desch], July 10, 1998," in possession of author; Vrooman-Langdon interview.

87. Klein-Langdon interview.

In July 1971, the UP notified the ICC that the company would dispose of its interests in IC Industries within 10 years of a merger with the Rock Island. See Frank J. Allston, *Conglomerate: A Case Study of the Innovative Leadership of William B. Johnson in the Formation of IC Industries during the 21-Year Term as Chairman and Chief Executive* (Naperville, Ill.: Illumina Concepts, 1992), 106.

88. Klein-Langdon interview.

89. "RI-UP Merger Chronology," Langdon papers; Cordtz, "The Fight for the Rock Island," 141.

90. Klein-Langdon interview.

91. Grant, *The North Western,* 213–14; Cordtz, "The Fight for the Rock Island," 141; "Why the Rock Island–Union Pacific Merger" (n.p., n. d.), Langdon papers. See also box 94, Rock Island Collections.

92. Klein-Langdon interview; *Chicago Tribune,* August 16, 1966; *Chicago Sun-Times,* August 11, 1966; *Wall Street Journal,* March 24, 1967.

93. Klein-Langdon interview; board minutes, July 17, 1967, 4, box 67, Rock Island Collections; Desch interview.

94. Vrooman-Langdon interview; Klein-Langdon interview; executive committee minutes, April 17, 1967, 3, box 67, Rock Island Collections.

95. Theodore E. Desch, "The Rock Island Merger Case: A Bureaucratic Debacle," in possession of author.

96. Jervis Langdon Jr., "The Union Pacific–Rock Island Litigation: A Lost Opportunity," *Trains* 42 (June 1981): 24–25; *Wall Street Journal,* February 3, 1967; *Daily Oklahoman* (Oklahoma City), April 4, 1967.

97. Desch, "The Rock Island Merger Case"; Vrooman-Langdon interview.

98. Notes in Langdon papers.

99. "One Railroad for the Entire U.S.?" *Trains* 28 (July 1968): 15; Jervis Langdon Jr., "Railroads," *Tenth Annual Transportation Conference* (College Station: Texas Transportation Institute, 1968), 6–8; *New York Times,* July 19, 1970.

100. Langdon, "Railroads," *Tenth Annual Transportation Conference,* 6–8.

101. Klein-Langdon interview.

102. *Chicago Today,* September 10, 1969; Grant, *The North Western,* 215–17.

103. Rock Island 1969 annual report, 4.

104. Desch, "The Rock Island Merger Case"; "Examiner Approves UP/RI Merger," *Railway Age* 168 (July 27, 1970): 14.

105. Desch, "The Rock Island Merger Case"; Saunders, *Merging Lines,* 348–53; Richard Saunders Jr., *Main Lines: Rebirth of the North American Railroads, 1970–2002* (DeKalb: Northern Illinois University Press, 2003), 19.

106. Desch, "The Rock Island Merger Case"; Jervis Langdon to Frank Richter, n.d. [1990], Langdon papers.

107. Dan Rottenberg, "The Last Run of the Rock Island Line," *Chicago Magazine* (September 1984): 197–201, 234–37; Klein, *Union Pacific,* 531.

108. Klein-Langdon interview; Vrooman-Langdon interview; Jervis Langdon Jr. to Thomas A. Stoery, September 2, 1998, Langdon papers.

109. Vrooman-Langdon interview; board minutes, July 31, 1970, 6, box 69, Rock Island Collections; *Philadelphia Inquirer,* July 28, 1970.

110. Durbala interview, September 29, 2005; "RI Names Successors to Langdon," *Railway Age* 168 (September 28, 1970): 8; *New York Times,* September 15, 1970; *Wall Street Journal,* September 15, 1970; David M. Cawthorne, "Approval of Rock Island Certificates Opposed by Chicago Industrialist," *Traffic World* (January 26, 1976): 66.

Rumors had floated through the railroad community that Alfred Perlman, former vice chairman of Penn Central, might become Jervis's replacement. Henry Crown, always the perceptive businessman, wanted Perlman, but other Rock Island board members lacked his enthusiasm. See *New York Times,* September 15, 1970.

5. Rerailing Penn Central

1. *New York Times,* June 21–23, 1970; *Trains* 31 (December 1970): 13; Joseph R. Daughen and Peter Binzen, *The Wreck of the Penn Central* (New York: New American Library, 1971), 6–7.

2. *Moody's Transportation Manual* (New York: Moody's Investors Service, 1970), 233, 235–39; David Vrooman, interview with Jervis Langdon, September 13–14, 1966, Railroad Executive Oral History Program #1, John W. Barriger III National Railroad Library, St. Louis.

3. Richard Saunders Jr., *Merging Lines: American Railroads, 1900–1970* (DeKalb: Northern Illinois University Press, 2001), 245–74; Charles Luna, *The UTU Handbook of Transportation in America* (New York: Popular Library, 1971), 170–71; Joseph Albright, "Penn Central: A Hell of a Way to Run a Government," *New York Times Magazine,* November 3, 1974, 17.

4. Alfred E. Perlman, "Penn Central," *Progressive Railroading* 11 (May/June 1968): 34; *The Penn Central and Other Railroads: A Report to the Senate Committee on Commerce* (Washington, D.C.: Government Printing Office, 1972), 544.

The designer of the new Penn Central logo in 1967 worked the P and C around each other in a protective embrace. "Although the design's slight angle enhanced a sense of motion," noted historian James A. Ward, "its square overall shape and the long bottom line of the C lent it a stability not reflected in the road's financial books." See James A. Ward, "On the Mark: The History and Symbolism of Railroad Emblems," *Railroad History* 153 (Autumn 1985): 61.

5. Interview with James Hagen, Harrisburg, Pa., September 25, 2005.

6. Interview with Charles Shannon, Arlington Heights, Ill., October 1, 1988; *The Penn Central and Other Railroads,* 18–19; Rush Loving Jr., *The Men Who Loved Trains* (Bloomington: Indiana University Press, 2006), 52–53; Saunders, *Merging Lines,* 387–91.

7. Stephen Salsbury, *No Way to Run a Railroad: The Untold Story of the Penn Central Crisis* (New York: McGraw-Hill, 1982), 140; Daughen and Binzen, *The Wreck of the Penn Central,* 70–104; Rush Loving Jr., "The Penn Central Bankruptcy Express," *Fortune,* August 1970, 107; *Wall Street Journal,* March 10, 1965.

8. Loving, *The Men Who Loved Trains,* 55–56; Michael Gartner, *Riding the Pennsy to Ruin: A Wall Street Journal Chronicle of the Penn Central Debacle* (Princeton, N.J.: Dow Jones Books, 1971), 4; Salsbury, *No Way to Run a Railroad,* 140–44.

9. Vrooman-Langdon interview; Gartner, *Riding the Pennsy to Ruin,* 6; Loving, *The Men Who Loved Trains,* 57.

10. Shannon interview.

11. H. Roger Grant, *Erie Lackawanna: Death of an American Railroad, 1938–1992* (Stanford, Calif.: Stanford University Press, 1994), 101–18; interview with Perry M. Shoemaker, Tampa, August 19, 1989.

12. Luna, *UTU Handbook,* 173; interview with Rush Loving Jr., Harrisburg, Pa., October 1, 2005, hereafter cited as Loving-Harrisburg interview; Gartner, *Riding the Pennsy to Ruin,* 7; interview with Harry G. Silleck Jr., Cleveland, October 19, 1988; Loving, *The Men Who Loved Trains,* 75–78, 87; Loving, "The Penn Central Bankruptcy Express," 164.

13. Gartner, *Riding the Pennsy to Ruin,* 13; House of Representatives, Committee on Interstate and Foreign Commerce, *Inadequacies of Protections for Investors in Penn Central and Other ICC-Regulated Companies* (Washington, D.C.: Government Printing Office, 1971), 1; Jim McClellan, "USRA Strikes Back" [letter to the editor], *Trains* 67 (May 2007): 7.

14. Frank N. Wilner, *Railroad Mergers* (Omaha: Simmons-Boardman Books, 1997), 165; interview with Judge Robert B. Krupansky, Cleveland, February 21, 1989; Daughen and Binzen, *The Wreck of the Penn Central,* 294–95; "Langdon, Three Others, Named PC Trustees," *Railway Age* 168 (July 27, 1970): 11; *Chicago Tribune,* July 23, 1970; Vrooman-Langdon interview; *Wall Street Journal,* July 23, 1970.

15. Hagen interview; interview with John W. Barriger IV, Cedar Rapids, October 14, 2006.

16. Interview with Irene Langdon, Elmira, N.Y., September 16, 2006; letter from Irene Langdon to author, May 23, 2007; Vrooman-Langdon interview.

17. Irene Langdon interview; *New York Times,* August 21, 1970; *Wall Street Journal,* September 15, 1970.

18. Irene Langdon interview; Jervis Langdon to David P. Morgan, January 25, 1977, Langdon papers; Loving, *The Men Who Loved Trains,* 135; *New York Times,* March 20, 1971; Hagen interview.

19. Hays T. Watkins Jr., *"Just Call Me Hays": Recollections, Reactions, and Reflections on 42 Years of Railroading* (Jacksonville, Fla.: R.E.B. Communications, 2001), 86; *Philadelphia Inquirer,* July 28, 1970; Loving-Harrisburg interview; Hagen interview; Vrooman-Langdon interview; *Wall Street Journal,* August 11, 1970.

20. *Wall Street Journal,* August 11, 1970.

21. *Wall Street Journal,* December 13, 1954; Vrooman-Langdon interview; *Philadelphia Evening Bulletin,* July 24, 1970.

22. Vrooman-Langdon interview; *New York Times,* October 17, 1971; Loving, *The Men Who Loved Trains,* 141; Hagen interview.

23. Loving, *The Men Who Loved Trains,* 137; Hagen interview; *Washington Post,* August 13, 1970; *New York Times,* August 13, 1970.

24. *New York Times,* August 13, 1970; *Wall Street Journal,* August 21, 1970; *Washington Post,* September 2, 1970.

25. Vrooman-Langdon interview; Jervis Langdon Jr., "The Struggle for Viability—First by Penn Central, Then by Conrail," *ICC Practitioners' Journal* (1982): 375; "Penn Central Files Preliminary Reorganization Plan," *Railway Age* 170 (February 22, 1971): 64.

26. Langdon, "The Struggle for Viability," 375; Jervis Langdon, "Draft-Plan Rationalization," February 16, 1978, Langdon papers.

The traditional framework in which Penn Central would be reorganized involved following Section 77 of the Federal Bankruptcy Act, passed in 1933. The plan would be to scale down the railroad's financial obligations under the supervision of the federal court and the ICC.

27. Jervis Langdon Jr., "Remarks of Jervis Langdon Jr., Trustee, Penn Central Transportation Company, Third Annual Delaware Valley Regional Transportation Conference, Philadelphia, Pa., September 12, 1972," Langdon papers.

28. *New York Times,* April 7, 1971.

29. Langdon, "The Struggle for Viability," 375–76; Vrooman-Langdon interview; *New York Times,* September 16, 1971.

30. *Washington Post,* November 17, 1970, July 29, 1973; *Trains,* December 1970, 13; Loving, *The Men Who Loved Trains,* 139–40; Penn Central news releases, November 17, 1970, June 7, 1971, box 1651, Penn Central Transportation Company papers, Hagley Museum and Library, Wilmington, Del.; Jervis Langdon Jr. to Robin T. Turner, September 30, 1971, Langdon papers; *Wall Street Journal,* December 16, 1970.

31. Hagen interview; Vrooman-Langdon interview.

32. Vrooman-Langdon interview; Loving, *The Men Who Loved Trains,* 142; *Wall Street Journal,* May 14, 1974; Penn Central news release, June 27, 1972; Hagen interview.

33. George W. Hilton, *The Northeast Railroad Problem* (Washington, D.C.: American Enterprise Institute for Public Policy Research, 1975), 31; Vrooman-Langdon interview; Jervis Langdon to Professor Michael Conant, January 19, 1977, in Langdon papers.

34. *Wall Street Journal,* January 14, 1972.

35. The arguments that Jervis put forward in the *Times* essay were not new. For some time he had urged railroad consolidation and even a single national carrier. See, e.g., his letter to the editor in *New York Times* for September 24, 1972.

36. *New York Times,* April 1, 1973.

37. Silleck interview.

38. Vrooman-Langdon interview; Langdon, "The Struggle for Viability," 389–90; Penn Central news release, January 2, 1973; *New York Times,* June 25, 1972, January 22, 1973.

39. Loving, *The Men Who Loved Trains,* 155–56; Hagen interview.

40. "Trustees Interim Report of February 1, 1973; District Court for the Eastern District of Pennsylvania, No. 70-347"; Penn Central news release, February 1, 1973.

41. Vrooman-Langdon interview; Loving, *The Men Who Loved Trains,* 157.

42. Loving, *The Men Who Loved Trains,* 158–59; *Washington Post,* February 10, 1973; *New York Times,* February 11, 1973.

43. *New York Times,* February 27, 1973; Vrooman-Langdon interview.

44. Vrooman-Langdon interview; interview with Gregory W. Maxwell, Moreland Hills, Ohio, August 23, 1989; Langdon, "The Struggle for Viability," 390–91; "ICC Opens Hearings on Liquidation of PC," *Traffic World* (August 20, 1973).

45. Loving, *The Men Who Loved Trains,* 159–63.

46. Vrooman-Langdon interview; Penn Central news release, June 29, 1973; "Jervis Langdon Jr. (1905–)," Langdon papers.

47. Vrooman-Langdon interview; *Wall Street Journal,* August 14, 1973; *Washington Star-News,* August 13, 1974; Penn Central news release, August 13, 1973; *Philadelphia Inquirer,* August 19, 1973; interview with Rush Loving Jr., Baltimore, June 23, 2006, hereafter cited as Loving-Baltimore interview.

48. Langdon, "The Struggle for Viability," 392–93.

49. Vrooman-Langdon interview; Loving, *The Men Who Loved Trains,* 162–63; Loving-Baltimore interview; Hagen interview.

50. *Washington Post,* November 1, 1973; *Annual Report, June 30, 1974, with a Supplemental Report through October 1974* (Washington, D.C.: United States Railway Association, 1974), 9; Loving, *The Men Who Loved Trains,* 164, 180; Langdon, "The Struggle for Viability," 393.

51. Vrooman-Langdon interview; Richard Saunders Jr., *Main Lines: Rebirth of the North American Railroads, 1970–2002* (DeKalb: Northern Illinois University Press, 2003), 105–108, 112–15.

52. Albright, "Penn Central."

53. Loving, *The Men Who Loved Trains,* 140–43; Hagen interview; Loving-Baltimore interview; *New York Times,* January 5 and 26, 1974; *Washington Post,* January 29 and April 2, 1974.

54. Vrooman-Langdon interview; Penn Central news releases, January 4 and May 15, 1974; *Wall Street Journal,* June 19, 1974; *New York Times,* December 29, 1972, January 5, 1974.

55. Newspaper clipping, "Jervis Langdon? He Turns Trains Around," in Langdon papers; Hagen interview.

56. Vrooman-Langdon interview.

57. Penn Central news release, October 30, 1974; interview with William J. Dixon, Sarasota, February 25, 2006.

58. Langdon, "Jervis Langdon Jr. (1905–)"; Penn Central news release, September 19, 1974; Vrooman-Langdon interview.

59. "The Other Side of the PC Story," *Railway Age* 175 (October 29, 1973): 78.

60. Jervis Langdon, "Penn Central's Operating Performance during Bankruptcy," manuscript in Langdon papers.

61. Vrooman-Langdon interview; Penn Central news release, March 21, 1974.

62. Penn Central news release, April 4, 1975; Jervis Langdon Jr. to Claude S. Brinegar, February 12, 1974, Langdon papers.

63. "Statement of Jervis Langdon Jr., President, Penn Central Transportation Co. to the House Interior Committee Regarding H.R. 1863 and Related Bills Amending the Mineral Leasing Act," Langdon papers; Penn Central news release, November 12, 1975.

64. Langdon to Morgan, January 25, 1977; Langdon to Conant, January 19, 1977.

65. Ken Smith to Langdon, March 21, 1976, and Joseph R. Coyne to Langdon, March 25, 1976, Langdon papers.

6. Still Railroading

1. David Vrooman, interview with Jervis Langdon, September 13–14, 1996, Railroad Executive Oral History Program #1, John W. Barriger III National Railroad Library, St. Louis.

2. Irene Langdon to author, February 14, 2007.
There is some doubt about the role played by Bob Blanchette. "Southern interests tried several times to enlist help from Jerv, but he was occupied elsewhere," recalled Irene. "The Alston, Miller offer came at an opportune time." Irene Langdon to author, June 20, 2007.

3. Interview with Bernard V. Donahue, Cleveland, November 14, 1990; interview with Harry A. Zilli Jr., Cleveland, February 4, 1992.

4. Interview with Harry G. Silleck Jr., Cleveland, October 19, 1988; Vrooman-Langdon interview.

5. Harold H. McLean, *Pittsburgh and Lake Erie R.R.* (San Marino, Calif.: Golden West Books, 1980), 129–47; *Moody's Transportation Manual* (New York: Moody's Investors Service, 1980), 767.

6. Vrooman-Langdon interview; McLean, *Pittsburgh and Lake Erie R.R.,* 199, 201–202.

7. Scott D. Trostel, *The Detroit, Toledo & Ironton Railroad: Henry Ford's Railroad* (Fletcher, Ohio: Cam-Tech, 1988); Don L. Hofsommer, *Grand Trunk Corporation: Canadian National Railways in the United States, 1971–1992* (East Lansing: Michigan State University Press, 1995), 83, 85–86; H. Roger Grant, *"Follow the Flag": A History of the Wabash Railroad Company* (DeKalb: Northern Illinois University Press, 2004), 220–21.

8. Vrooman-Langdon interview; Hofsommer, *Grand Trunk Corporation,* 86–92.

9. Don L. Hofsommer, *The Tootin' Louie: A History of the Minneapolis & St. Louis Railway* (Minneapolis: University of Minnesota Press, 2005), 263–66; *Moody's Transportation Manual,* 931.

10. Hofsommer, *The Tootin' Louie,* 266; Vrooman-Langdon interview; *Wall Street Journal,* January 14, 1981.

11. Jervis Langdon Jr. to Hays Watkins, January 18, 1981, Langdon papers; interview with Robert Downing, Harrisburg, Pa., September 30, 2005; *Wall Street Journal,* April 1, 1976; interview with Paul Reistrap, Baltimore, June 24, 2006.

12. Interview with Bill Collins, Loudonville, N.Y., February 26, 2007; Delaware and Hudson Railway Company, press release, February 28, 1979, Langdon papers; *Sunday Telegram* (Elmira, N.Y.), March 4, 1979; *Wall Street Journal,* March 2, 1979.

13. Collins interview, February 26, 2007; Jervis Langdon Jr. to Robert Blanchette, January 31, 1981, Langdon papers; *Journal of Commerce,* April 7, 1981; interview with Bill Collins, Loudonville, N.Y., June 1, 2007; Bill Collins to author, August 1, 2007.

The extension of trackage rights to D&H gave the appearance of enhanced rail competition in the Northeast, an alternative to the failed efforts by the USRA to create two large railroads from the former bankrupts and to have involvement from both Chessie and the Southern. The reality, however, was somewhat different. Once the trackage rights plan went into effect, which was concurrent with the startup of Conrail, the Albany-based road found its trains routinely discriminated against by Conrail dispatchers. Conrail trains received priority, thereby adversely affecting D&H service and increasing its operating costs. Jervis noted publicly that "these D&H extensions . . . were over the tracks of its principal competitor—a competitor with a grudge."

14. Collins interview, February 26, 2007; interview with Kent Shoemaker, Minneapolis, November 4, 2005; D&H press release; Irene Langdon to author, March 7, 2007; Collins to author.

15. Collins interviews, February 26 and June 1, 2007; Shoemaker interview; Collins to author; *Patriot-News* (Harrisburg, Pa.), November 19, 1985; Jervis Langdon Jr. to Andrew L. Lewis, January 24, 1981, Langdon papers.

16. Collins interviews; Shoemaker interview; *Wall Street Journal,* September 18, 1981, July 29, 1982; Jervis Langdon Jr. to Louis Rossi, August 25, 1985, Langdon papers.

17. Collins interviews; interview with Mortimer B. Fuller III, Greenwich, Conn., April 20, 2007.

18. Collins interview, February 26, 2007; Langdon to Rossi; *Moody's Transportation Manual* (New York: Moody's Investors Service, 1988), 284; *New York Times,* January 11 and June 9, 1990.

19. Edward A. Lewis, *American Shortline Railway Guide,* 5th ed. (Waukesha, Wis., 1996), 128–29; Fuller interview; interview with Mark Hastings, Greenwich, Conn., April 6, 2007.

20. Interview with William McKnight, Harrisburg, Pa., September 28, 2005.

21. Langdon to John H. Burdakin, Detroit, May 20, 1983, in possession of William McKnight, Northville, Mich.

22. Vrooman-Langdon interview.

23. Interview with Chris Burger, Cedar Rapids, October 12, 2006.

24. Jervis Langdon Jr., "Jervis Langdon Jr. (1905–)," Langdon papers; Reistrup interview; "Memorandum on Monongahela-Conrail," September 26, 1987, Langdon papers.

25. Irene Langdon to author, February 14, 2007.

26. *Washington Star,* July 26, 1978.

27. *Wall Street Journal,* February 7, 1979; Jervis Langdon and William Dixon, "Nationalization of Rails Inevitable, but Example of Canada Offers Hope," *Money Manager* 7 (April 3, 1978): 1–4.

28. *Washington Post,* October 16, 1980; Rush Loving Jr., *The Men Who Loved Trains* (Bloomington: Indiana University Press, 2006), 196, 223; Jervis Langdon to Hays Watkins, January 19, 1981, Langdon papers; Vrooman-Langdon interview.

29. Vrooman-Langdon interview; *Washington Post,* June 31, 1983.

30. Langdon to Watkins; *Traffic World,* July 4, 1983, 55.

31. Richard Saunders Jr., *Main Lines: Rebirth of the North American Railroads, 1970–2002* (DeKalb: Northern Illinois University Press, 2003), 233–38; Frank N. Wilner, *Railroad Mergers: History, Analysis, Insight* (Omaha: Simmons-Boardman Books, 1997), 285; *Washington Post,* July 23, 1984; *New York Times,* February 9, 1985.

32. *Washington Post,* October 25, 1984, May 15, 1985; Loving, *The Men Who Loved Trains,* 253; *New York Times,* December 13, 1984.

33. Jervis Langdon Jr. to Mario Cuomo, July 14, 1985, Langdon papers; Jervis Langdon Jr. to L. Stanley Crane, July 15, 1985, Langdon papers.

Jervis knew how to work the political system. He made certain that copies of his letter to Governor Cuomo went to others, including Stan Lundine, who represented the Southern Tier counties in the House of Representatives.

34. L. Stanley Crane to Jervis Langdon, April 13, 1987, Langdon papers.

35. *Wall Street Journal,* March 26, 1987; Saunders, *Main Lines,* 240, 340–45.

36. Undated manuscript in Langdon papers. See also "Barron's Mailbag," *Barron's,* August 11, 1986.

37. Jervis Langdon Jr., "An Old Railroader Tries to Look Back," manuscript, April 8, 1987, Langdon papers. A revised version appeared in *Trains* (August 1987): 66.

38. "To the Editor of *The New York Times,*" Nov. 7, 1993, Langdon papers.

39. Autobiographical sketch, 1996, in Langdon papers; *Journal of Commerce,* May 25, 1995.

40. Irene Langdon interviews, August 5, 2005, September 16, 2006; Irene Langdon to author, March 7 and May 23, 2007; Jervis Langdon, "Mark Twain in Elmira," *Chemung Historical Journal* (October 1987).

At the heart of the Langdon–Elmira College agreement for Quarry Farm were these restrictions on the use of the main house:

> No industrial or commercial activity shall be pursued on the property, which shall be used solely as (1.) A center for the study of Mark Twain, his works, and influence upon his and later generations and (2.) a temporary home for such students of Mark Twain as may be designated from time to time by the President of the College as the Grantor.

41. *Mark Twain Circular* 18 (April 2004): 1; Irene Langdon to author, May 23, 2007.

42. Irene Langdon interview, September 16, 2006; Fuller interview; Hastings interview.

43. Irene Langdon interview, August 5, 2005; Irene Landon to author, May 23, 2007.

44. E. R. Lichty to Jervis Langdon, May 4, 1990, July 23, 1990, Langdon papers; McKnight interview.

45. Collins interview.

46. Irene Langdon interview, September 16, 2006; E. Ray Lichty, "If Only He'd Had Some Money," *Sentinel* 26 (Second Quarter 2004): 30; *Elmira Star-Gazette,* February 17, 2004.

Books in the Railroads Past and Present Series

H. ROGER GRANT, Kathryn and Calhoun Lemon Professor of History at Clemson University, is the author or editor of 24 books, most of them on railroad history. He has written company histories of the Chicago & North Western, the Chicago Great Western, the Erie Lackawanna, the Georgia & Florida, and the Wabash railroads.